Praise for

CREATED EQUAL

"We are familiar with movies that are based on books. Now comes a book that is based on a movie. If you were riveted by the film *Created Equal: Clarence Thomas in His Own Words*, as I was, and you wanted to hear the stories that were left on the cutting room floor, as I did, you will want to get this book."

— **Randy E. Barnett,** professor of constitutional law at George-town Law, coauthor of *The Original Meaning of the Four-teenth Amendment: Its Letter and Spirit*

"Every great historical figure ought to get an opportunity to share his life with future generations. *Created Equal*, the film and now the book takes us on an exciting journey that starts in Pin Point, Georgia, and ends with Clarence Thomas, who has become an American hero to millions of people. Justice Thomas's life story and his judicial opinions have helped shape our nation. I highly recommend this book because it is Justice Thomas's recollection of his life and the people and circumstances that helped make him the giant he is today. It is certain to become an invaluable resource for historians, students, and other readers who will recognize it as the definitive work on Justice Thomas's life."

— **Carol M. Swain,** Distinguished Senior Fellow for Constitu-tional Studies, Texas Public Policy Foundation

"A compelling, must-read book that shows us how greatness comes from unflinching courage in the face of adversity. Clarence Thomas is a national treasure."

— **Laura Ingraham,** host of *The Ingraham Angle* and former Thomas law clerk

"Few life stories are as authentically American as Supreme Court Justice Clarence Thomas's, yet you'd never know it from the way he is often portrayed in the media. Michael Pack and Mark Paoletta's *Created Equal* goes a long way toward correcting the distortions. They succeed in presenting the essence of Thomas—his modesty, graciousness, wit, humor, and unflinching honesty. We owe the authors a debt of gratitude for this profound and moving book."

    —**Jason L. Riley,** author of *Maverick: A Biography of Thomas Sowell*

"While I have known Justice Thomas for more than twenty-five years, I learned a great deal more about him in this compelling, book-length interview. Justice Thomas tells the riveting story of his life journey from Pin Point, Georgia, to the Supreme Court. He also explains his views on our nation's founding principles and the process by which he approaches his work on the Supreme Court. This is a must-read!"

    —**Mike Lee,** U.S. senator and former clerk to Justice Samuel Alito

"Clarence Thomas's inspiring story is vitally important to this moment in our nation's history. Every American should read this exceptional book."

    —**Mark Levin,** host of *The Mark Levin Show*

"The story of Clarence Thomas's rise from a poor Gullah boy growing up in the Jim Crow South to one of America's most influential intellectuals is without a doubt one of the most inspirational stories in U.S. history. The fact that so many people who claim to care about racial inequality have spent decades dismissing and lying about Thomas because he insists on thinking independently is just further proof his story needed to be told—and finally, masterfully, and elegantly, Michael Pack and Mark Paoletta have given Thomas's life story the respect it deserves."

    —**Mollie Hemingway,** editor in chief at The Federalist, author of *Rigged: How the Media, Big Tech, and the Democrats Seized Our Elections,* and coauthor of *Justice on Trial: The Kavanaugh Confirmation and the Future of the Supreme Court.*

"This new book about Justice Thomas tells the quintessential success story of a journey from abject poverty to intellectual leadership on the highest Court in the land. The justice had the good fortune of a grandfather who insisted that he be educated by nuns, thus laying the groundwork for a career of pathbreaking scholarship. Like the trajectory of most judicial giants, many of his dissents have become majority rulings. And his honesty, humor, and generosity have graced everyone he meets, from janitors to presidents."

—**Ambassador C. Boyden Gray,** counsel to President George H. W. Bush

"Supreme Court Justice Clarence Thomas is rightfully known as a towering figure in American jurisprudence. *Created Equal* builds upon this conventional wisdom, amplifying Justice Thomas's own words to reveal how his grandfather's moral guidance, an enduring faith, and a stellar education helped him develop the mindset of an Overcomer that propelled him from humble beginnings in Pin Point, Georgia, to the very pinnacle of the American Dream."

—**Ian Rowe,** senior fellow at the American Enterprise Institute and co-founder and CEO of Vertix Partnership Academies

"In *Created Equal* Michael Pack and Mark Paoletta have provided a fascinating account of an extraordinary man who rose from the most humble beginnings to become an associate justice of the Supreme Court of the United States. Based upon Clarence Thomas's own words it also offers an incisive commentary on some of the critical issues of our time: the Constitution and the rule of law, race relations, and our legal and judicial system."

—**Edwin Meese III,** former U.S. Attorney General

"The story of Clarence Thomas needs to be told. It is the story that of a man of integrity who embodies the best of our national character. Michael Pack and Mark Paoletta have done the country a great service by bringing out the story in Justice Thomas's own words.

This book is must-reading for anyone who wants to understand the principles of our nation and the nobility of the American character."
   —**The Very Reverend Paul D. Scalia,** son of Justice Antonin Scalia and episcopal vicar of clergy for the Diocese of Arlington

"The interviews with Clarence Thomas collected here—excerpted from twenty-five hours of conversation over six days—are assuredly the most intimate ever conducted with a sitting Supreme Court justice. The revelations are personal and historical, with bracing lessons for students of the law, politics, race relations, the media, and human nature. Skillfully structured by Michael Pack and Mark Paoletta, *Created Equal* brings us deep inside the soul of an American icon: an essential document of a life at once unique and emblematic of a nation."
   —**James Rosen,** chief White House correspondent for Newsmax and author of *Cheney One on One: A Candid Conversation with America's Most Controversial Statesman*

"An essential, revealing, and intimate portrait of a great American life. In *Created Equal*, the authentic voice of Justice Thomas shines through with all its intelligence, originality, charm, and wit as Michael Pack and Mark Paoletta humanize one of the most consequential Supreme Court justices in history. To know the real Clarence Thomas, you must read this compelling and important book."
   —**James L. Swanson,** bestselling author of *Manhunt: The 12-Day Chase for Lincoln's Killer*

CREATED EQUAL

CREATED EQUAL

CLARENCE THOMAS IN HIS OWN WORDS

MICHAEL PACK & MARK PAOLETTA

Regnery Publishing
WASHINGTON, D.C.

ISBN: 978-1-68451-270-6
eISBN: 978-1-68451-310-9

Published in the United States by
Regnery Publishing
A division of Salem Media Group
Washington, D.C.
www.Regnery.com

Manufactured in the United States of America

10 9 8 7 6 5 4 3 2

Books are available in quantity for promotional or premium use. For information on discounts and terms, please visit our website: www.Regnery.com.

I dedicate this book to my wife, the love of my life,
Gina Cappo Pack, who never gets enough credit for the work
we do together, this book no less than all the other projects.

—*Michael Pack*

I dedicate this book to my wife Tricia. Every day
I wake up, I consider myself the luckiest guy in the world
because she decided to share her life with me.

—*Mark Paoletta*

CONTENTS

CONTENTS

INTRODUCTION

This book is not a conventional biography but the record of a long biographical discussion. As such, the authors know that the book will be read by different kinds of readers and used in different ways. This introduction is intended as a guide.

WHY THIS BOOK WAS WRITTEN

The impetus to write this book came from the success of our documentary, *Created Equal: Clarence Thomas in His Own Words.*

In our two-hour documentary, Clarence Thomas looks directly at the camera and in his own words tells the audience the story of his dramatic and inspiring life. He begins with how he grew up in the segregated South and ends with his years on the Supreme Court. His life is a great American success story, with many twists and turns along the way.

Created Equal first played in more than 110 movie theaters from January to March 2020—a wide release for a documentary—until theaters were forced to close on account of COVID-19. Then, that May, PBS broadcast the film nationally in prime time. The *Washington Post* called it "a marvel of filmmaking." The *Washington Examiner* declared that "everyone interested in the truth and a great story should go and see it." *Time* magazine dubbed it "a rare insight into the mind of a justice."

Created Equal was released digitally in October 2020 and is still streaming on many sites. Our website, ManifoldProductions.com, links to the streaming services where it can be viewed. Ironically, Amazon chose to cancel the film during February 2021, Black History

Month, sparking a firestorm of controversy. In spite of this attempt to suppress the film, it remains quite popular.

Many viewers have asked for more—more details about Justice Thomas, more of the interview. An unprecedented number of viewers have approached us, both at in-person and virtual screenings and through our website. A surprising number have seen the film multiple times. Some wrote to protest the Amazon cancelling. Many told us that they wanted the film to be longer (a rare complaint about a documentary), and some even wanted to see the entire thirty hours of outtakes.

Public recognition of Clarence Thomas's importance has been steadily increasing. Many call the current Supreme Court "The Thomas Court," pointing to him as the most influential justice, even though he is not the chief justice. For years, he has written the most opinions in each Supreme Court term. His powerful dissents have slowly shifted the court in his direction. Justice Thomas's life and his opinions seem to speak to this moment and beyond.

To satisfy the public's interest in our film and Justice Thomas, we offer this book, selected excerpts from our extended interviews with Justice Thomas and his wife, Virginia. Over 90 percent of the material in this book did *not* appear in the film.

THE AUTHORS AND JUSTICE THOMAS

Michael Pack

I first met Justice Thomas in the context of the film. Some mutual friends, including Mark Paoletta, were interested in having a documentary made about Justice Thomas. They were tired of the numerous films, books, and articles that have lied about and distorted his life and work, and they wanted to correct the record in film.

At the time the idea of a possible documentary was brought to my attention, I knew little about Clarence Thomas. Like everyone of a certain age, I vividly recalled being glued to the television, tuning into C-SPAN to watch Anita Hill's shocking charges and Thomas's full-throated rebuttal. But I knew little else, and—as I later realized—I had inadvertently absorbed some the media's biased narrative and hidden assumptions about Justice Thomas.

Our mutual friends arranged a meeting. One meeting and a little research was all it took to convince me that Clarence Thomas had a great story to tell. His was a story of overcoming great obstacles, of resilience and moral courage. I very much wanted to tell that story, a story the American people needed to hear.

Mark Paoletta was a key part of the production process throughout, especially in confirming the factual details. Justice Thomas's wife, Ginni Thomas, often says, "Mark knows more about our lives than we do." Really he was an unsung, uncredited executive producer of the documentary. Now he is a close friend.

Originally I planned a traditional documentary, including many interviews with friends and enemies, covering all the phases of Justice Thomas's life and all sides of the issues raised by his jurisprudence and his career, from busing and affirmative action to the Anita Hill charges. Eventually, I realized that this project would become unwieldy and that Thomas's own unique voice would be lost. Plus, he is the best storyteller of the events of his own life. So ours would be a subjective film—not the objective truth but Justice Thomas's own story, told his way. Audiences could choose to accept or reject it, based on what they heard from him and the many other sources out there.

In the end we settled on a documentary based on long interviews with only Justice Thomas and Ginni Thomas, both talking directly to the camera, looking the audience in the eye, as if chatting across a dinner table. I interviewed them for over thirty hours, from November 15, 2017, to March 14, 2018. No filmmaker has ever been given such access to a Supreme Court justice. The film, and now this book, is based on those interviews. Of course, there was also extensive use of archival footage, vintage photographs, and expressionistic re-creations.

As is our standard practice, neither Justice Thomas nor Ginni Thomas had any editorial control over the film. In fact, Justice Thomas's only suggestion was to include Ginni. He was to be the only interview subject, but he correctly saw that Ginni could talk about his (and their) states of mind in difficult moments in a way he could not. Ginni's interview was so compelling that we have added an appendix with selections from it.

I am forever grateful for the trust the Thomases placed in me and my team to tell their stories fairly and honestly. Working on this film and now this book has been one of the great privileges of my career. I was honored to be able to share their stories with you, the viewer, and now you, the reader.

Mark Paoletta

I first met Clarence Thomas in October of 1983 at an event in Bridgeport, Connecticut, when he was the chairman of the Equal Employment Opportunity Commission and I was a senior in college. Along with a few others, we chatted for a little more than an hour. He was engaging and full of energy and opinions. He made a huge impression on me.

In March of 1989, I was a young lawyer serving in the George H. W. Bush White House and working on the team that vetted individuals for possible appointment as federal judges. The White House was interested in selecting Clarence Thomas for the D.C. Circuit and wanted to do due diligence on his record. Based in part on that 1983 conversation, I volunteered to reach out to Thomas to obtain copies of his speeches and writing.

What I read was electrifying. Here was a guy who stood up for what he believed in and called it like he saw it. He took on the civil rights establishment and Congress. I spoke with him several times, and he was the same as the man I remembered meeting six years before. I hoped the president would select him because he had been through the fire as a black conservative in the Reagan administration and seemed to have a steel back bone toward *anyone* who tried to tell him what to think or do. But given his public opinions I was not sure he would be confirmed by the Democrat-led Senate. The president did select him, and Thomas was confirmed in March 1990 to the U.S. Court of Appeals for the D.C. Circuit.

When President Bush announced on July 1, 1991, that he was nominating Clarence Thomas to the U.S. Supreme Court, I was thrilled that I would be part of the White House team working to get him confirmed. At that announcement, Thomas spoke those uplifting words, "Only in America" in his brief remarks, capturing so eloquently the hope and promise of our extraordinary country.

But immediately the left began an all-out assault to destroy this good man for no other reason than that he did not conform to the beliefs he was assigned by virtue of his race, and that he would not back down from those views. Out of that terrible ordeal, a friendship was forged.

Several months after he was confirmed, I was diagnosed with cancer. As I went through surgeries and chemotherapy, our bond grew deeper. Justice Thomas visited or called me every day, particularly during my rounds of chemotherapy, focusing on my health challenge and always cheering me up. When my treatments were done and my hair had grown back, he signed a photo of us with the words, "Great hair, buddy! We survived!" We have been close friends ever since.

Clarence Thomas is an American hero, representing the best of America. He is our greatest Supreme Court justice. As exceptional a public figure as he is, he is an even better friend, and not just to me.

Justice Thomas's wife, Ginni, is also a dear friend and an inspiring figure in her own right.

Over the years, I have been angered by the vicious, racist, and false portrayals of Justice Thomas in articles, books, and films. After the anti–Justice Thomas HBO movie *Confirmation* was released in 2016, I was determined to help bring about a film that portrayed the real Clarence Thomas. It was in that context, and with the help of some friends, that I began working with Michael Pack. We were blessed that this A-list documentary filmmaker turned out to be interested in making a film about Clarence Thomas. Michael Pack truly understood the monumental importance of Clarence Thomas's life journey, his ideas, and jurisprudence. It has been one of the greatest joys in my life to be able to work with Michael on the film. Michael has made a masterpiece that every American should watch.

How to Use This Book

We designed this book to be used two ways.

First, you can read it straight through, as Clarence Thomas's life story, with a clear beginning, middle, and end. In this way, the structure of the book parallels the structure of our film. The actual interviews, like most conversations, meandered. Justice Thomas might circle back to reflect on an earlier phase of his life or flash forward to something more recent. We have smoothed all this out for the book, as we did for the film.

To help place you in time, we have provided a chronology, a timeline of the major events of Clarence Thomas's life. As you read along, you can always refer back to the chronology to get your bearings.

Second, we expect some readers will want to go to the topics and incidents of interest to them, to skip around—say from affirmative action to the confirmation hearings. The index is designed to support these readers. We also offer very detailed chapters and subchapter headings, which appear in the table of contents and can guide the reader to the sections of most interest.

However you use the book, we hope that learning more about Justice Thomas's life and ideas will be as inspiring to you as it has been to us.

TIMELINE

KEY EVENTS IN CLARENCE THOMAS'S LIFE

JUNE 23, 1948—Clarence Thomas is born in Pin Point, Georgia, to Leola Williams and M. C. Thomas.

1951—M. C. Thomas leaves the family; Clarence Thomas's parents are divorced. Clarence lives with his great-aunt Annie Jones (Leola Williams's aunt) in her home in Pin Point with his two siblings, Emma Mae Thomas and Myers Lee Thomas.

1954—Clarence Thomas starts first grade at the segregated all-black school, Haven Home, in Pin Point.

WINTER 1954—Aunt Annie's home in Pin Point burns down. Clarence Thomas and his brother move to live with his mother in Savannah. His sister Emma Mae stays with Aunt Annie in another home in Pin Point.

SUMMER 1955—Clarence Thomas and his brother Myers move to live with their grandparents Myers and Christina Anderson at their home in Savannah, Georgia.

FALL 1955—Clarence Thomas is enrolled in the second grade at St. Benedict the Moor Catholic School in Savannah, the segregated school for black students run by the Missionary Franciscan Sisters of the Immaculate Conception.

CHRISTMAS DAY, 1957—Grandfather Myers Anderson takes Clarence and his brother out to Liberty County to work on the family farm, where they will spend their summers for the next ten years.

1962—Clarence Thomas graduates eighth grade at St. Benedict's and begins his freshman year at St. Pius X High School, the all-black Catholic high school in Savannah.

1964—Clarence Thomas transfers to St. John Vianney Minor Seminary, a boarding school outside of Savannah on the Isle of Hope. He repeats the tenth grade to complete an extra year of Latin. St. John's has just been desegregated, and Clarence Thomas is one of the first two black students to attend the school.

1967—Clarence Thomas graduates from St. John Vianney and begins attending Conception Seminary College in Conception, Missouri.

1968—Clarence Thomas withdraws from Conception at the end of his first year. In the fall he begins attending Holy Cross College in Worcester, Massachusetts, as a sophomore.

SPRING 1971—Clarence Thomas is awarded his B.A. from Holy Cross College on June 4. He marries Kathy Ambush on June 5.

FALL 1971—Clarence Thomas begins attending Yale Law School in New Haven, Connecticut.

FEBRUARY 15, 1973—Clarence Thomas's son Jamal Thomas is born.

SPRING 1974—Clarence Thomas is awarded a J.D. from Yale Law School.

1974—Clarence Thomas begins working as an assistant attorney general for Missouri Attorney General John Danforth, a Republican, in Jefferson City, Missouri.

1977—Clarence Thomas begins working in the legal department of the agricultural company Monsanto in St. Louis.

AUGUST 1979—Clarence Thomas begins working for Senator John Danforth in Washington, D.C., as a legislative assistant on energy, environment, and public works issues.

DECEMBER 1980—Clarence Thomas attends the Fairmont Conference in San Franciso, organized by Professor Thomas Sowell. There he speaks with *Washington Post* reporter Juan Williams, who writes an op-ed, "Black Conservatives, Center Stage," which appears in the *Post* on December 16, 1980.

JUNE 19, 1981—Clarence Thomas is confirmed as assistant secretary for Civil Rights in the Department of Education in the Reagan administration.

MARCH 31, 1982—Clarence Thomas is confirmed as chairman of the Equal Employment Opportunity Commission (EEOC).

1983—Clarence Thomas's grandfather Myers Anderson dies on March 30; his grandmother Christina Anderson dies on May 1.

JULY 1984—Clarence Thomas and his wife, Kathy Ambush, are granted a divorce.

1986—Clarence Thomas is confirmed to another term as chairman of the EEOC.

1987—Clarence Thomas marries Virginia Lamp in a ceremony at St. Paul United Methodist Church in Omaha, Nebraska, on May 30.

MAY 1989—Clarence Thomas is nominated by President George H. W. Bush to the U.S. Court of Appeals for the D.C. Circuit.

FEBRUARY 1990—The Senate Judiciary Committee votes 12–1 to recommend Clarence Thomas.

MARCH 6, 1990—Clarence Thomas is confirmed to be a judge on the D.C. Circuit Court of Appeals by a voice vote in the Senate.

JUNE 27, 1991—Justice Thurgood Marshall announces his retirement from the Supreme Court.

JULY 1, 1991—President George H. W. Bush announces he will nominate Clarence Thomas to be associate justice of the Supreme Court.

SEPTEMBER 10-16, 1991—Clarence Thomas testifies before the Senate Judiciary Committee.

SEPTEMBER 23, 1991—Anita Hill submits a confidential statement to the Judiciary Committee.

SEPTEMBER 25, 1991—The FBI interviews Clarence Thomas about Hill's allegations.

SEPTEMBER 27, 1991—The Judiciary Committee votes 8–8 on the Thomas nomination and sends it to the full Senate, which is expected to vote on his nomination on October 8.

OCTOBER 5-6, 1991—Anita Hill's allegations are leaked in stories in *Newsday* (October 5) and on National Public Radio (October 6).

OCTOBER 7, 1991—Anita Hill holds a press conference at the University of Oklahoma Law School.

OCTOBER 11-13, 1991—The Senate Judiciary Committee reconvenes the hearing to consider Anita Hill's allegations.

OCTOBER 15, 1991—The Senate confirms Clarence Thomas as associate justice of the U.S. Supreme Court by a 52–48 vote, with eleven Democrat Senators voting for Thomas and two Republicans voting against him.

OCTOBER 18, 1991—Clarence Thomas is sworn in by Justice Byron White, who administers the constitutional oath at a ceremony at the White House.

OCTOBER 23, 1991—Clarence Thomas is administered the judicial oath by Chief Justice Rehnquist and takes his seat on the U.S. Supreme Court.

1996—Clarence Thomas issues his hundredth opinion on the merits.

2003—Clarence Thomas issues a dissenting opinion in *Grutter v. Bollinger,* which is extensively discussed in the interview for *Created Equal.*

2004—Clarence Thomas issues his three hundredth opinion on the merits.

2013—Clarence Thomas issues his five hundredth opinion on the merits.

NOVEMBER 14, 2017-MARCH 14, 2018—Clarence Thomas sits for six interviews, and Ginni Thomas for three, for the documentary *Created Equal: Clarence Thomas in His Own Words.*

2020—Thomas issues his seven hundredth opinion on the merits.

CHAPTER ONE

CHILDHOOD YEARS

"They had faith in this country"

MP (Michael Pack): Justice Thomas, what are the lessons of your life, when you look back over it?
CT (Clarence Thomas): I don't consider myself someone who reflects on that stuff a lot. We tend to make life pretty complicated. Poor people don't have that luxury. They can't start debating the number of angels on a pinhead. No offense to St. Thomas Aquinas, but they can't be Thomistic. Things are simplified. They are not gray. They're black and white. You either fed the hogs or you didn't. You fed the chickens or you didn't. You repaired the roof or you didn't. You put the fodder or hay in the barn or you didn't. Whether you did it or didn't do it makes the difference between survival and not surviving. So that's something my grandfather taught us. There was always right and wrong.

I went off to school and I took all sorts of philosophy and took history, took theology. You read, you thought about things. Later in life, I was thinking back on my life, and I thought after all of that, the person who had the greatest influence and probably the most accurate

1

was Sister Mary Dolorosa in the second grade in 1955 as we were beginning the Baltimore Catechism.[1] She would say, "Why did God create us?" And the answer was pretty uniform—a whole group of second graders answered in unison: "God created us to know, love, and serve him in this life and be happy with him in the next." So that's pretty simple. After all the existentialism, having studied metaphysics, nihilists, you've been through all these, and you come back to Sister Mary Dolorosa and the second grade in September 1955.

It seemed to me in a lot of ways that life was a circle that you started in one place, went away, and came back.

MP: To your grandfather's values, to the nuns' values after a journey away from them?
CT: In my youth, there are still freed slaves around, alive. They're elderly, very, very old, but they're still alive. So, that's the world that you're bridging. These people had a faith in the future and in a set of values that you needed, to pursue that unknown future. But there's a way you had to conduct yourself. They had faith; they had hope; and they had charity. They were kind to each other. They were a community. They had hope in the future. That's why my grandparents invested so much in us.

They had faith in this country and that if they did the right things, it would all work out, even though they could not see the progress. And that's where hope comes in. I mean, think about it: you're uneducated people in Georgia during very difficult times. And yet they still had faith, hope, and charity. Compare that to today and how many people actually convey any of those virtues to you? They convey, "Oh we all need to have a sense of community," that sort of thing, but that's not quite charity in any case.

There are lots of lessons that were learned. And there was always an honesty. People were always honest with us. I mean, there was a trust. You can think of today and contrast it. From the house I grew up in, it is three quarters of a mile almost exactly from my school,

St. Benedict's.[2] Imagine a kid that's quite a bit under a hundred pounds, and in the pre-dawn time frame walking to serve the 6:00 Mass at the convent there. And my biggest fear was stray dogs; not being robbed or molested or abducted. Stray dogs. Now how many kids today would be allowed to walk the inner-city streets in the dark, or any time for that matter, at the age of seven, eight, nine, ten? We walked to school every day, and no one ever bothered us, an occasional bully or something, but that was a part of life. But there was a trust. And my grandparents had a faith and a belief and trust in the community that nothing would happen to you, that it was perfectly safe.

Pin Point
"We were those people back up in the woods"

MP: Justice Thomas, let's try to retrace your journey, starting at the beginning. How did your people end up in Pin Point?[3]
CT: As best we can tell, our forebears were brought over in the mid-eighteenth century, and more precisely, some people think it was in the 1760s, to Ossabaw Island, which is one of the barrier islands.[4] Some members of my family were on that island for more than a century and came to the landward side after that. My grandfather is from the landward side in Liberty County. As far as we know, virtually all of my family members were in that region.

MP: What was Pin Point like?
CT: Pin Point is hard to describe because it's kind of gone away. People would have said back then, "We were those people back up in the woods." We were isolated. It was a community. It wasn't a town. You could see the river from there. You hear of the song, "Moon River"? Johnny Mercer's from Savannah.[5]

It was close to Savannah but in a sense far away. There was one way out; it was a dirt road. All your family members were there. You played, you ran, you knew everybody. For me it was idyllic, but it was isolated, and I didn't know how isolated it was until years later.

MP: What does it mean to be Gullah Geechee?[6]
CT: What does it mean to be Gullah Geechee? You know, I never thought about it when I was a kid. It was just a distinctive culture, West African. It had a mixture of English and other words that was somewhat difficult to understand. The closest thing I can think of today would be if you went to the Caribbean. The dialects are close, or if I saw someone from West Africa, the accents are close to what I grew up with. Back when I was a kid, to be called Geechee was a put down. It would be years later that they would begin to celebrate it.

MP: Tell me about when you were born, a little about your mother, and your other siblings.
CT: I was born at home, right on Shipyard Creek in 1948. My mother always said I was too stubborn to cry. And I guess that was sort of an indication of the person I would be. Ms. Lula Kemp, the midwife, came over from another little community, Sandfly, and brought me into this world, and that was June 23, 1948.

I am a middle child. My mother had had all of us, we think, before she was twenty. She was not educated. And then she and my father separated when I was a toddler. So I would have no early memories of him. I have memories of other family members but he wasn't there—he wasn't among the family members.

MP: What was growing up in Pin Point like?
CT: Our home was just a shack. No one had running water. You had a woodstove in the kitchen, you had kerosene lamps for illumination,

and I still have a memory of one light bulb in the living room area. And of course, if there was a hole in the wall people covered it up with different things. They used newspaper or old catalogue pages.

But for us it was home, and it was well kept. I always remember on Saturdays, which was always a big day, because people cleaned and cooked and prepared themselves for the Lord's Day. It was really a big deal. So you would have to rake the front yard. Well, the front yard didn't have any grass. It was just dirt, and it was always interesting to see how neatly people would rake. And you see the marks of the rake in the front yard in an area that was not grass. It was just dirt. That's just how fastidious people were about keeping things up even though the house itself was not something you would consider an elegant house. And the rule was: well, it's yours, you have to do your best.

People raked oysters and they caught crabs and they fished. The women picked crab, people like my mother and my relatives did that at the crab factory, which was just there in Pin Point. And they also shucked oysters—all of which is hard work and requires a lot of manual labor and dexterity and standing up.

Well, when they were gone we were on our own. We were off on our adventures. We would catch minnows in the creek. We'd walk along the water's edge throwing oyster shells. If you sail an oyster shell you can make it skip on the water. And so then we would see who could make it skip the most.

Most people didn't have store-bought toys. So you made them. You made pluffers which was a weapon we made. Chinaberry, you would put it in a bamboo tube and you create a vacuum and push the berries through and made a popping sound. And then we would have a war with each other. The rims from old bicycles were also a great source of fun. You would take the rims and we would take a stick and you get all the spokes out and you would push it along the dirt road with a stick in the groove.

We would roll tires. In those days you had lots of old tires that had gone bad. If you go back to the movie *To Kill a Mockingbird*, Scout, the young girl, when she is pushed into Boo Radley's yard, she's in a tire.[7] I have no idea how kids today can have any idea what they were doing with her inside a tire. We always did that. Inside the opening in the tire where the rim would normally go and you're rolling down the road inside a tire. Well, if someone lets that go downhill, you could wind up rolling into somebody's yard or down into the river.

We connected old cans and made what we called trains with coat hangers and things like that. But you name it, we did it. I remember years later reading *Huck Finn* and *Tom Sawyer* and wondering what the fuss was about. We had done a lot of those things.

MP: As you tell it, it does sound idyllic.
CT: There was always plenty to eat. You lived on the water, so that was a cornucopia. Some people made turtle stew. It was called kudda. They'd have raccoon or some people ate possum. There was lots of fish. They made conch. Someone killed a deer. Someone killed a wild hog. Someone came back with a big flounder, someone went way out and got whiting or mullets. So there was always lots of food. Now you may not like the way it was fixed. You may not like that particular food, but there was always lots of food. And it was peaceful.

When I was six years old, in those days the schools were still segregated. The school that blacks in Pin Point attended for grammar school was called Haven Home, which doesn't exist anymore. You went to the head of Pin Point, and you walked down the road and the bus came, and it was exciting to be big enough to go to the first grade. And the first day of school in those days was a huge event. All my cousins were there. It wasn't like you were going with a bunch of strangers. It was like a family outing for the kids. There were all your relatives there. It was safe. It was my complete world.

MOVING TO SAVANNAH
"THAT IS THE WORST PLACE I'VE EVER LIVED"

MP: Why did you and your family leave Pin Point?
CT: The house burned down. One day I came home, someone said there had been a fire, and we get there and this little shack that we had all been living in was just ashes and twisted tin. Everything that you ever knew in life is just there. I mean it's smoldering. I had lived in that house in Pin Point with my mother's Aunt Annie until that house burned down in the winter of 1954.

They left my sister [Emma Mae] in Pin Point with Annie. She was the oldest. My brother was five years old and I was six. We went to Savannah to live with my mother who was working as a maid.

My mother lived in one room in an old tenement with an outdoor bathroom. That is the worst place I've ever lived.

Whenever you flushed the toilet, or someone else flushed, it didn't actually go in the sewer system—it went in somebody else's yard. My all-encompassing word is gross. I mean, it was putrid. It was the smell of raw sewage. There were these boards, people would make these sort of makeshift paths to get across the gross wetness in the backyard.

We lived upstairs and one of our chores on the weekend was to empty the chamber pot in the outdoor toilet. In the summer in 1955, I was carrying the chamber pot down and had a significant amount of stale urine in it. I tripped at the top of the stairs and I fell all the way down. And then the pot and its content emptying out followed me and then washed me. It underscored all that had happened moving from Pin Point to the west side of Savannah.

And so you had the contrast between rural poverty, which is what we had in Pin Point and which was very livable. Then you had urban squalor and that was horrible.

I was supposed to go to school in the afternoons in those days and my mother wasn't there to make me go, because she had to go to work, so I wandered the streets by myself. I was six. That was a hard year. You were hungry and didn't know when you'd eat, and cold and didn't know when you'd be warm again. My mother didn't have money for kerosene. We had a kerosene stove in the room but there was never any kerosene so it was just whatever the weather was outside is what you got inside. She and my brother slept on the bed, and I slept on a little chair that was too small.

WALKING TO HIS GRANDPARENTS' HOME
"THE LONGEST AND MOST SIGNIFICANT JOURNEY I EVER MADE"

MP: In 1955, you moved to live with your grandparents. How and why did that happen?
CT: My mother had difficulty with two little boys and working as a maid which required some unevenness in her hours because not only was she cleaning, she was raising other peoples' kids. So that meant babysitting and things like that. So she asked my grandparents for help. And my grandmother, who did not have children, she was my mother's stepmother, suggested that she let her raise these two boys.

And one day, one Saturday morning we woke up and my mother said, "Put all your things in the grocery bag," and remember the paper grocery bags in those days, and my brother took one and neither one was full. All of our items, just imagine everything you have, in less than a paper bag. So we took our grocery bag each, and walked the couple of blocks from Henry Lane to East Thirty-Second Street.

That was the longest and most significant journey I ever made because it changed my entire life. And that walk along East Broad Street was a walk that I would replicate literally hundreds of times in the years after that. But I would always remember the first walk.

And that's how we went to live with my grandparents.

MP: What happened on the other end when you showed up to your grandparents' house?
CT: My grandfather was this myth. We saw him maybe once or twice when we lived on the west side. He was very stern. And he sat us there at the kitchen table and he said, "Boys, the damn vacation is over." He said from then on it was going to be "rules and regulations and manners and behavior." Oh my goodness. And he meant it. And he just explained what the rules were: my grandmother was always right, that he was in charge. He made it very clear that it was by grace that we were there, his grace. And the door in 1955, when we went to live with him, was swinging open inward. If we didn't behave ourselves, there'd be a day when it would swing outward and we'd be asked to leave.

MP: Could you describe your grandparents' house?
CT: They lived in this new house, and it was beautiful. For us, it could have been a palace. My grandfather and his cousins built that house. He didn't believe in mortgages and debt. That house cost him six hundred dollars. The floors were hardwood and had beautiful fixtures. To me it was a luxury.

We had never been in a house with a bathtub, a beautiful white porcelain toilet. My brother and I, one of our activities was to flush the toilet every time we had a chance. I mean we would walk by and flush the toilet. And my grandfather would chastise us and, as he would say, "You're runnin' up my damn water bill." It was the most amazing thing to us. We'd never been someplace where you had a working toilet. Beautiful, as we used to say back then, modern kitchen with a refrigerator, et cetera, and lots of food.

It was the first time we had ever had our own toothbrush. We had our own room. My brother and I had twin beds. My grandmother made these wonderful bedspreads. They would eventually buy us a desk. My brother and I shared a bureau. We shared a closet. It was like the most beautiful place we had ever lived. They had all the appliances. He had a freezer for food. He had the Magic Chef stove. We never lived any place with a hot water heater. There was plenty of food.

And my grandmother would just lavish you with those things. My grandmother was as sweet as she could be. She would always be saintly.

GRANDFATHER MYERS ANDERSON
"I WILL NEVER TELL YOU TO DO AS I SAY. I WILL ALWAYS TELL YOU TO DO AS I DO"

MP: Would you describe your grandfather, what he looked like, how much schooling he had?
CT: My grandfather was West African, obviously. He was illegitimate and never knew his father. He was born in Savannah. His mother died when he was seven or eight years old. When his mother died, he was raised by his grandmother, who was a freed slave.[8] She raised him on the family farm in Liberty County, which was twenty-five miles south of Savannah. The farm was a stone's throw from where we were living

on the farm. It's the same land that's been in the family since after the Civil War.

His grandmother was really hard on him. His grandmother would go to the dirt road and then spit on the dirt in the summer, and he would have to run way down the road to the store. And she said, "You better be back before that dries." So that doesn't sound exactly as someone who is warm and fuzzy.

His grandmother died when he was around fourteen, and he went to live with one of her sons, Uncle Charles, who was more of a fisherman. He was a hard man. He had twelve or thirteen kids of his own and even though he'd been hard, I remember when Charles died, it affected my grandfather greatly and he felt obligated always to look out for his widow. We built a house for her, and we always made sure that when we had produce, that she got some of it. She lived right next to us where we farmed in Liberty County.

My grandfather had a total of nine months of education. He went to one of those one-room schools in Liberty County. He went to the third grade, but school was three months out of the year because you had to work.

My grandfather was almost six feet tall. He was muscular, a very strong and lean man, and hardworking. He had lost a finger working on a lumber boat or something going up and down the Intracoastal. He didn't worry about it, but he always talked about it. Somehow, he must've gotten his glove caught up in some machinery and it pulled his finger off. He didn't allow us to wear gloves much as a result of that when we were working.

My grandfather had worked at various things. He'd moved houses, worked various jobs, and decided he wasn't going to work for anybody. He got an old truck and started selling wood. He would go in the woods at night to cut the wood, come back and sell it during the day. Then he added to his delivery business selling ice and then coal. Eventually the ice business went away as a result of refrigeration and his coal and wood morphed into a fuel oil delivery business. By the time we went to live with my grandfather he was delivering fuel oil.

In our neighborhood, you have these old houses, and my grandfather bought some of those and he used those as rental property. There was another business that he'd been involved in that he would tell us about occasionally. At some point in the late forties or early fifties, he bought a cinder block–making piece of equipment. I don't know exactly what that was, but he had a building for it, which would eventually become one of the garages that was made out of the cinderblock. He made the cinder blocks for some of the houses that he built behind us. And he made all the cinder blocks for the house we grew up in. He tried to get a permit to expand that business from the city of Savannah, but they declined, and he sold the machinery to a white man who went on to do very well.

MP: Please tell me about your grandmother, Aunt Tina.
CT: Aunt Tina was a small woman, about 5'2" or so, very slight, and I think she must have had some mixture with Native American blood. She, even to her death, had perfect teeth. She had been a maid, like most black women had been, and she worked for people at different places. She was from a county just north of Liberty County, Bryan County, in the Richmond Hill area. Aunt Tina had had a child early before she met my grandfather, but the child died shortly after or in childbirth. She had no children. I don't think she could have children, and she always referred to us as her boys. She and my grandfather were married almost fifty years. They both died in 1982.

She was a saint. She taught me how to sew and how to cook. Most people don't know how to thread a bobbin, and she taught me how to do that. She taught me how to cut out patterns. She made dresses and things for people. She taught me how to reupholster furniture, how to upgrade venetian blinds. Fruitcakes. Not a lot of people know how to make fruitcake. Well, I do. Not a lot of people want to know how to make fruitcakes. But she taught me how to do that. She taught me how to clean. She nursed us when we were sick, made us take castor oil once a year, cod liver oil every Friday night to clean out our system. She was a wonderful lady, and she was the person I would go to when my grandfather was such a difficult person.

MP: How did your grandfather raise you?
CT: My grandfather said, "I will never tell you to do as I say. I will always tell you to do as I do." Years went by and I thought about who would put that burden on themselves because a kid sees all, and a teenager sees and knows even more. And that's the burden he put on himself. I asked my brother when we were both in our forties, "Did you ever think he was a hypocrite because of what he said, 'Do as I do?'" My brother without hesitation said, "No." Whatever mistakes he made, he admitted them, and he just said follow me. He made us follow him. He wouldn't let us play organized sports. He wouldn't let us stray. He kept us close to him as though we were his apprentices in life, that we were adults in training. He was the one who was going to train us, so we were to follow him. Watch how he did it. "Watch how I live my life and you will learn."

You could never just have something and enjoy the mere having. He would always connect the dots for you. He would say, "There was a reason why I have this house. One, I don't throw money away on Cadillacs, clothes. I don't waste money. I don't drink excessively." (He took one drink a day.) You had to work for it. Everything was about work. "Why do I have this car? One, I don't waste money." He didn't believe in debt so he didn't buy a car on time. He didn't buy anything on time. To save money, you pay cash. So he said, "Because I work hard I can have this; because I don't waste what I earn, I can have this. Now if I went out and I wasted my money on drink, I couldn't have this and I couldn't send you all to school. I couldn't raise you all." He would always go the next step and explain to you why this is possible.

He would often talk about the difference between what you're supposed to do and what you wanted to do. He would say things like, "Don't confuse want and need. You may want a new suit, but you don't need it. You may want a new car, but you don't need it." So you were constantly being exposed to this dichotomy between what you might desire, or what you might feel like at the moment and what you need. And he would constantly tell you that.

MP: What was it like working with him on the oil truck?
CT: If you look at an oil truck, even today, it has a hose on the back. My grandfather's rule was once you reach that point, and I think for us that was about nine or ten years old, where you could pull that hose, then you were required to be on the oil truck. So the rule was, we got out of school at 2:30. You had to be home, dressed, and ready to be on the oil truck by 3:00. If you wanted a snack, you grab that on the run, and you got dressed, ready to go. And that's the way it worked. And even in spring, you got home, and you have to be ready to work. He had other chores for you. On Saturdays, invariably, I was the one who went on the oil truck with him, and that was all day.

When you rode with him, he was the professor, and you were to be seen and not heard. You could not initiate a conversation unless you wanted to clarify an instruction he had given. You were constantly getting this one-way input. And you couldn't get away from him because you always had to be around him.

MP: Didn't your grandfather even take the heater out of the truck?

CT: In 1956, my grandfather bought a new GMC truck. He removed the heater and plugged up where the heater was. And his thinking was this: having heat in a truck during the winter when you have to get in and out to deliver oil, one, it made you lazy. It made you not want to get out in the cold. And two, you might catch cold from going from hot to cold, back and forth. So he put that heater on a shelf in the garage, and there it rotted while I froze in that truck.

HIS GRANDFATHER'S WISDOM
"IF YOU DON'T WORK, YOU DON'T EAT"

MP: Could he read the Bible?
CT: He could make out certain words in the Bible. When he got a portion of it, like most of the people I knew, most were uneducated and most were functionally illiterate and many were totally illiterate, they would get a part of the Bible that they would memorize or that would become a part of their lexicon.

MP: What was some of the advice your grandfather would give you?
CT: He had lots of sayings. Some of them weren't exactly complimentary. He was without education so he had to learn things the hard way. He had to learn through experience in the school of hard knocks, and he was passing it on.

He thought that we were destined to have to work for everything because of what happened in the Garden of Eden, and because of our fallen nature. And we would have to earn everything by the sweat of our brow—that was biblical. And we would have to work from sun to sun, biblical. "If you don't work, you don't eat"—biblical. The philosophy of life that he had came from biblical sources.

He was a literalist. I guess today they would say he was an originalist or he was a textualist, but he was literal in that sense like people arguing over a literal notion out of the Bible.

We would often say we couldn't do something; he would make us. I mean, he pushed you to the limit. And when we went to the country to work on the farm, you got up at 4:00. And then when you didn't want to do work, he'd say things like, "You have no trouble with work. You can lay by it all day and never touch it." I think of course the proper English is lie by, but he just says, "Lay about all day and never touch it." Or if you don't work hard enough, or you're not making much effort, he just looked at you and he said, "Boy, you're worth a carload of dead men to me."

MP: Didn't he say, "Hard times make monkey eat cayenne pepper"? What did that mean?

CT: He would say to us ominously, "There are things in your life that are hard, that one day you're going to have to do." We were sitting at the table, I sat at one end of the table, my grandfather sat directly across in front of me at the longer end at the other end, and my brother sat to one side and my grandmother on the other. I spent every meal that we had at that table looking at my grandfather. And in those days when you were a child, you were not permitted to initiate conversation. You are to be seen and not heard. You are to speak when you're spoken to. That was it. And that was enforced.

We're Catholic, so we ate fish on Friday. So my grandmother served us fish early on. It had a head on it. Well, we got to the head and we wouldn't eat the head and we definitely weren't eating the eye. My grandfather, staring at us, said, "Why aren't you eating the head?" I'm not eating that. And he goes on this lecture about, "You all got it too good. And if you were starving, you'd eat it." And then he tries to persuade us to eat it by telling us about his grandmother and that she ate cow eyes. Now, I don't think it is a persuasive argument to tell a kid that somebody else ate cow eyes and therefore you should eat a fish head. No, it did not work.

Now I'm definitely not eating fish head or cow eyes. So it's in that context that he would say, "Hard times make monkey eat cayenne pepper." But it has a larger meaning. He didn't say cayenne. He said, "Hard times make monkey eat Carrie-Anne pepper." And it would be years later when I was in the grocery store that I bought cayenne pepper. When people can't read and don't see the written word, they repeat derivations or mispronunciations if not malapropisms that they hear from others. So "cayenne" from someone who has never seen the actual word becomes "Carrie-Anne." So at any rate we knew what he meant. You will eat very, very hot peppers if you have no choice. But I'm not eating a cow eye.

MP: Did he ever use corporal punishment with you and Myers?
CT: You got whippings. When we were kids, we all received our just deserts. We've confused or conflated punishment and abuse. What used to just be punishment has now become the equivalent of abuse. All corporal punishment is abuse today.

It may be abusive to send undisciplined kids in the world. My grandfather was never abusive—ever. He never hit us in anger. He never punched us or anything like that. He would tell us, "If you do 'A,' you're going to receive this just punishment." He was never abusive. He was hard but never really mean.

MP: A very good distinction.
CT: Someone asked about whether the nuns gave you corporal punishment. And my answer normally is, "Not as much as I deserved." My grandfather was a just and honest person. I remember there were few times, and since I was the older brother, not by much but I was

the older brother, I would sometimes be held responsible for my brother and me. And there were times that I would say that, you know, I didn't do certain things and then he would agree, "Maybe you didn't do it." And I had already been punished. And he would say, "That's for the one you got away with." If you're Catholic, you examine your conscience. And we have Catholic guilt anyway, so, yeah, I haven't gotten all I deserve. I'm lucky to get away this easy.

The Nuns
"You knew they loved you"

MP: How did your grandfather become Roman Catholic?
CT: My grandfather wasn't much for it. He said his father was a jackleg preacher. That's self-taught. My grandfather thought his father took advantage of his mother and that's how he was born. So that was one problem he had.

Most of the religions around us that blacks were involved in were more evangelical. My grandfather wasn't into a lot of jumping and falling out and expressive stuff. And he certainly wasn't into being in church all day on Sunday. He would say to me, "Boy, if God knows everything, why you've got to be in church more than an hour?"

Of course, I couldn't say anything, but my question is, "Why do you have to be in at all if he knows everything? He knows what you're thinking and you can just call it a day." But I wasn't going to say that—that would have gotten me in trouble.

Sometime in the late forties or so, Mr. Sam Williams—who was another black gentleman who was a friend of my grandfather's and another black businessman, and they were in business together for a while—he was a Catholic convert, and he persuaded my grandfather to attend St. Benedict's. And he liked it. He liked the order, he loved the liturgy, he liked the discipline. He converted, and he was a very devout Catholic.

When we went to live with him, my grandfather took my brother to St. Benedict's, and my brother hadn't started school yet. The nuns of course admitted him immediately.[9] Then he took me, and they looked at my attendance record and that was, oh boy. I hadn't really gone to school very much. I was nominally a second grader. There was some doubt, but they liked him. They allowed me to start second grade on his word.

Now the curious thing about going to live with my grandparents was nobody ever exchanged any papers. I was never adopted, they never got formal custody. There was never any guardianship papers. And yet they could put me in school; they could take me to the health department. They could claim me on their tax return. It was a different era.

MP: What was Catholic school like for you?
CT: Fabulous. When we started, you had to invest in school uniforms. We wore blue pants, and they were gabardine or something, and a blue tie and a white shirt. The rule was, in our house, you wore the shirt two or three days. And because they were all cotton they had to be ironed. My grandmother made our lunch, usually bologna sandwich or ham. You had egg on Fridays or fish, obviously non-meat. And she'd make a peanut-butter-and-jelly sandwich as dessert. She made it every morning, every single morning. And then my grandfather left us money for milk. And usually in the early days it was, I think, a nickel. There would always be two nickels, one for my brother, one for me. He would leave it every single morning. It almost brings tears to your eyes.

The Catholic schools were very orderly. It was segregated. The nuns didn't much appreciate the fact that blacks were treated that way. They were mostly Irish nuns and they were outspoken too. Oh God,

I love it. They were on our side from day one. We would start lining up in the school yard two by two, grade by grade. And you said the Pledge of Allegiance. And then you walked in.

MP: And was there discipline and hard work?
CT: It was very disciplined. There were about forty kids per class and no noise. My brother used to say, "When you walked in there, you could hear a gnat tiptoeing across cotton." It's an old building with double hung panes, and even compared to the black public schools, these schools were in bad shape as a physical plant. They were old buildings. But the education was fabulous.

You knew the nuns cared about you. They lived at the convent, across the street from the school. You knew that the nuns cared enough to live there. They didn't come in from suburbs. You knew they loved you. When you think somebody loves you and deeply cares about your interests, somehow, they can get you to do hard things. I found that even in the worst days, even when I had fallen away from the Church, I would go visit the nuns. Somehow, I would find a way back to go sit and say hello.

MP: The nuns were called racial slurs sometimes, including being called the "n——er nuns"?
CT: They were called a lot of things. Because they worked with black kids, and they thought that these racial barriers were wrong. Some people called them pejoratives, including the N-word. They never backed down when it came to us. And I think they wore that as a badge of honor.

MP: Who was Sister Virgilius? Why was she important to you?
CT: Sister Mary Virgilius Reidy became the embodiment of what they were. Sister Virgilius was from Kerry, Ireland. She was scary because

she was the principal of my grammar school, and she was a tough Irish nun. But there were other nuns who had influenced me before her. Sister Mary Aquin, my seventh-grade teacher who trained me to be an altar boy and was as sweet as they came. Both she and her blood sister, Sister Mary Daniel, were down there, and I got to know them. They became like my favorite aunts over the years. Sister Mary Katherine was in the sixth grade. She was as sweet, as kind as they came. She was older. Sister Mary Francis Paul was in the fifth grade. She was tough and beautiful, and young and energetic. Sister Mary Geraldine was fourth grade, just a very kind person. That's when you started learning geography. Sister Mary Chrysostom, she was third grade. She made us memorize the multiplication table. In those days you had to memorize it up to twelve; that took a total in my life of less than an hour, I think. And then we spent the next month and a half or so waiting on other people to do it. Sister Mary Consuello was in charge of the convent. She was always generous beyond perhaps their means.

Sister Mary Virgilius, my eighth-grade teacher, when she saw my entrance exam scores to high school, she looks me in the eye in 1962 and says, "You lazy thing, you." In other words, I was underachieving. It was actually accurate, and I've never forgotten it.

About twenty years later, I sought her out, tried to find my nuns, and she was in Boston, Massachusetts, retired from teaching. I went by to see her, and I sat with her, and I thanked her for teaching me and making me believe that we could learn, and for not letting me slip into victim status and forcing me out of it.

She had a tough edge, but they were like your favorite aunts, all the nuns. And then I started wondering, like I did with my grandfather, what did it take for them to be so tough, when underneath it was just warm and fuzzy and kind. To have that kind of discipline. I got to know them as a non-student, as an adult, and they were the sweetest loving people. Think of what love it took for them to force us not to fall into that victim status and to demand much from us, to keep a game face on. I got to know them later in life; they didn't have to have a game face, and they were totally different.

MP: What was your grandfather's attitude towards your going to school?
CT: My grandfather understood that education was the key because he didn't have it, and that's what held him back. He wasn't going to let that happen to his boys. And he said that he went to third grade, but school was three months out of the year because you had to work. Education wasn't some social experiment. It wasn't a lot of this drivel you hear today. It was the key. It was something that had to be done. Reading, writing, arithmetic, and, by golly, you are going to learn it. You were never going to miss a day of school. And he made that very clear. Remember now I am seven years old, my brother is six, and he says to us, "You are going to go to school every day. And if you are sick, you are still going, and if you die, you will go. I will take your body for three days and make sure you're not faking." And he meant it. The thing about it is, it's one thing if somebody says that and you think they're exaggerating. He wasn't that kind of guy. In your mind you knew he had laid down a marker. Nothing you did or said was going to get you out of going to school. You were going to go dead or alive. Well or sick. And that's the way we went.

CARNEGIE LIBRARY
"THIS WONDERFUL OASIS OF LEARNING"

MP: You loved going to the library. Why was that important to you?
CT: We're little kids in the summer of 1955, still living on Henry Lane with my mother. Half a block over is Henry Street, right on the corner

on Henry Street near East Broad is the Carnegie Library.[10] On Saturdays, someone told us, "Carnegie Library has a reading session, all you got to do is go over." They had little chairs and a lady read to you. Most importantly, they gave you cookies and juice afterwards. Of course, because of my desire to learn, I went over for my cookie and juice. And that's when I was introduced to Dr. Seuss at that library.

Under the front of the library, there's a basement area and I would go there. I would continue to go there when I lived with my grandparents. Then about the fourth grade or so, they allowed us to go upstairs to the real library where the big books are. It was everything. My grandfather, who threw up every roadblock to prevent you from being on a sports team, who would always find something for you to do if you were just sort of sitting around, if you announced you have to go to the library, he would suddenly say you don't have to work today, and he would drop you off. It became this world that, despite anything else was going on, you could go to a library.

A few years later, when they desegregated the Savannah Public Library, I must have made a hundred trips over there. I was a regular over there. You walked through white neighborhoods, black neighborhoods, night, day. Nobody ever said or did anything to me. My view of libraries, particularly the Carnegie Library, is just this wonderful oasis of learning, of peace, of quiet, of just wonderment.

MP: The Carnegie Library was segregated, right? What were some of the books you read there?
CT: Everything was segregated. It was a way of life. You went on with your life. Any book you wanted you could get. It would be like being in a regional library. You couldn't get "book A" because, "We don't have it here today, but it'll be here tomorrow." It was like a branch library. Is it right for it to be segregated? No, but you could get every book.

I loved the Horatio Hornblower books. Why I was interested in that is beyond me, but they were interesting. I loved any sports book. My favorite is *Crazy Legs McBain*.[11]

One of the advantages of the library being right there in my neighborhood, and as a result of being segregated, one of my classmate's mother, Mrs. Cameron, was one of the librarians. And they lived up the lane from us. We were on the farm during the summer, so I couldn't get to the library. Mrs. Cameron would make it to the 8:00 Mass, which is the one we went to, and she would bring me more library books, four or five, every Sunday. And I would read those four or five and then exchange them with her again the following Sunday. Now if I were at Savannah Public Library [the whites-only library], I couldn't do that. But I was able to do that because Mrs. Cameron was my friend's mother, she was a neighbor, and she was a fellow Catholic.

LESSONS FROM WORKING ON THE FARM
"OLD MAN CAN'T IS DEAD, I HELPED BURY HIM"

MP: I wanted to ask about the farm. When did you go there and what were your grandfather's plans for you there?
CT: We had spent many years going out to the country. It was customary in those years in the fifties to take rides on Sundays. It was a day of rest, the Lord's Day. The streets were pretty much empty. There were no businesses open.

My grandfather would take us for Sunday afternoon rides. You went to 8:00 Mass. We would take a ride out to see my grandmother's folks in Bryan County, and my grandfather's folks in Liberty County. We would also do that on certain holidays, especially Christmas. We would ride out and spend time with Cousin Hattie and Cousin Robert Chip in Liberty County.

On our second Christmas with my grandparents, toward the end of that day, my grandfather said, "Let's go over to where I grew up on the farm." And that was right next to his Uncle Charles, where he was raised ultimately. He drove up on now fallow fields, and we walked across this field to where there was an oak tree, and he looked around, and pulled out some old cord, and twine, and some sticks, and he marked off where he was going to build a house. We stepped it off, and he marked it off.

Then we started bringing cinder blocks out, and it became every weekend, and every day off, and he started building a house. And that house is still there. We finished that in May of 1958, and every summer after that we farmed. I turned ten in 1958. You started clearing land and we started building garages, and built barns, chicken coops. We had to dig a well for water. We built a pump house, screened in the porches. It was constant activity. He said that even if all we could do was hold a nail, we were going to be there to hold that one nail.

Then we started farming. We started plowing with Cousin Jack's horse, Lizzie, which was a very spirited animal. We would go running behind them. When you were on the farm, we were barefooted and the horses were plowing up the dirt, and we're running along behind them, and occasionally they plowed up a snake. We'd scurry a little bit. And he said, "You all need to worry about those two-legged snakes out here. That snake's not going to bother you." And then we started doing corn and beans and peas, and okra.

MP: What was the reason he gave for why he brought you out to the farm?
CT: My grandfather thought that we were, as he said, "getting up in age," and he thought we needed to be kept busy during the summer. And he didn't want us around our "no good friends" in the city, "that riff raff." He said, "Idle hands are the devil's workshop." That was

reiterated every place you went. He wasn't going to have us with idle hands. He wanted us also to experience the way he grew up, in the ways, he said, "of slavery time."

He thought that the best way to do that was on the farm. Your time is dominated by labor, and there's a lot of it, from sun to sun. You woke up at "fo day," which means "before day." And you labored. You would always find there's always more work than you had time. Even if we couldn't do much, he would make us go. We put up fence lines, we cut down trees, and he would always do it manually. You didn't use a chainsaw, you used to crosscut saw. It seems like everything was done to be doubly hard.

You're a little kid and you say you can't do it. And he would just say over and over, "Old man can't is dead, I helped bury him." And that wasn't just him sitting down and explaining something to you. That was his reaction to your desire to quit. "You can't quit." And he would say it.

A Metaphor for Life
"You start out with something hard, you get blisters, you get the pain, and then you become toughened to it"

CT: You're building a fence line. You had to learn how to stretch barbed wire.

If you did something stupid, he would say to you, "You know what? If I could cultivate your head down to the size of your brain, a peanut hull would make you a sun hat." Now that's not exactly a compliment.

You had to learn how to gut fish. You don't want to be there and up to your eyebrow in scales and fish guts, and the smell. And then the accompaniments: the flies, the gnats, the mosquitos, et cetera. And you'd say you want to give up. And he said, "You can give out, but you can't give up."

My grandmother would say, "You should give them a compliment." And he said, "No, that's their job to do it right."

He had total control of us and the environment. Today people don't have control of their kids' time, at any time. They're on the Internet. They have cell phones. Well, he could monopolize it all. We didn't even have a phone out there. He dominated our time, and in the long run that was good for us. He was able to teach us things that way.

You've got to put up a hog pen, a chicken coop, or something. First, you've got to clear undergrowth, you've got shrubbery, you've got trees. You never cut a live oak tree. That is a mortal sin. You cut other trees, pines, things like that, little scrap trees, but never a live oak.

How do you clear land? How do you clear out all that shrubbery? You see what I'm saying? You use an axe. You use a bush hook. You use a crosscut saw. We had the one with two handles on it. So now your little hands are learning how to use a bush hook. A bush hook handle is longer than an ax handle, it has a beak on the end. You have to bend down because you have to cut low to the ground. If that tip catches something, it wants to twist. When something torques like that, it causes a blister, it rips the skin off.

At the beginning of every summer, with the axe, the cross-cut saw, the sling, the bush hook, the carrying of things, pulling of things, no gloves, your hands at the beginning get this blister, then you get blood in that blister. Then the blister becomes hard. By the end of the summer your hands all the way across underneath your fingers are all calluses. That became for me the metaphor about life, or at least an example of life experience. You start out with something hard, you get blisters, you get the pain, and then you become toughened to it. You get calluses, and you're able to work even more.

MP: You've mentioned that your grandfather had some interesting sayings when you were on the farm.
CT: When you weren't shoveling a whole lot, he would actually take the shovel from you, and hand it to somebody else, and say, "Go put the shovel up and bring me a teaspoon because for the amount of work he is doing all he needs is a teaspoon."

Or if you do something really stupid, he would say, "You know what boy? I'm a ship your head off to J. Edgar Hoover to see what's wrong with your brain."[12]

He was not promoting your self-esteem. He wasn't there to boost you up. He wanted his work done. My grandmother would say, "Myers, you should give these boys a dollar for every A they get in school." "No. I pay the tuition. Their job is to get an A."

When I got a little older, I was kind of feeling my oats. He told me do something, I don't even know what it was, and I told him, "Isn't slavery over?" And his response was, "Not in my damn house."

MP: You have said that working on the farm and in the oil truck were the most important classrooms to you.
CT: Because it was with him. When we went to live with him, he said, "I'm going to tell you to do as I do, not as I say" and so he was a teacher. Years later, my brother and I were talking on the phone. It was probably 4:00 in the morning. We groused about my grandfather because he got us up between 2:30 and 4:00 every morning. "Time to get up!" If you try to sleep late on Saturdays till daybreak, he would yell at you, "You all think y'all rich!" My brother and I were on the phone and he said, "Can you imagine? We are having a call at 4:00 in the morning. And when we were kids, we swore that we would never get up at the time that man was waking us up."

Growing Up in the Segregated South
"You were never allowed to walk to the interior of that park"

MP: Your grandfather was a supporter of the NAACP.[13]
CT: My grandfather was a lifelong member of the NAACP. That's back in the day when the NAACP was fighting the segregation laws, and segregation in schools, and jobs discrimination, the black codes, that sort of thing. He was one of the few who actually went to virtually every Sunday meeting. When I was in high school, especially when I was in seminary, he would make me go with him. And I was shocked at how few people were actually at those meetings. He didn't work for the school system, or the government in any way. He didn't work for the university. He worked for himself. Because of that, he could use his property. When you had the students at Savannah State College sitting in at the lunch counters at Kress and places like Woolworth, he could use his property to bail them out of jail. He and Sam Williams and Mr. Ben Wise, because they were businesspeople, they were more independent and were able to decide whether to be involved in civil rights. People make it seem as though the Civil Rights Movement was this wave that swept across all black people. That's nonsense. There were different pockets of that. There were some who were more involved than others. And my grandfather was one of the most involved and committed.

MP: Didn't the Ku Klux Klan march through Savannah in 1960?
CT: It was annual. The Ku Klux Klan march, to my knowledge, was an annual event. You were told about it and that day you didn't go downtown. But some blacks were down there. There may have been confrontation. I just don't remember hearing much about it. There

seemed to be more confrontation during the St. Patrick's Day events than it was during that. But it was downtown Savannah.

MP: The South is segregated in these years. What does that really mean? And how did you experience it?
CT: It's really interesting. People would ask me things like, "How often did you run from the Klan?" And I said, "But I've never seen the Klan." You knew they were downtown once a year or something, or in some of the rural areas. You'd read about it. I followed *Crisis* magazine.[14] I have a real issue with the Klan. But that wasn't in my day-to-day life. My day-to-day life was going to school, playing with my friends when my grandfather didn't have us under his wings. It was what kids did. You watched Roy Rogers on TV, watched Hop-along Cassidy, and you watched the Cisco Kid, and Superman.

I think sometimes in retrospect people talk of that era as though it was all about civil rights. And that it was all that happened in your life. Well, that's not true.

Civil rights was, for kids, it was a minor part of your life. Doesn't mean it wasn't important. I think that the technological developments going on in life, and the world at that time, have been important in our lives, like the space program.

Segregation meant we lived in our neighborhood. It was a safe neighborhood. The neighbors were fabulous people. I mean, everybody knew each other. I walked to school every day. You walk past these businesses. First would be Madden Brothers right behind our house, that was a meatpacking company. I think he was Jewish. Then it was Mr. Ben Wise, black gentleman. Then, Reverend Bailey. Mr. Moon, another Black gentleman, all of them are black. And he had a fish market. Then the next business was Mr. Goodman, Jewish. Then across the street there was Mr. Lee. And for years, we all thought he was Chinese, and they would refer to him as Chinese.

In my thirties, I went over and he would always come out and hug me, and in his accent he would talk with me. I asked him in the 1980s, "How did someone of Chinese descent wind up in Savannah, Georgia?" And he said, "I'm not Chinese. I'm Korean." Mr. Grady, at the gas station, he was a white gentleman. That was my neighborhood. You never thought twice. I mean, where you ran into segregation was in schools. Neighborhoods were more checkerboard. There were two white ladies who lived at the end of our block. The next street over was white. The next block up was white.

I couldn't go to the Savannah Public Library early on. But then I got the right to go. The irony: what is interesting about life is that people will complain about not having the right to go, but never complain about the fact that when people have the right, they don't go. My grandfather was an adamant man. So when he got the right to vote, I mean he protected that right to vote. He would vote if you were voting on a dogcatcher. He would be the first at the poll. He would be there when the polls opened. And you're talking about learning from somebody, I still do that today. I will comfortably wait until a few people now get there first. But I just like to vote early. And I just think that if you have the right, you're obligated.

MP: How were you treated when you went to the Savannah Public Library?
CT: The interesting thing is nobody ever said anything to me. Initially they stared at you, and there might have been a few people who were gruff and tried to make you uncomfortable. Well, good luck with that. I recently ran into a lady who really got emotional when she saw me, and she's quite elderly now, and she said, "I helped you at the public library when you were a kid." To me that pretty much said it all. There were a lot of people who helped me. For example, at the little bookstore in Savannah, there were these white ladies and they showed me the *Funk*

and Wagnall's Dictionary, which I still have. It doesn't have a cover on it anymore. They showed me the preparation books for the SAT's. They were the ones who showed me vocabulary-building books when I was trying to build a vocabulary to learn Standard English. They were the ones that probably introduced me to Ralph Ellison, to Ayn Rand.

At the same time, I'd go to the Carnegie Library, which was black. And those ladies were nice to me. So, you know, yeah, there was segregation. It was absolutely wrong. Now, if you went downtown shopping, there were rules and there was some conflict, not conflict really, there could be unpleasantness. There were some restaurants you couldn't go to, which was wrong. One of the major parks downtown is a rectangle, much like this table, Forsyth Park. And the rule, I never saw it written any place, but the unwritten rule that was passed on to us, that we obeyed, was that you were never allowed to walk to the interior of that park. You were only allowed to walk around the perimeter. And that's how I learned the word "circumnavigate." So, you could walk around this all you want. You could not go across the park. And there were other practices or customs that prevented us from doing all sorts of things. But just as a kid growing up, I did not run into conflict with a lot of those.

MP: When did you start to run into this type of conflict?
CT: Where I began to run up against those was when I went to seminary in 1964, and now I'm in an all-white school. Now if you have white classmates, and you're in a predominately white school, let's say for example, we went to Shoney's Big Boy restaurant on Victory Drive in Savannah. And I remember walking in there. I'd never been in there. I knew it had been segregated. I walked in some time '65 or '66. And the place would get, oh my goodness, you could hear a pin drop. That was, that was difficult. There were some other unpleasantness like that, being with a white group crossing lines, because

my white classmates did it. But when you grow up in an all-black environment, you live in a world that's separate from that.

COLORISM—A DIFFERENT KIND OF DISCRIMINATION
"THERE WERE CLASS DIFFERENCES AND COLOR DIFFERENCES"

MP: Let's talk about another kind of racial prejudice that you have written about as well and that is within the black community.
CT: People don't like to talk about it. They try to mask it with what they call solidarity. And we're not supposed to air our dirty laundry. Those are all those things that minimize or mask those differences. But obviously there were class differences and color differences.

When I was in school, people called it a "paper bag test," or "cafe-au-lait test." If you want to go to certain colleges, your skin color had to be the color of a paper bag, a brown paper bag, or cafe-au-lait. You had to be light skinned.

My granddaddy said, "You had to be light, bright, and damn near white" to go to some of these schools. There was a color line, and a class line. And they had their organizations, whether it's Jack and Jill, or The Links, or whatever. They had their cotillions and their little groups, their fraternities, and sororities that were based on class and color. Now that may have evaporated or disappeared over the years. But just like some of the unwritten rules in Savannah, there were these. There were places you were not wanted within the race. You can sort of excuse it and say they were mimicking general society. Well, that's a poor excuse because my reaction would be, if what the others are doing to you is wrong, then you don't do it to yourself.

My grandfather was very firm about those class things. If there was something that really got under his skin, it would be that—that he was being put down by people who thought they were superior to him within our race.

MP: What did "ABC" mean?
CT: America's Blackest Child. In the sixties and the fifties, people would insult you by calling you black. Since I'm dark skinned, I would be easy pickings. And there were people who were loudmouths and perhaps fair in complexion. One of their insults would be ABC, America's Blackest Child. And that was supposed to be an insult. But it never really got under my skin that much. I'm black. So how is that insulting?

MOVIES TO REMEMBER
TO KILL A MOCKINGBIRD AND BARBERSHOP

MP: You mentioned that Aunt Tina's favorite book was *To Kill a Mockingbird*.[15]
CT: The movie came out sometime in the sixties, and it was black and white, with Gregory Peck. And I must have saw that three, four, maybe five times. And I swear that was my first idea of becoming a lawyer. To see Atticus Finch defend that black gentleman. Who's the mob today? Who is burning torches? Who is going to convict people without a trial, to indict people without evidence? Doesn't mean you're going to be victorious. But it means you've done the right thing. And that's when I read the book. One of the things I do regret is that I wish I'd gotten to meet Harper Lee before she passed away.[16] There's a lot in that book. I don't know how you understand it if you didn't grow up like that. So much in that movie brought back the relationships, the complicated relationships.

MP: You saw your culture in the book. Is that the way you read it?
CT: It's closer to the way. Movies like the most recent movie on the black women at NASA [*Hidden Figures*].[17] That's more of what I grew up with, women like that. Families like that, fighting odds, believing that you could do any job. Or a movie [called *Something the Lord Made*] about the guy who helped to operate on blue babies.[18] Those are the kind of black people I grew up around. The environment you see in the South was like that. People were positive, hard working. There was discrimination, and bigotry, and things like that. But their reaction to it was it was something that elevated you. That made you want to be better than you thought you could be. And that's what I think of my grandfather and my nuns. They made you want to be better than you thought you could be.

MP: You also talked about the movie *Barbershop*.[19]
CT: The movie *Barbershop* reminds me of the barbershop when I was a kid. There was every opinion, all sorts of people, from the most devout Christian, the most erudite minister, to scam artists, to the numbers runner. I loved it. They'd have *Ebony* magazine and they'd have *Jet*. And you're listening to the conversation. But there are signs on the wall like, "Old man credit is dead. Bad pay killed him." Or, "If you have nothing to do, don't do it here." Sitting in the barbershop, you had opinions, you had arguments, you had people with different beliefs, and it had humor. There would be some guy coming in, and they would exchange pieces of paper, and I would tell my granddaddy about it, and he'd say, "That's the bolita man" [numbers runner], something like that. And it was just really fascinating. I loved it. Every two weeks we got a haircut.

The opinions went from [Marcus] Garvey to debt and religions, from Catholic to the United House of Prayer, Seventh Day Adventists. Everybody was there. Politically, a lot of blacks were Republicans; the

Republican Party was the anti-slavery party. This is before the War on Poverty and the Civil Rights Movement sort of blending into the Democrat party.[20] They would give Catholics—they thought we were worshipping the pope and idols in church—all that sort of thing. But it was really vibrant. I loved going to the barbershop.

CHAPTER TWO

IN THE SEMINARY

"I'm the new kid, so I'm the outsider, and I'm black.
So, obviously I didn't fit right in"

**MP: How did you come to your decision to go to minor seminary
and become a priest?**[1]
CT: That was a natural progression. You went to Catholic schools.
You became an altar boy. In those days, you had to memorize Latin.
And you had to have the capacity to memorize it. And you have to
have people like my grandfather who would make sure you got there
in time to serve the 6:00 a.m. Mass. It was a big deal to be an altar
boy. When you became the lead altar boy, you were serving the high
Masses, which I eventually did.

When they had events at the cathedral, you went there. One of
the events they had as a part of that, for altar boys, was an event at
the minor seminary for the Diocese of Savannah.[2] It was just out on
the edge of Savannah, on the Isle of Hope. I had never been there.

It was one Sunday afternoon and may have been a bit of a recruiting
event. So I went and played sports, and they had different things. I saw
the school, and I said, "Wow, this would be perfect for me."

So I told my grandfather, who wasn't initially all that excited because it was expensive. And I remember when he took me to the front porch to have a talk, and I told him that I thought I had a vocation, and it would be great, and he said, "Well, if you go, you know you can't quit."

MP: Tell us a little about the minor seminary you went to. It just started to admit black students, so what was it like?
CT: I showed up one Sunday evening with my grandfather. He drove me there and he dropped me off, and then he left. And so I'm there by myself, and I look around. Most of the kids there are all white in my class, and they all knew each other because they'd been there before as freshmen. I'm the new kid, so I'm the outsider, and I'm black. So, obviously I didn't fit right in. So, I was like, "What the heck?"

That evening, I saw that there was another black kid there, Richard Chisholm. He was in the freshman class. His sister had been a classmate of mine at St. Benedict's, and then again at St. Pius.[3] So, at least I wasn't the only one, but we were the first blacks at the school. And to their credit, they did not make a big deal of it. In any world there is going to be some uncomfortable moments. And some kids are better than others. But for the most part, there was nobody chasing you. There was nobody yelling at you. There was no real fanfare about it. There were no parents protesting, none of that happened. And it's just the early difficulties that you would have at that age, and at that time.

MP: The school was demanding.
CT: It was the first time I was in an environment where you were surrounded by people, constantly, who were educated and who could help you. Throughout the years I had been in school, no one in our household could help me with a single thing in homework. You learn how to do things on your own. From third grade on, I was the best reader in

the house. No one can help you with math. No one can help you with the multiplication table. All they can do is tell you to do your homework. When you were in the seminary, you were always around people who knew some of the answers. When you were taking Latin, if you didn't know a declension, or conjugation, or an exception to a particular rule, or a certain vocabulary word, or didn't know the syntax of something, then someone was there who could explain it to you.

The other thing that was different, was what I was doing after school. When I lived with my grandparents, I was working and then I was studying in the late evening. Now, you have structured two hours of studying. You have to be at a desk in the study hall. You had an assigned desk, and you would sit at that desk, and that's where you would do your work. And there would be an older student sitting at the front of the room, watching to make sure you weren't sleeping and were doing your homework, or not goofing off. There was a lot of focus on you studying at the appropriate times, and that emphasis showed me the level at which you had to engage in preparation in order to excel. And then when you saw how much the better students were studying, you could see a model. Here's what I need to be doing. So if I'm studying at level five, and I see someone studying at level six, then I would have to up my game.

MP: Were you worried in this more demanding academic environment that you wouldn't succeed, initially? Did you have a fear of failure in the early days there?
CT: Virtually anybody who winds up in a situation in which they think that there's a possibility they may not get through it, I worried about that, to some extent. That would haunt me throughout the rest of my academic career.

We're sitting on the front porch, and I'm telling my grandfather I want to go to the seminary, and that's a big deal. This is religiously a big deal, racially a big deal, family-wise a big deal, financially a huge deal. This is not just, "Oh my kid is going off to become a priest." This is huge on every front.

And one aspect of that was the racial part. Savannah is still a segregated city. My grandfather is active in the NAACP. There is this firm belief, almost of biblical proportions, that if we had a chance as a race, we could do as well as anybody else. Heard it at home. You heard it from other blacks, the older blacks, whether they were working as maids. It was absolutely universal. If we had a chance, we could do as well as anybody else. To my nuns, it was almost a matter of religion that this was the case.

One of the sayings among blacks at that time was, "We had to work twice as hard to get half as far." The idea that you had to make double the effort was an accepted way of life. And that you would get one half, if you're lucky, of the results, was an accepted way of life.

When I first got there, and it's an unknown. You're a kid. It's a new world in every way. It's a foreign world. The work is much more demanding than even St. Pius was. It's pretty aggressive. So obviously that would create the sense in you that I may not be able to live up to the expectation.

We got report cards after every six weeks. Father [William] Coleman was the head of the school, and we had to sit outside of his room. And I was sitting on the floor that Sunday evening, students going in, getting their report cards, and some coming out pretty sad. And then it was my turn, and I was scared to death. I did fine; I never had academic issues.

Father Coleman said to me that I would not be considered the equal of whites if I didn't learn how to speak Standard English. And I can remember, to this day, going back to the chapel and praying. I said, "My God, that was a put down." But one of the things he did was offer to help me. He was from Connecticut, so he offered to help me speak Standard English. Again remember, I'm someplace between my dialect and quote unquote, "talking Southern," but certainly nothing close to Standard English.

MP: You were hurt by his comment?
CT: I went to the chapel. But internally I vowed to learn English, and that no one would be able to ever say that about me. As much as it hurt, there was some truth to it. I did not speak Standard English. I found the English language almost indecipherable. If I were reading a book of modest difficulty, it would take probably, ten, fifteen, twenty minutes. I had read someplace that you never skip over a word you don't know. And I began the practice of writing down every word I didn't know on that page, underlining it, writing it down, looking it up in my *Funk & Wagnalls Dictionary*, and then trying to memorize the definition.

MP: You mean ten or twenty minutes per page?
CT: Ten or twenty minutes per page. Now when one reads at that pace—when you're looking up words, trying to write down definitions, it is not leisurely reading. And it would take years before I had a vocabulary that was significant enough and large enough to be able to read a page without looking up words.

RACIAL DIFFICULTIES IN THE SEMINARY
"THESE WERE CHALLENGING TIMES"

MP: In addition to your challenges with your studies, you also had some unfortunate episodes because of your race. I recall one involving a spelling bee contest.
CT: Like the old spelling bee, we had our Latin Bee—you stand around the room, it was declensions, conjugations, things like that.

It was just like any spelling bee, you make a mistake, you sit down. I was the last person standing. The prize was a St. Jude statue. It wasn't an expensive statue. And I won that. That statue, more than any award that I've gotten in life, was probably one of the most important, if not *the* most important. It certainly was at that point, the most important. St. Jude is the patron saint of hopeless cases.

I put it on my bureau in my dorm, left to do something else, and came back and the head was broken off. No one would say who did it. I glued it on, came back another time, and it was broken off. There were a couple of guys smirking, and you sort of had an idea of who was involved. And I glued it on again, and never had another problem. I always kept that St. Jude with the broken head with me. I took it to every job. I always made sure it was in my office, always around me. I loaned it to a friend when he was going through some difficulties, since I was on the Court, and unfortunately it got lost.

MP: How did you feel when your classmates broke the head off the statue?
CT: Well, not happy about it. Your initial reaction is one of disappointment. And then you're angry. One of the things I learned from my grandfather about these emotions, they can control you, or you can control them. And I watched that great man who could get really upset about things from time to time, control his own passions and his emotions, so that he could do things that he needed to do. You can indulge yourself with your emotions. You're angry, and you can feel really empowered by your anger. Well, your anger can also be your undoing. So, I just go to chapel, and pray. And I stayed focused on what I was there to do.

MP: Justice Thomas, can you share with us the story about the comments about the great running back Jim Brown?

CT: We were sitting there watching the NFL championship and Jim Brown was having one of his patented games, and he broke away on a run, and one of these guys says, "Look at that n—a go." Well, I got up and left. And it was just horrible. Yeah, and then of course, I did go to chapel, because you know anger is one of those things, if you let it consume you, it just eats up everything.

There was another experience which stands out. After dinner one night, in the spring, we all were at the basketball court, and there was an uneven number of us. We went to shoot; whoever makes the basket, you decide which team, you choose your players, you choose up sides, and you play two on two, or three on three, whatever it was. Well, I made the first basket. And then the other guys went off and decided among themselves to play each other. And then I was the odd person out, and I can still remember making that long walk across the field, all the way to the front of the seminary. That these were people who would, for whatever reasons, could be racial—that they would exclude me—they would violate the rules that we agreed on, to choose up teams in this way, was hard.

But what I chose to do, and others could say they would have done it differently, was to make the long walk and just go to chapel, because there would be other times in my life when things like this would happen. These were challenging moments.

I think that sometimes you can react to things in a way that actually winds up making your point a lot better than just returning negative behavior with negative behavior.

MP: That's clearly the long view. It's hard to have that at fifteen or sixteen years old.
CT: We were actually taught to have the longer view, and that was my grandfather. Think of his entire life. What was going to school? The longer view. What was going to church? The eternal longer view.

What was self-discipline? The longer view. When you talked about deferred gratification, the longer view. So the summers were spent planting, the longer view. Raising a hog or chicken, the longer view. You're storing up. The whole life was to take a longer view, to prepare for the rainy day, to prepare for the future, to think ahead. So I guess, yeah, in your youth, your longer view may not be so long, but it's not instant gratification, which would entail yelling and screaming and carrying on.

MP: What about the time one of your classmates wrote you a note about Martin Luther King Jr.?
CT: One day we were sitting in class, I don't know, maybe history class, or something. And these are small classes, and people pass notes from time to time. So I get a note; the note said, "I like Martin Luther King," and then you open up the inside, and it just had the word: "dead." You have a range of emotions—disappointment, anger. You want to lash out. You want to yell.

FINDING COMMON GROUND
"I'M BLACK. I'M DIFFERENT; I GOT THAT PART. WHAT DO WE HAVE IN COMMON?"

MP: How did you deal with going to a school where you are in the distinct minority in the class?
CT: When I was in the seminary, you just walk in the room, look at your classmates—they're white, I'm black. I'm different; I got that part. What do we have in common? That's what I started thinking through. We're Catholic. We're all about the same age. We're all males. We all think we have a vocation. We all have to take Latin. We all are scared to death of Father Coleman, who

headed up the school. And then you go down the list. So, I began to focus more on what I had in common with people than what our differences were.

Now I can pluck out of that a lot of challenging experiences. There were a lot of experiences. Latin was a difficult experience. In the summer of 1965, school is ending, we're leaving, and Father Coleman pulls me aside and says, "I just want you to know that we're having algebra 2 next year." I said, "Father, I haven't had algebra 1." He said, "We're having algebra 2." And then he told me where the algebra 1 books were, where the answer book was, and over the summer on the farm, I taught myself algebra. Was that difficult? Yes. Was it challenging? Yes.

Maybe disadvantages are actually advantages, particularly after you get over the disadvantages, because you see life a totally different way. It isn't supposed to be all rosy. And you see that it's going to have ups and downs, and you know how to survive those downs. And you know how to work uphill and into the wind.

How do you go through life without having ups and downs? Who's that person who has not had a time when they doubt themselves? Who is that person? Who has never had someone slight them, or disappoint them, and then had to regroup? Every human being is going to have a moment, or moments, of unfairness, of things beyond their control, that are hurtful, or painful, or difficult. And then the question is: How do we deal with all of that? Yes, it was horrible. But you're sixteen years old.

After my first year in seminary, Richard Chisholm, the only other black kid, left. The next two years I'm the only black kid there. You don't hear me complaining about those years. I'm not going to say, "Oh, woe is me." I'm not going to do that. It had its ups and downs. What I did say later on was, to people who then thought that integration was the panacea, "Look, that's not so easy." I'm the one who said—I gave cautionary words—that it is fraught with challenges, it is not a panacea, it's not the magic ointment to all that ails. It is really, really hard. I don't think it was easy. I don't think it was a cakewalk. It was very, very challenging. And not everybody was going to be able to do it.

MP: Along these lines, you were very struck by Robert Frost's "The Road Not Taken" poem.[4] **How did that affect you?**

CT: In English class, we were doing Robert Frost, and we came across this poem: "Two roads diverged in a wood, and I—I took the one less traveled by. And that has made all the difference." And what I was thinking was some place in my life, the roads had split off. I was no longer in the world that was my comfort zone, my neighborhood, my family, my school, my routine. Two roads had diverged in a wood, and I took one less traveled by. I had gone to the seminary. I had gone to all-white schools. And it's made all the difference. What was that difference? That, I didn't know.

MP: Didn't you receive some racially charged comments in your yearbook?

CT: After my first year, again just disappointment. I was perplexed. One of the older students signed my yearbook, "Keep on trying, Clarence. One day you'll be as good as us." This was more racial. But that was probably one of the last of the bad things. That was again by the end of my sophomore year.

MP: In a later yearbook, you have a really positive caption.

CT: Well, just think about it; think of the difference in the years. The caption, "Keep on trying, Clarence. One day you'll be as good as us," is the end of my sophomore year, that's 1965. The captions you see in my yearbook my senior year are my friends. These are kids I've been with for three years. We've grown up and gone through trials and tribulations together. We are now reduced to nine kids in my class. So we've gone to less than a third of the class that was there when I was a sophomore. They know more about me as a person. I mean, think about it. You work with somebody for nine months, you know them at one level. You work with them for twenty-seven months, you know them at a different level.

I had gone from a student with grades in the 80s, to a student with grades in the 90s. It's been a constant increase. Academically, I did very well. And year after year, I've been among the best athletes in the school. I'm not going to study hall; I'm monitoring study hall. I'm not learning Latin; I'm helping other kids learn Latin.

MP: So what was the caption alongside your photo in your senior year book?
CT: I think it's, "Blew that test, only a 98." And that came from the fear of failure. You can ask anybody who constantly pushes themselves. They always fear they're not doing enough. It may not be a morbid or pathological fear of failure, but there's always this uncertainty. "I've got to get up. I've got to go over something." It's always, "I haven't really done enough" or it is, "One more thing I need to think about." When I would get chemistry, or physics, or whatever, get an exam back, Latin, and I'd have a 98 on it, it would be, "God, I blew that." And here's my thinking: You have to work twice as hard to get half as far. You assume you're going to be discriminated against, or at the very least, you're not going to be treated the same way as whites. So, I can't get a 98. And if I'm going to force someone to have to discriminate against me, then I have to have a hundred. In other words, leave them nothing but race, and force them, it's sort of like, check mate. Okay? I wasn't leaving any room for error.

LEAVING THE SEMINARY
"THE WORLD WAS CHANGING"

MP: Your next choice is to go to major seminary. How did you make that choice?
CT: We made that choice as a group. They were good classmates, they were bright, they were energetic. When the time came to go off to major seminary, we decided we were going to go to the same seminary—Immaculate Conception in Missouri.

Immaculate Conception was great. I loved the contemplative life. I loved lauds, which was the morning prayers, vespers, evening prayers. I love the Gregorian chant. I love being a part of it. I love going to the basilica. I loved my friends there. I did very well again, academically and athletically. But the world was changing.

Probably the first omen was the summer of 1967. I worked at the seminary at St. John's. It was the first summer since 1958 I had not gone to the farm for the summer. And instead, I worked for my little $45 a week. I was sort of the grounds guy and the handyman, and factotum at Camp Villa Marie, which was on the grounds of the seminary. I stayed with my mother in her apartment, and I caught the bus and went to work that summer.

You began to see the society changing in the summer of 1967. You read the daily papers, or back then everyone watched the evening news. You began to see some fragmentation. One of the things that happened that summer as I was living in Savannah was, I got to see a number of my black friends that I had grown up with. Because of being at the seminary, I rarely saw the kids I grew up with anymore.

In the summer of 1967, because I was staying with my mother, after church on Sunday, I could see them. One of the people that I had grown up around, and gone to school with, was a kid named Tommy. I saw him a bit that summer, and did some things with him, and then

I went on to Immaculate Conception seminary, and while I was there, Tommy was murdered. Later on that year, I thought everything was coming apart because Otis Redding died.[5] Then they released his song *Sittin' On the Dock of the Bay* posthumously.[6]

MP: Did you sense that you may be losing your vocation?
CT: You're nineteen years old, and you're wondering why the Church isn't more vocal on discrimination. You're wondering what your role is. I mean, all these kinds of questions you have when you're nineteen. That's a part of it. Then I met an older black seminarian there named Dolis Dural. He eventually became a priest. Dolis was a bit more cynical and more well-heeled, and he introduced me to Nina Simone's music. And that was kind of hard-edged, and he got me interested.

You start seeing things in a different way. I'd been in the minor seminary. I was almost cloistered. And now I'm reading different things. I'm talking to different people. First time I've ever been this far west. I'm west of the Mississippi River. All of this is new and suddenly I'm thinking about the world differently.

Dolis is asking me questions. I'm reading things, and suddenly I'm getting more upset about the whole racial situation in our country. We react differently at nineteen to the inflow of complicated and really hard problems like that. It makes you react more emotionally.

Interestingly, my uncertainties were never deeply religious uncertainties. It was not uncertainty about the faith. It was uncertainty about how those people lived out the faith, how they lived as Catholics, and the stands they took. When you go to a devout Catholic church, you get people who will pray to end abortion, pray for religious freedom. If we had constantly prayed for the end of bigotry, the end of racism, the end of discrimination, the end of segregation, and that became a central part of what we were approaching God and intercessors for, then that might have made a difference. But it was no place to be found at the time—except with my nuns and the priest in my parish in Savannah.

MP: Let's talk about your reaction to the shooting of Dr. Martin Luther King Jr. What happened that day?
CT: I went home for Christmas my first year of college in Immaculate Conception, and I came pretty close to leaving then. It was really a very emotional and difficult time. I talked to my grandmother, I talked to my parish priest about it. He said, "Finish out the year, and see what you think." And I went back, and things were going fairly well, but I was still ambivalent. And I wasn't certain about leaving.

In the spring, when I was walking back into the hall, we lived in Benedict Hall, someone was down watching TV, and he yelled out from the basement as I was walking in the dorm, he said, "Martin Luther King has just been shot." And the seminarian in front of me said, "That's good. I hope the son of a bitch dies." And that was pretty much the end of me. That was it. Because that was the opposite of what I thought you said about a man of God, and what a seminarian, or the Church should do. And that, if to the extent that I had any ambivalence, it ended that day.

CHAPTER THREE

RADICAL YEARS

*"For the first time in my life, race and racism
explained everything"*

MP: You said your vocation was over?
CT: It was done that moment he said, "I hope the son of a bitch dies."
That was it. The question becomes what do I do? I did not want to
be in an all-white school anymore. I didn't want to be doing all of this
anymore. I was not obsessed with the fact that I was black and my
classmates were white. I didn't have any great academic difficulties. I
don't have any problems getting along with my classmates. None of
that. But I understood this was different.

One of the things that I think that people don't quite focus on is
that when you come from a certain environment and you cross barriers to another world, not only aren't you going to be a part of the
world you're in, I was never going to be a part of that world. I was
never going to be white, and I never expected to be. The problem is,
I can never go back completely to the world I came from.

I'll give you something very simple, superficial almost. When I
left home, the only music I ever listened to was R&B and gospel.
That's what we had. By the time I had been through four years of

this, and I also listened to Peter, Paul and Mary, and Simon and Garfunkel because I had been exposed to people who listened to that. I wasn't a folk music fan, but I had listened to it, and I kind of liked "Homeward Bound" by Simon & Garfunkel—particularly when we were headed home.[1] So in a sense I couldn't go back. I was different. I could go back to that world, but I was no longer of that world. And I can survive in the world that I was in, in the seminary, but I was not of that world.

And the question then becomes, "What do I do?" I was not going to an all-white school again. I was adamant about that. I was not carrying this burden again. I was going to go back home and possibly go to Savannah State College, a local black college. Well, my chemistry teacher from the seminary who is also a Franciscan nun, Sister Mary Carmine, had a classmate of mine from St. Pius, Robert DeShay, who was now at Holy Cross College in Worcester, Massachusetts, send me an application because she had heard I was having doubts about the seminary, and she wanted me to apply there. Out of courtesy, I filled it out within an hour or so. I had my transcripts sent. But my mindset was, I was going to probably go to Savannah State. I was not going to go to a white school. I wasn't headed off to some foreign land again. I had been there, done that. And I was not a happy camper.

MP: How did your grandfather react when you said you were leaving the seminary?
CT: It was as though the bottom had fallen out, there was nothing positive anymore. The priesthood had been my only goal. And when that went away it was like I was in a freefall. I go home and now I face my grandfather.

And I'd like to say, "It was facing the music," but it wasn't music, it was a stony silence almost, and it was a coldness. So he took me to the living room, and he said that, as he had promised when we came to live in 1955, the door opened inward then, now it was opening outward. And I was to leave his house. Since I had made decisions of a man, I should live like one. And I said, "When?" And he said, I will never forget it, "to-day, this day." I think I was fumbling around, and said, "Well, are you still going to help me with college?" He said, "No. You're a man. You figure it out."

My mother had an extra room in her apartment, so I went over there.

MP: I think you've said it felt like you were reversing your first walk to your grandfather's.
CT: I was going from 1955, when I had come to this wonderful place that was a sanctuary, and now I was going back to live with my mother in her apartment.

The bottom was falling out, I was falling apart. And then that summer I pretty much stopped going to church. I was angry at everybody, angry at the world. Summer of '68 was when you had a lot of the riots. I mean I thought everything was coming apart.

MP: '68 was also the time that Bobby Kennedy was shot.
CT: The Kennedys were heroes in our house. And I can't say I understood all the politics, but we were all Democrats for whatever reasons, even though the Republican Party was the anti-slavery party. I think it had more to do with Roosevelt than anything else. But Kennedy was also Irish Catholic, and the nuns were Irish Catholic. We were Catholic. When John F. Kennedy was assassinated, that was one of the darkest moments ever.[2] And then Martin Luther King was assassinated.[3] And then Robert Kennedy.[4]

I was getting ready for work one morning, and I was listening to the radio while I did that. And they announced that he had been assassinated. Well, I mean, I dropped to my knees, I said, "It's over."

All steam left me then. I don't know how I even got it together to go to work. But it just seemed to me that bad things were happening. My grandfather had kicked me out. Kennedy was assassinated. I remember sitting there, "Kennedy, King, Kennedy. KKK." I remember writing it. Oh my God there it is! "KKK" you know. And it was, it was, that was probably the last straw. I mean, I didn't need a last straw but that was it. That was the nail in the coffin for me.

MP: It's surely a dark moment.
CT: It was a dark moment, but it was a hope-depleting moment. I was giving up on the very things that had been the guiding lights in my life. I've given up on faith, my church. I'd given up on this hopeful outlook. I had walked away from my grandfather, or I had been thrown away from him, because of my actions. I had given up on the only dream I'd ever had. The things that have been the inspiration for doing things were now gone.

Robert DeShay gave me a copy of *The Other America* by Michael Harrington, who had gone to Holy Cross.[5] And that was sort of the beginning. Suddenly that made sense to me, and for the first time in my life, racism and race explained everything. It became, sort of, the substitute religion. I shoved aside Catholicism and now it was this. It was all about race.

I was very, very upset. Once you allow yourself to be angry, you give yourself license to feel all that anger. There's a lot of it. It's about even things that didn't happen to you personally, but just kind of an aggregate, collective injustice.

I was pretty upset. And so all that emotion, all the passion, all the things that you had been willing to modulate, "to control yourself" as my grandfather would say, you felt now that it was okay to let it just come to the surface, and almost dominate your thinking, and dominate your life.

I'm angry with my grandfather. I'm angry with the Church. If it's a warm day, I'm angry. If it's a cold day, I'm angry. I'm just angry. I'm angry. I'm sort of flying, lashing out at every single thing. Nothing is right. I'm staying in a room with a mynah bird, with my mother, with her two big dogs. But the one out that I do have is that I was accepted to Holy Cross. I've got one door is open, only one. And that was Holy Cross.

I didn't have a number for Holy Cross, and I called a long-distance operator, and I said, "I'd like to get the number for Holy Cross College in "WOR-CHESTER," Massachusetts." And she said, "What?" I said, "Wor-chester." You know, W-O-R-C-E-S-T-E-R." She said, "WOOSTER." I said, "Okay well, whatever, it's Worcester."

At Holy Cross College, Mr. Wood was the financial aid director, and they pieced together the standard package, and with work study, and guaranteed student loans, a little bit of grant, and that was the tuition, and what I saved up working.

THE HOLY CROSS YEARS
"IT IS AT ONCE EMPOWERING—YOU FEEL LIKE SUPERMAN, YOU CAN TAKE ON THE WHOLE WORLD"

MP: You have talked of feeling like Clark Kent tearing off his suit in a telephone booth.
CT: In that era, we had come to believe that people like my grandparents had been too submissive, that they had been too weak. That lack of emotion or lack of lashing out was a sign of weakness. And there's a strange thing about anger. It is at once empowering—you feel like Superman, you can take on the whole world. But it also flames out pretty fast. It's self-destructive, it's destructive of whatever's flaming. And you did feel it. I mean suddenly you felt like you were unleashed.

I just turned twenty. Yeah, I mean you feel empowered, you feel invigorated. You suddenly are like "The Man." You're ready to go take on the whole world. I'm tough now and then I'm bold and can get in people's face. That sort of thing.

MP: And the anger was at "The Man," right?

CT: Whoever that was. And that was whites, people who discriminated; that was the system. And I think sometimes we have to have something that embodies all of the things that we think are wrong. And I think that "The Man" is that person. I used to ask people, "Where does he live?" Because "The Man" is doing all sorts of things to me. You go to school, and someone said, "No need for you to go to school because 'The Man' isn't going to let you do anything." Or you work hard at your job, they said, "That doesn't make a difference because 'The Man' isn't going to let you get promoted." Where is he? "The Man" was this all-encompassing or perhaps embodiment of all that was wrong, of all the ills in society, and all the racism, all the oppression, all the discrimination, all the evil—"The Man."

MP: What was Holy Cross like for you?

CT: Holy Cross was almost salvific. It was the one chance I had. I didn't have any place else to go. When I got to Worcester and went up on campus, I had never been to New England. I liked it from the beginning. I liked the way it looked. It was Jesuit. My roommate was also a transfer student. We were both sophomores. He from Northeastern, I from Immaculate Conception. He was a biology major, and I decided to major in English literature because English was my worst subject, and the hardest thing for me.

MP: How diverse was Holy Cross when you arrived?

CT: This was the era when a few blacks were on these campuses. There were almost no blacks at Holy Cross. I was the sixth member of my class out of five hundred fifty. One of the vice presidents, Father Brooks (who would eventually become president of Holy Cross) decided to go around to the Catholic schools on the East Coast and recruit blacks.[6] So the freshman class, I think, had seventeen blacks in it. But my class, again, I was the sixth man. I think there were two or three in the junior class, and I think one senior. So that's not a lot.

THE BLACK STUDENT UNION
"WE'RE SUPPOSED TO BE REVOLUTIONARIES"

MP: What was your involvement with the Black Student Union (BSU) at Holy Cross?
CT: When I arrived at Holy Cross, Arthur Martin was a track athlete and just a nice guy who was in the junior class. Art Martin decided to start a Black Student Union, and he had some ideas, but I could type. The same summer I taught myself algebra, I taught myself how to type. I said, "I'll type it up." I had my trusty Smith-Corona typewriter with automatic return. I sat in my room in Hanselman on campus and typed up the constitution and bylaws of the Black Student Union. I said, "What do you want in it?" He said, "Anything you put in." So I typed it up, and that became the Black Student Union.

MP: One thing they did was create the black corridor. What was that like?
CT: That was an odd deal. Creating black corridors and black dorms became fashionable. I didn't agree with that. Why did we come to a white school to segregate again? And I just came from segregation,

and I don't care who chooses to do it, we're still segregating. And so, to my recollection, I was the only vote against that. But for solidarity, I went and I lived up there. And I don't think that was the right decision, in retrospect. But you're a young man and they're your friends, and you understand what they're doing, and you're not so certain whether you're right or not.

I said I'll live with them, but I didn't want to change my roommate, so my roommate came and lived with me. He was John Sirocco. Great guy. Because of John, I was a better student, and I attribute much of my academic stability in those years to John Sirocco.

MP: In your new radicalism, how did you dress?
CT: We're supposed to be revolutionaries. You go to the local Army Navy store in Worcester, and you get Army fatigues and boots. Why that was the dress is beyond me, but that's the way we dressed, and I wore, like carpenter's pants, and things like that, bib overalls.

MP: To go back to the BSU, there was a walkout on campus. What happened during the walkout?
CT: These were buddies of mine. This is solidarity again, and friendship. This was the era of the anti-war movement, the Vietnam War. It's like everything was coming apart in society. And GE [General Electric] was recruiting on campus. Holy Cross was a fabulous place to recruit, and some of the students protested them because they were making jet engines or somehow supporting the Vietnam War effort. They protested them, and they were warned, and then they got in trouble. Some of the black students were identified through photos, and we thought that they were profiled. That was before you said those words. They were easier to identify because there's only a handful of blacks. And so there was a hearing, and we all protested that, and then there were some sanctions against them. I think they were booted out.

Once that was handed down, we had an emergency meeting. And I remember blurting out, "Well, if they don't want us here, we should all just leave." And we left. We were all in our suits, our finest wear, and we left. And as soon as I left, I started thinking, "Now what do I tell my grandfather?" And I was horrified. This is the second time. So it looks like now I'm definitely coming home with my tail between my legs. This is really not good.

We were over in Clark University (that's a local university), we were over there with some friends, and thinking this whole thing through, and there were negotiations. And thank God, after a while, we were let back in. And I vowed then, this is it. I will never leave again. And I went back to Holy Cross with a renewed dedication to never quitting. But that didn't stop me from continuing my protesting ways. I continued to be very upset about a lot of things.

MP: A Black Panther came to Holy Cross, but you were not so impressed by that guy.
CT: That was pretty scary. We went to one of the rooms in the campus center, and he was railing, and called us cowards and wimps, and said that we were there in school thinking that we were revolutionaries, and that the only way we were going to have a revolution was at the point of a gun. And he whips out this gun and starts waving it around. Today, he'd probably get arrested. Boy, that showed me something. Not only was I not impressed, I mean, it was clear that this guy was not someone who was about to persuade you. And he was almost like he was a criminal.

MP: What did you think of the other sort of more radical black leaders of the time, like Malcolm X and the Nation of Islam?
CT: I was not into them. I had friends who were schoolmates at Holy Cross who were black Muslims. The one thing that we did agree on

was that we should have self-discipline and solve some of our own problems, like you solve the problem of not doing your homework by doing your homework, and that sort of thing. Do what's in front of you. I had just gotten out of Catholicism, and I didn't agree with their outlook and their religion, so I didn't get into that. Malcolm X, I admired because we were young and he was in your face. We were for anybody who was kind of in your face. It could be Stokely Carmichael, it could be H. Rap Brown, it could be Angela Davis, it could be Huey Newton, It could be Eldridge Cleaver. So the more radical tended to be the people we gravitated toward.

MP: Did you feel that way about the anti-war movement?
CT: The anti-war movement, they were friends of mine, and I was anti-war, but I didn't really know why, because the next week I was a hawk. Then I even toyed with the idea of joining the Marines, which I still regret that I didn't. I vacillated on that, but I participated in a lot of the anti-war activity but didn't quite understand it. Came down to D.C. for an anti-war march, but I can't say I felt as strongly about that as I did about the race issue. It's almost as though you were with them as much because they were with you. It was kind of a correlation. But, if I were to think about it in a rational way, I think I would've probably been more pro-U.S. on that. But, again, I was confused. I was twenty something years old.

MP: Many of your friends of that era, and this is the era of Woodstock and other large gatherings of young people, regularly engaged in what we could call the sex, drugs, and rock 'n' roll aspect of the sixties. Why didn't that appeal to you?
CT: I'm a kid from Savannah, Georgia. I just came out of the seminary. If I fail, if I have one big mistake, who rescues me? I saw my life in school, as literally, and I would picture it this way, it was a high

wire act with no net. How many times do you get to fall? That's the way I saw it. One fall, and I am done. It's a one and done.

MP: But other black students got involved in Eastern religions and they got involved in drugs.
CT: I would never indict those kids. It's really hard. We used to say being up at Holy Cross was a crusher. It would crush your spirit. It was a lot. To be out of your element, to be in that cold weather, to be in an academically demanding environment, especially some of these kids who came from inner cities. Remember the advantage I had. Today people talk about white privilege. Well, I had Catholic privilege. I had been in the seminary. I had been to all male schools. When I was in my first year in college at the seminary, I took twenty-one credit hours a semester. At Holy Cross, I was only taking fifteen. But now imagine if you came out of an inner city, in Philadelphia, or in New York or D.C., think of the shock. Or think of the shock coming from Savannah. It was hard on some of these kids. Some, it knocked them into a tailspin, much the way I was in a tailspin after I left the Church and after I left the seminary.

You listen to jazz, you listen to Sonny Rollins, you listen to blues, or you listen to gospel, you hear it. You hear the disappointments. You hear the hurt. And it's sort of a wailing. You read Richard Wright, or Ralph Ellison, or any of these guys, you could feel it in there.

MP: You mentioned music. What were you listening to these years at Holy Cross?
CT: I don't like people telling me what to do. My view to everyone was that Lincoln freed the slaves, and I like to take full advantage of that. People would tell you, because you were black, you have to listen to a certain kind of music, like Hugh Masekela or something like that. I wasn't against Hugh Masekela. I wasn't against jazz. I like jazz. I

wasn't against blues, or R&B, all of the above I like. But when someone comes to you and says, "blacks like" or "blacks listen to this, listen to that." So then I listened to classical music. I liked classical music. Think about it. I'm a black kid from Savannah, Georgia, where my grandmother listened to gospel; my grandfather didn't listen to music. So where would I get an exposure to classical music? Cartoons. It was Looney Tunes. So I started listening more to classical. I particularly like Mozart. And then I listened to Wagner, but it got a little tough for me. Then I decided I was going to listen to country music, because it was close to blues, and because people said I shouldn't. And then I found out I like country music, so I listen to some of it. I listened to virtually everything when I was there. I was transitioning to being more eclectic by then.

BOOKS WITH AN IMPACT—*INVISIBLE MAN,* *NATIVE SON, THE FOUNTAINHEAD*
"PEOPLE WANTED YOU TO BE A STEREOTYPE"

MP: You mentioned too that you read the book *Invisible Man.*[7] What was that experience like?
CT: I reread *Invisible Man* because *Invisible Man,* like *Native Son,* like *The Fountainhead* and *Atlas Shrugged,* are books you can read as a teenager, and then you reread them in your twenties, you reread them in your thirties, your forties, your fifties.[8] And each time you see more. So it's almost as though it's an onion and you continue to peel. *Invisible Man,* I finally realized that [Ralph Ellison] was right, that people wanted you to be a stereotype. They wanted you to embody their stereotypes of a race: that I'm black, and that there are these stereotypes and myths they have about blacks, which music, what your beliefs are, your politics, then you're supposed to act it out even if you

don't believe it. And then that person, a white person, is supposed to act out their stereotypes. As Ralph Ellison says, you're lying to each other; we're supposed to lie to each other. And then we realize that people will treat you badly if you tell the truth. So his only way of being truthful, and being honest and being himself, was to be invisible.

MP: You also have written that you identified with the character Bigger Thomas in *Native Son*?
CT: Well, I mean, you're young. I read that many times since then. And yeah, Bigger Thomas did some bad things. But Bigger was unencumbered by good judgment and things that would modulate his passions. And he would lash out. One of my concerns with him was eventually circumstances would control him. That if you are sliding down the side of a mountain, once you start, you don't get to control it anymore. And he started down a mountain. So you always worried that you would start. You were talking about not getting into a lot of things like drugs and stuff. I always worry that if you start something, how do you control it? How do you control the consequences of it? So yeah, you feel that freedom of lashing out, or the empowerment, or whatever. But there's a price to it. It builds, then it has its own momentum and has its own life. And you have no control of it. So Bigger, it consumed him. Eventually it destroys him.

And there's also these really wonderful debates between Ralph Ellison and Richard Wright over being the angry black man versus the individual. I tend to side with Ellison. You know, in my youth I was more of Richard Wright. In later years, even in my thirties, I was more toward Ellison.

MP: Were you influenced by Ayn Rand's libertarian philosophy?
CT: Ayn Rand and *The Fountainhead* started in high school, and this would play out later in law school. I would describe myself as a lazy

libertarian. And it was because I was looking at structures, or restrictions, on me, whether there were religious restrictions, or structures or strictures on me. My grandfather and his rules, society and its rules, and I guess in a sense, I was saying, "All of you, leave me alone." In fact, my mantra when I was in law school is "Leave me alone." It wasn't, "I want to do this to dominate the world." It's "Leave me alone." I remember glibly telling one guy I was in law school with that I'd rather go to hell on my own than to heaven with his advice. It's because people love to tell you what to do. And so, as a libertarian, you get a framework within which to tell people to leave you alone, that you prefer to make your own decisions. If you look at *The Fountainhead* (that's what I make my clerks watch), there's a great line by Dominique Francon in *The Fountainhead* when she says, "We both have strength, but not courage."[9] You know a lot of people have the capacity to do things, but they don't do them. And sometimes when you're an individual, you've got to muster the courage to go it alone, to do it yourself. To say that you'll fight the whole world.

And that became particularly important because a lot of times, people had these very uniform—if not universal—expectations, or stereotypes, or demands, or commands of what I was supposed to do. What if I rejected it? What if I don't agree with that? What if I am the *Invisible Man*? Do I go underground? Do I hide? Do I pilfer other people's electricity? What do I do? How do I stay above ground and be an individual? So that demands, okay, maybe I have the capacity, but also the courage to do it. And then when you do it, what happens? There is going to be a price to pay. What does Ralph Ellison say in *Invisible Man*? The worst I've ever been treated was when I told the truth. Okay. And so that's what happens. And so now how do you accept that truth? That was always a question. Do you run from it? That's the whole point. Like with Dominique Francon, what are you afraid of? You see what I'm saying? And so when you read these books, you say [like Howard Roark in *The Fountainhead*], "I'll become a day laborer rather than be told what to do. . . . I'd rather be a total failure in your world, than to be told what to do or to be made to do something that I think is wrong."[10]

MP: Frederick Douglass made the phrase "Leave us alone" famous when he said: "The American people have always been anxious to know what they shall do with us. . . . I have had but one answer from the beginning. Do nothing with us! Your doing with us has already played the mischief with us. Do nothing with us! If the apples will not remain on the tree of their own strength, if they are worm-eaten at the core, if they are early ripe and disposed to fall, let them fall! . . . And if the negro cannot stand on his own legs, let him fall also. All I ask is, give him a chance to stand on his own legs! Let him alone! . . . Your interference is doing him positive injury."[11]

CT: I started quoting that speech back in the '80s. Frederick Douglass had depth and content, and the courage of his convictions. He reminds me in a lot of ways of my grandfather. You know there were many times my grandfather—I still think he is the greatest man that I've known—my grandfather would say when people were upset with him, just simply, "He's got a lifetime to get pleased." It wasn't his problem. He had his opinion.

I think we've lost the capacity in our society to accept the fact that there are people who have a different opinion. That used to be one of the features of liberalism. Civility was one way of us navigating between those differences and getting along. I think we've lost that. People started this imposition of views on me. You'll see throughout my life that there are people who have this notion, and I remember going through confirmation, Senator Heflin said, "Judge, people who know you, say you're a good guy. People who don't know you, say you're a bad guy. Who am I to believe?"

And then people have the preconceived notion, this stereotype of what one is supposed to be. And then again as Senator Heflin said, I was "an enigma" because this is what I was supposed to think, and this is what I thought. And there was a conflict between what I was supposed to think and what I thought.

We can actually sit here and have a conversation about a perception of what I'm supposed to think because I'm black and what I actually think as a reasoning human being. It's the most absurd thing in the world. I always like to know, what is the black version of nuclear physics? What was the black viewpoint on analytical geometry, or something?

We've gotten away from the individual. So yes, I did like Richard Wright. I like the passion, I read *Native Son, Outsider, Black Boy.*[12] I read all that in high school. But then I read *Invisible Man*, too. And then to try to understand that. And then you get Ayn Rand.

I prefer to think for myself. The strongest person I've ever known was my grandfather. What if he had succumbed to the circumstances around him? What if he said, "Look, I was born in 1907 with no education; that determines the outcome in my life." Okay? "I'm a beaten-down black man in Georgia." He never looked at it that way. He rose above all that.

MP: That's perhaps a flaw in *Native Son*. I think Wright wants to say that Bigger Thomas had no choice. His crime was inevitable.
CT: In a sense, he didn't once it started snowballing. See at some point when you're on the edge of the mountain, in a foot of snow, you can choose to go down another twenty feet, but you may never be able to come back up. So you make your choice way up here.

As my granddaddy used to say, again smartest man I've ever known, he said, "Son, when you jump off a building, flying is nice. Landing is hell." Okay? He said, "Halfway down you can't decide."

So once you jump off, you have pre-determined the outcome on something. So there is an inevitability to that leap. It's not every instance that you can turn around. And maybe to some extent, in defense of Bigger Thomas, and I'm not going to defend him completely, as he did some bad things to his family and his girlfriend, and he put himself in the situation, but what got him ultimately in trouble was not necessarily something of his own doing.

But once you go over a certain cliff, there's an inevitability of it that we're trying to avoid, every one of us from the South: Where's that cliff? Where's that ledge? Where do I fall off? Where is my destruction inevitable? When does it become inevitable? So I'm not going to totally defend Bigger, but I can see what happened to him. I can understand that.

HOLY CROSS AND THE JESUITS—
HONEST LIBERALS
"THEY DIDN'T ACCOMMODATE THE MEDIOCRITY"

MP: *Time* magazine called Holy Cross and the Jesuits there "the cradle of the Catholic left." Was that your impression?
CT: They were still priests. The thing I liked about them was, yes, they may have been ideologically to the left, but then I was way off to the left, too. Despite all of that, they still wore the Roman collar, and they were sensible. They would actually engage you. So yes, they may have been to the left, but they would reel you back in. They would force you to do your economics homework. They would force you to do well because you could flunk out. They didn't accommodate the mediocrity. They required you to learn English and to learn it well. They required you to take the core courses: metaphysics, philosophy of man, ethics. You couldn't skip steps with the Jebbies.

One of the reasons I left the Church was because I thought no one was responding to what was happening morally on the race issue. The Jesuits were different. They responded. They forced you to think about how you respond. Father Brooks got in his car, drove the East Coast, and recruited black students. He responded. He reached out to us. The Jesuits may have been to the left and may have been what I call, "liberals." I don't think they were hard left. I think they were just liberals, and they were good for me. Father Brooks was the best. Father Brooks was the glue. Father Brooks was the person that never forgot you. He didn't solve your problems, but he didn't forget your problems. He didn't dismiss you. He held you accountable, but never in a callous way.

Father Brooks reminds me of my nuns. I would ask Sister Mary Virgilius what it was that was the key to their success. She said, "We loved you." And I think that was true of Father Brooks: You always got a sense that he truly loved you, and he always had your best interests at heart, that you weren't a part of some scheme he had. It was how he felt about you.

MP: You have noted that the first group of black students at Holy Cross were successful. But as they admitted more and more, it didn't work out as well.
CT: It did up to a point in the early years, but someone asked Father Brooks about that before he passed away in the last year of his life, why was that group so successful and that success never replicated. And as only he could, and someone unburdened by what other people think and political correctness, he answered candidly that, today the Ivies would swoop up all those kids, and Holy Cross would never get them. He said, "We could never get them today. That's why we were never able to replicate it."

For years we understood the sort of misplacement of students. That students would be one or two levels above where they should be, and it was a point I argued vehemently when I was on the board of trustees at Holy Cross. That certain students that would do well at Holy Cross, wind up at Harvard. And students that would do well at maybe another school, wind up at Holy Cross. And they wind up at a school where it's much more difficult, if not impossible, for them to excel. And that would be true for any student.

MP: My friend Stuart Taylor wrote this book *Mismatch* analyzing that in the end, it's unfair to the very students that the system intends to benefit, because then they flunk out, or they feel badly, or they feel not as good as the other students, and they carry that with them.[13] **Whereas if they had been not mismatched, but properly matched, it would have a positive empowering effect and they would be primed to succeed.**
CT: Stuart Taylor was being honest, and so was Father Brooks. And when I was on the board of trustees at Holy Cross, I asked a simple question, "Would you do this to your own child? Would you put your child in a school where you know the chances of his or her success are minimal, if not improbable or impossible?" And most people would say they wouldn't do that to their own children. So why would you do that to this poor black kid? I mean, why would you do it to a kid, who, like only a fraction of our race, is able to go to college? Why would you make it harder, if not impossible, for them to do well? So that you can feel good about yourself?

You're for diversity. You're for integration, or whatever. We were down that road with school busing. So think of it, just think of it, a second. Can you honestly say that school busing improved the education of black kids? And if so, how is that quantified? Now, you say, well, we think that there should be diversity. Fine. We all do. But that's not why you sent your kids to school—to be diverse and not to be math-educated or to be literate. You didn't send your kids to school for that. That was Father Brooks's point—when we got the kids that we thought should be here, the first year, look at how well they did.

ATTENDING AN ANTI-WAR RIOT IN BOSTON
"BEGINNING OF THE SLOW RETURN TO WHERE I STARTED"

MP: During this period, you attended an anti-war protest in Boston that had a big impact on your life.
CT: In the spring of 1970, this is after we had the walk-out in the fall semester, I decided to go in April for a protest to Boston. It was an anti-war thing. There was an escalation in the Vietnam War and the bombing of Cambodia so I went for that, not quite understanding it all, but it was an opportunity to protest. And then unbeknownst to me, we get steered off to Cambridge, to another protest.

On the way to Cambridge, we stopped at this liquor store, and this poor guy, he saw us, and he gave us the liquor. I think he gave us some potato chips, or something, too. But he said, "Just go." And then on the way we consumed this liquid courage. So we walk over to Cambridge, this time to free political prisoners.

Then we proceeded to be back and forth in Cambridge all night. And this turned into a full-scale riot. I mean, there was tear gas and sirens. It was bad. I saw what I had become. I didn't even care about it, didn't care about getting hurt, or anything else, or what was happening to other people.

We were headed back after a long night of rioting. This is the wee morning of April sixteenth, we're walking back to where we had parked the car and some of the police officers, the riot police officers, they came toward us. They had those long riot sticks, and all their gear on, and one said, "This must be the n——er contingent from Roxbury." And that was the first time in my life anyone had ever addressed me, other than a black person, using that word. Never in Savannah; it was in Boston, Massachusetts. And, of course, we decided then that it was not prudent to respond. So we kept walking, in hopes that they wouldn't follow us, and they didn't. And when I made it back to Worcester, I was exhausted, emotionally spent. And couldn't sleep, even as exhausted as I was. I just got out of bed and walked over to the dining hall to get something to eat, because I hadn't eaten all day, the day before. And on the way, you passed the chapel. And I remember standing right in front of the chapel outside and I asked God, "If you take anger out of my heart, I'll never hate again." And that was the beginning of the slow return to where I started.

MP: You've spoken of releasing "the beast" of rage and resentment before that moment at the church. What did you mean?
CT: I had become something that was a caricature of who I was. I had become the antithesis of what I had been in the seminary. And I saw what that could lead to—that I was spiraling out of control. And that was the beginning of not allowing "the beast" to roam unfettered. It was an opportunity from God to see what I had become.

When I would go back home, the exchanges with my grandfather were really horrible, because I'd talk about the revolution and about how awful this country was, and racism. And I would be drinking, and wouldn't comb my hair, and it was bad. And he looked at me and he would say, "I didn't raise you to be like this. After all our sacrifices, this is what you've become." My conduct was just not good.

I thought he was weak. And he thought I'd gone up North and become "one of those damn educated fools"; that I went up North and they put all that foolishness in my head. It was a recognition that I had become something other than who I really should have been, and what I was raised to be, and what I was really like. It was almost as though you become the worst you could be rather than the best you can be. I had become so unlike anything that he thought I would be or wanted me to be. He didn't say I had to agree with him. Here's a man who was raised by freed slaves. What could I tell this black man, born in 1907, growing up in Georgia, about race?

I think it was the pain I caused him. When we went to live with them, they would say over and over and over that they weren't going any further in their own lives, that they didn't have the education, that they were in their mid- and late forties, but that they were going to use the rest of their lives to raise their boys. And my brother who came back from the Vietnam War didn't like it.

MP: What did he say?
CT: He told me that all of us should leave the country.

MP: All you radicals?
CT: All of us, to leave the country, and he had no use for any of us.

MP: He never wavered in his patriotism?
CT: Oh God, no. He was over in Southeast Asia. And he was a patriot. He said that when he came back in the early seventies from his time in Thailand. He was there around a year and a half or so and he was in the Air Force. And when he came back, he said that he would never leave this country again—this was the best country in the world, and he was never leaving again. He wasn't going to Mexico, the Caribbean, to Canada, or any place else. And he never did. He died in January 2000, jogging. But he never wavered.

MP: Did this strain your relationship with him?
CT: My brother was my brother. The hardest part about being his brother was when he died at fifty. Particularly when I was at Yale, he was a beacon of stability. He wasn't my grandfather, but he basically reflected his views.

MP: When did you first meet Kathy Ambush, and what was she like?
CT: I met her in my sophomore year. Our politics overlapped, our politics tended to be more radical, to the left. We started dating and would date throughout my time at Holy Cross. And then we got married the day after I graduated.

CHAPTER FOUR

LESSONS FROM
YALE LAW SCHOOL

"If you're black, you didn't really quite belong there.
So we'll discount that a bit"

MP: How did you decide you wanted to be a lawyer?
CT: I had quit the seminary. I'm not going to be a priest. What role, what job, or what profession, could I be engaged in that would allow me to do some of the things I was interested in? Perhaps someone comes with a problem. How do you address it? You look around society and you see its laws. Laws affect everybody. It has an influence on everyone's lives. If you're poor and you look at people like my grandfather, I think of when he came home one day, and he was very upset, and he was taking a drink. He never took a drink in the middle of the day. Well, what had happened was, he was driving the oil truck, a police officer stopped him. I think he fined him like $40 or so, and it had to be paid in cash on site. And he had stopped him for having too many clothes on, and that's ridiculous.

Just the thought of it is ridiculous. But what do you do? My grandfather is this black gentleman. It's Savannah. It is either the late fifties or early sixties. He has no way of challenging that. So he ran into the law, and he always was afraid of that. You couldn't walk across certain parks, you couldn't go to certain schools, people's property being taken, people taking advantage of him because they could say, "The law did this or did that." So, I thought maybe the law would be a good path, and it would allow me to do a variety of things. So I decided I was going to go to law school.

MP: You get admitted to Harvard Law School. How did you feel? How do you tell your grandparents?
CT: Part of my goal to go to law school was that you always had to have, at least at that point in my life, this rabbit to chase. And so just out of the blue, I said, and maybe not out of the blue but for some reason, I'm going to go to Harvard. So that set that rabbit. It didn't mean I was going to get to go to Harvard. But it gave me something to aspire to.

When I was admitted in my senior year, I called my grandmother up. In those days you call long distance; it wasn't as easy as today. I had to call collect. You call a long-distance operator, and they put you through, and someone has to accept the collect call, and it was my grandmother. And I told her I'd just gotten accepted to Harvard Law School. She was a sweet, sweet woman. And she said, "That's wonderful, if that's what you want. But when are you going to stop going to school?" And I understood that. She didn't know what Harvard was. It wasn't a part of her lexicon. It wasn't a part of her world. What difference does it make to her? So you realize that the things that might be important to you, in the scheme of things to the people who are important to you, they're not a big deal. It's just more school. Plus, I had devalued the education in New England a bit because I had become so negative, and had such a bad attitude, and with left-wing ideologies, with sort of this radical disposition, and rudeness toward my grandfather, in particular, and disavowing the things that I had been raised to cherish.

MP: It seems also to confirm a point you made earlier, that the gap was widening between you and where you were from. She didn't know what Harvard Law might mean to you and your future.

CT: In high school, I was living near Savannah, and even though I was there, there was this gap that was occurring between my grandfather, my grandmother, my family, my cousins, and even my brother and me. The world that I was spending the bulk of my time in was different from the world that we all had in common. And when I went to New England, it totally broke the connection. Not only was it foreign, it had turned me into, I think, someone that part of my family would have considered objectionable—certainly my grandfather would have considered objectionable. So not only did the distance increase geographically, but it also increased ideologically. I'd stopped going to church, I did not go to Mass anymore, which was anathema. I mean, the idea that I would be home in Savannah, and not go to Mass, a kid who had just been, a little before that, in the seminary. So I had become a different person. I was becoming a stranger in our household.

MP: And then, in the end, you decided to go to Yale.

CT: I had applied, again in an ill-informed way, to three law schools. And I can't explain why. I was a young kid, had very little input from adults. I applied to the University of Pennsylvania, Harvard, and Yale. And when I was admitted to Harvard, there wasn't much need to apply to a lot of other schools—remember the rabbit I was chasing. But then when I visited, I decided that it was too big and too conservative for me. The University of Pennsylvania was smaller, and I thought I'd go there. Yale was kind of your reach school. There's no way I'm going to get in, but I'm going to give it a shot. And when I didn't get a letter of acceptance, I assumed I was rejected.

Apparently, what had happened was, my grandmother in one of my phone conversations with her said, "Some papers came here for you." So that explained the delay in hearing from Yale. And in those days, when you got a thick envelope from a law school, that meant you were accepted because they were sending you a packet of materials for you to review, including a catalog and housing options, things like that. When you got a thin envelope, that was a rejection because there was no need for additional information. Well, the letter from Yale was thin. So I assumed, that was that. And it turned out, that it was an acceptance letter. But it explained the late arrival.

MP: In the summer before attending Yale Law School, where did you work?
CT: After our wedding, we moved to New Haven immediately. Again, I didn't have any money, so I needed a job. And once again, Father Brooks, this great man, he was like a father, and when I told him I was going to New Haven, he called up a Holy Cross alumnus, Judge Angelo Santaniello, who was a local judge in Connecticut. And Judge Santaniello, he would eventually go on to be on the Supreme Court of Connecticut, called up someone at the New Haven Legal Assistance, and they gave me a job. I would work for them for the entirety of my time at Yale.

We got a one room apartment—not one bedroom, one room—an efficiency apartment. And we lived in the inner city across from Hill House High School. And I started at New Haven Legal Assistance.

MP: What did that experience working there teach you?
CT: New Haven Legal Assistance provided me the opportunity to meet some fabulous people, the most interesting of whom and most important for me was a woman who would become my son's godmother, when he was born. Pearly Carter lived in the housing projects on Dixwell Avenue, which is right in the heart of the inner city of New Haven, and just a few blocks from Yale. When she met me, she saw

me as a starry-eyed black kid who had these pie-in-the-sky ideas about how you could help in the community. And she said, "I'm going to school you." And she would take me into the neighborhoods, into the projects. We would remain friends until her death.

MP: Were you still a radical?
CT: I was cynical. I don't know what I was. I had a lot of questions. Remember, I had been at Holy Cross; I had been going to marches, we've done the free breakfast program, been to the meetings at the radical bookstore, wore the garb, had the attitude, had *Ramparts* magazine, hung out with the SDS [Students for a Democratic Society], you'd done all of that.

When I came back from the march in Boston on April 16, 1970, something had happened, where I wasn't going along, just to be going along. But I wasn't moving very fast in any particular direction. If anything, I was probably chasing my own tail and going in circles.

But I had taken a course my last semester of my senior year at Holy Cross. I was in the Honors Program, so you get to arrange certain courses. I had always been fascinated by Richard Wright and Ralph Ellison, and the way they progressed in their own thinking, or didn't progress. And I saw myself moving away from sort of the anger of Richard Wright and more toward the individuality that I saw in Ralph Ellison's *Invisible Man*. But it was not a straight line. I think sometimes, in retrospect, in our lives, people tend to smooth out all the edges. They tend to make it seem as though they weren't zigzagging, and backtracking, and losing their direction, and make it look as though they walked absolutely straight from Point A to Point B. Well, that's not life, and that's certainly not what happened with me. I can't say I was radical. I was confused to some extent. While I was at Yale, I voted for George McGovern.[1] A lot of people today think he was really liberal. When I voted for him, my sense was he was a bit too conservative for me. But he would do; I mean, he was the least bad.

MP: Yes, I agree that intellectual journeys are rarely straight lines. Did your work at these grassroots community groups help inform you in this journey?
CT: I got better informed about the inner city of New Haven. Someone comes in, and it's about a driver's license, it's about a divorce, I mean, they were about just regular things that happen in a low-income area. It's really sad. There was a lady who came in one day, a white lady, and she needed a pair of shoes, a special pair of shoes and we find out she's got a very prosperous son in Hartford. She started crying and saying she didn't want to burden him, for fifteen or twenty dollars for a pair of shoes. But it was her son, and I just thought it was really horrible. But it was that kind of thing that you saw day in and day out. It's someone who lost his driver's license, and now can't get to work, but it's his third drunk-driving ticket. You saw a very real thing.

The two groups that you saw at Yale, and I think you may see a bit in society. The first group are those who actually are there, who see the day-to-day and who see the individualized problems that people have. And then there's another group: it's those people who see it in theory, they have a macro theory, some sort an overarching theory. You never saw them in a community office. You never saw them actually talking to the people. They say their theory will help. And so you had, at that time, the law reform crowd. So the reformers wanted to form the overall theory and approach of law, and then apply it to these people. We wanted to help the people, and to do that, you had to understand the law and the people.

People had very grand visions about school busing, and school integration, and none of that seemed to be working. The anti-poverty programs didn't seem to be changing much. You had all these ideas that had given hope, and it didn't seem to be going any place. I remember meeting the heads of these community offices, but by the end of that summer, I realized this is not going to go anyplace. These people will spend more time talking about their offices and their budgets, and what they want and the personality things, and again rarely do you hear about actually helping people. And that bothered me. I don't think that it was changing me so much ideologically as that I was becoming informed.

MP: How were your impressions of Yale?
CT: You know what Yale was back in the 1970s. Yale was four generations of Groton and Phillips Exeter, and "my father's grandfather was here." And there were secret societies, and all that sort of stuff. It was a different world, and it was a world that I didn't quite understand.

THE BIRTH OF HIS SON
"NOBODY WAS GOING TO HAVE SOME SOCIAL
EXPERIMENT AND THROW MY SON IN THERE"

MP: Your son Jamal was born during your time at Yale.
CT: When Jamal was born in February of my second year of law school, it woke me up about the direction that we were headed in our country and what the prospects would be for him.

You are in New Haven, and you get the news from New York and New England, and one of the big issues was school busing in Boston. I watched busing on TV, and busing was a big deal, remember because it was so violent in Boston. I'd been to South Boston, and I was scared to death to be over there, and the schools were as bad as the schools in Roxbury where the black kids were from. So why were you sending a kid through all that trouble, to go to a school that's as bad or worse? That didn't make any sense to me.

I saw that they have these theories and these overarching agendas and did not think of the little kids. What are they going to do with my son?

But I knew one thing, nobody was going to have some social experiment and throw my son in there. Someone has a theory, and then they insert human beings into their theory. To me that was always ghoulish, and we talk about Frankenstein monsters, but what about these social projects? I was going to school not for some theoretical reason, but in order to start with the individual, help that person, and then use the law, and other processes, to help that individual. Not to show you that I have this macro theory about society, and I just insert individuals, you know, sort of like, "Have theory. Add people." You know, it's like instant coffee or something, "Have coffee. Add water." So I wouldn't do that. I think that's wrong.

I understand the theory, but to what end was all of that? I understand that segregation is wrong. I grew up under segregation. I always thought it was wrong. But that's it.

Ending segregation and school busing are two different things. Segregation can be ended by simply saying, "You will be allowed to attend school where you live." That you'll be allowed to go to whatever school you want to. That's the end of segregation.

MP: Did many black people agree with you about busing?
CT: Putting kids on a bus, and busing them from Roxbury to South Boston, to what end? What was the purpose of that? Most blacks agreed with me on busing. There's a reason why I like to be with regular people. Those are my people, and they don't get to delude themselves and to pretend. Things have to work, things must be what they are. They can't be pretend, especially poor people.

If you're in a position of leadership, my question has always been: If you're walking on the edge of a cliff, why won't you walk carefully? Isn't every step a measured step versus you're just walking on flat ground? If you're walking down a corridor, you're not looking at the surface, not looking at the wall, you might be reading something, and today, people are on their cell phones. But if you're on the edge of a mountain, you're hiking in the Rockies, and going along the edge, you are really careful.

Why aren't we that careful when we deal with poor people? These people are on the edge. You make a mistake, it destroys them. They can't recover. The people whose kids were being bused, for whom education meant everything, they didn't see the point of it. Now, if the leadership told them to do it, they went along.

In the South, kids had been bused for segregation purposes. Savannah had the black high schools, and they were busing the black kids to either one of those schools. But they were passing white schools to get there. To get to Sol C. Johnson, many blacks in the city passed Savannah High School, which was all white, and some would have to pass Jenkins High School, which was white.

Busing was a constant. So my grandfather's question to us is, "What difference does it make if you turn the bus around and sent it in the opposite direction?" His parting shot on busing was, "Ain't nobody never learned nothin' on no damn bus." That was the end of it. His point was, the bus was irrelevant. He thought you should be able to go to the closest school, and it should not be based on race. And the schools should not be segregated.

MP: If most poor African Americans felt this way, why didn't you see this point of view on the local news?
CT: Well, it's because poor people don't hold the cameras, and poor people are not the ones sought out to be on *Meet the Press*. They're not

the opinion-makers. When I went back home, you heard from people who couldn't articulate things in the way that the more elite blacks, the so-called leaders, could. I was very fortunate in my life because I got to live in all of these worlds. I got to be a part of the poorest world, that's my world. The least educated, that's my world. I'm a direct descendant of slaves. I don't have to pretend. I don't have to tell you, "I knew somebody who was a descendant of slaves." It's a direct line. But on the other side of that, you have the exposure to Yale and that world, and all that entails—the exposure to the most literate people and the most well-heeled. So the people that I have the most affinity for are the poor, the poorest. I mean, those are the people I'm from. No one consulted them. Nobody asks them, "Do you want your babies bused to South Boston?" They did it, for the most part, because they thought it would help their children. And I think that's the failing. When you lead, you're obligated to not lie to them and to look out for their children.

Yale Law Graduate Who Can't Get a Job
"They smile in your face, but they feel exactly the way the guy feels with the 'No Coloreds Allowed' Sign"

MP: When you graduated from Yale, did your grandparents attend the ceremony?
CT: Yale was the end of the line, and I made it through. So I really wanted my grandfather to be there to witness the end, to witness that the kid that he took in in 1955 crossed the finish line. My grandfather did not come. He always had a reason. I think he was upset with me. I can understand that. And I certainly had not given him many good reasons to have any deep and warm fuzzy feelings about me, or my graduation. So nobody could come.

That was probably more difficult for me, and embittered me, more than anything else.

MP: How did you go about looking for a job after law school?
CT: I interviewed for jobs in D.C., Atlanta, New York, L.A.—with anyone, anywhere who might hire me.

The bottom line is the same, no matter what the reasoning is, the people looking at you for a job do not believe that you actually achieved what your resume said you achieved. Everything now is discounted. If you were black and you were at Yale, the presumptions were quite different than if you were white. So if you're white and you graduated from Yale, the presumption is what? It is that you are really among the best. On the other hand, if you're black and you're there, you didn't really quite belong there. So we'll discount that a bit. They can say ten percent, five percent, whatever. But the reality was the discounted approach resulted in certainly me not being able to get a job.

MP: How did your experience with this kind of racism up North compare to what you went through down South?
CT: In the South, they said, "No Coloreds Allowed," that sort of thing. Well, that's unpleasant. But they told you what they think. If someone made a negative comment, did not speak to you when you spoke to them, that's a negative. You don't like it, and it's wrong. But you know where they stand.

The same people, the hard ones in New England, and especially among the liberal elite, they smile in your face, but they feel exactly the way the guy feels with the "No Coloreds Allowed" sign, but they're smiling at you. So if you had to deal with unpleasantness, with someone who had a negative opinion of you, would you prefer to deal with the person who told you outright or the person who deceived you that they didn't feel that way, but in fact, felt exactly the same way?

MP: Your grandfather, I believe, compared them to rattlesnakes and water moccasins?
CT: I prefer not to be around either. But if you have to, if it's a binary choice, I prefer the rattlesnake, because unless you run up on it, it always warns you. Hence the rattle. It's basically saying to you, "Look I'm over here. I'm minding my business. Give me a few minutes, I'll get out of your way. But if you don't, you're going to have a bad day." The moccasin, on the other hand, never warns you. It sits there. It does not leave. And it says, "You are about to have a really bad day, because I'm not going to warn you, and I'm going to smack you."

Being from Lowcountry Georgia, we had both. We have the canebrake rattlers, which can be as long as six feet, and you have water moccasins. If you go back in those swamps, that's what's back there. And they can put a hurtin' on you. But the moccasins were more of the liberals in the Northeast; the rattlesnake was more of the Southerner and they warned you. You don't want to encounter either negative person. But if you have to choose one, if you have to run into a pit of vipers, would you prefer a rattlesnake or the moccasin?

And my grandfather always talked about that. He says, some people are water moccasins, that they just sit there. They don't tell you what they think. They don't give you a warning, and then they smack you. Maybe they smile in your face like a cottonmouth, got a big old wide smile on his face. But the rattlesnake gives you an opportunity to leave: "No Coloreds Allowed." Now, I'm not saying that's pleasant. Not saying it's right; in fact, I think it's wrong. I think it's all bigotry when it comes from whites, or blacks, or Asians, or Hispanics. All bigotry is just wrong. But, the choice is between the deceptive form of bigotry and the open bigotry. What would you pick? For someone trying to navigate his way through the uncertain world, I like a bright red light that warns me of danger, as opposed to inviting me in, and then closing down on me like a steel trap.

GOING TO WORK FOR MISSOURI ATTORNEY GENERAL JACK DANFORTH
"THE IDEA OF WORKING FOR A REPUBLICAN WAS REPULSIVE AT BEST"

MP: Eventually the Missouri Attorney General Jack Danforth offered you a job.
CT: Frank Washington [a classmate] had heard from then-professor [Guido] Calabresi that a friend of his, who had been at Yale Law School with him and who was the new attorney general of Missouri, was hiring students from Yale Law School. There was a posting on the bulletin board. I got [Jack Danforth's] number, called up and found out that he would be in New Haven. I set up an interview with him and that was the beginning of a new chapter in my life.

I had had really bad luck in some interviews, and you knew you were never going to get the job, not in a hundred years. And he was clapping his hands and he was all happy, saying, "Clarence, plenty of room at the top, plenty of room."

For me, I am thinking, "That's easy for you to say. You're the rich guy, and you're white, and you got it all." He was in his thirties and just pleasant. Maybe seeing the look on my face, he said, "I have never been in your shoes, and so I don't really know." He said, "I was born"—he didn't say silver spoon—he said, "I was born with a platinum spoon in my mouth. I really can't say how you feel," but then he went on to promise me, "Clarence, I promise you more work for less money than anybody in the country."

I told him, I wasn't interested in just being a token, just being there to fill a box. The pay was $10,800. And it was the only job offer I got. It was the quintessential Hobson's Choice. The hardest part about taking the job was he was a Republican, and the idea of working for a Republican was repulsive, at best. I was a registered Democrat. I was left-wing. As nice as he was, he was still a Republican. Putting that nicety aside, I wound up going.

MP: What did your friends say about working for a Republican?
CT: One of the students to whom I mentioned I finally got a job, and that it was the attorney general's office in Missouri, said, "What a waste of a Yale Law School education." And I said, "I'll see you in twenty-five years." That was that.

MP: It's a waste because it's thrown away at a Republican?
CT: It was a "nothing" job, he thought, because it wasn't New York, it wasn't D.C., it wasn't for a judge, I wasn't clerking. It was a job that you could get going to law school at University of Missouri–Kansas City, University of Missouri, Kansas University, or St. Louis University. But Yale was above that.

MP: What was it like working for Jack Danforth?
CT: Jack Danforth was the best boss I've ever had. Jack was just a good man. You can agree or disagree with him, that doesn't matter. He's just a good man. He never asked you to do anything unethical or wrong. He never asked me to do anything political. He respected your judgment. He was honorable. People often say, "No man is a hero to his valet." The familiarity with him, actually, has shown me just how decent and good a person he is. I've come to appreciate that more. That office was honest; it was understaffed. We had thirty-something lawyers, we probably needed a hundred. The work was

thrown at you, much like that television skit between Ethel [Mertz] and Lucille Ball in the candy factory, where the belt keeps speeding up, and they kept stuffing candy in their pockets. And the work was coming in like that, furiously. So it was indiscriminately and fairly assigned. No one lorded it over you. They expected you to do your work, and as a result of that, when you did a good job, it wasn't that you got any higher pay. What you got was the respect of your colleagues.

MP: You have written that, as a radical, you had concerns about cases where the Attorney General's Office was arguing to uphold convictions of black defendants.
CT: Cases poured through there; in those days, the Attorney General's Office handled all the appeals from the local prosecutors across the state. At the time, my thinking was that all blacks were political prisoners. That's sort of the sophisticated level at which I looked at the criminal justice system.

I worried about what I would do when I got a case involving black defendants. And then it happened. This guy was sitting on a bench and this black woman comes by. He's black, she's black. She's got her two- or three-year-old kid in the car with her. In those days, most people didn't have air conditioning. So, the windows are down. He comes up to the car at the stopped light, with an old-style can opener with a point, puts it to the kid's neck, and forces his way in the car, threatening the kid. And then he takes her to a remote location, rapes and sodomizes her.

Then she had to even stop for gas at one point. Throughout all of this, the can opener is at the kid's neck, and he takes her to another location, and rapes and sodomizes her again. And for that he received, I think, two twenty-five-year sentences. And I remember thinking: I thought that blacks were victimized by history, but to the extent that blacks are victimized by history, this woman was twice victimized.

And then I began to look into violent crime, and the intra-racial nature of violent crimes, rapes, murders, robberies, et cetera. And for the first time I realized that virtually all violent crime, and certainly the overwhelming majority of violent crime, is intra-racial, not inter-racial. So we can, at the margins, make race into an issue. But for the most part it's intra-racial, and it's black-on-black crime. And for most people, that would be obvious. For me, it was one of these "Road to Damascus" experiences.

MP: It sounds like you enjoyed working in the AG's office?
CT: The great thing about that job in Jeff City was that there was so much work. I'd invariably start work around 4:30 in the morning, and that was to get an extra four hours in. Others came in around 8:00. I had a lot of work to do, and I also had a lot to learn. In my mind, I figured, look if I'm traveling at the same rate of speed or slower than the other guy, and I've got to get farther, what are my choices? I've got longer to travel, so I just got to work earlier so eventually I will be farther.

I had wonderful friends. One of them was a quadriplegic, Richard Weiler. He's since passed away. He made you think about things differently. He got polio at fifteen, but he never would allow himself to be treated as a victim. He didn't want to be characterized, as, he called it, a "cripple." He didn't want to be called that. He also didn't want you to stereotype him with that. He was from West Point, Nebraska. He went to University of Missouri Law School. When he got polio, he lost the use of his limbs, and was in an iron lung in Warm Springs, Georgia. He would graduate from the University of Missouri Law School with honors. He put a stick in his teeth, and he would put a pen in that. With that stick, that's how he wrote. And then we would do e-mail years later and he would type with a rubber point on the end of that stick. He would type on the computer, and that's why I started doing email, because we would email together.

Richard would challenge you about being defined by bad things that have happened to you for being black. And I'm looking at him, and he's in a wheelchair. He can't move a limb, and he refuses to be defined by it. He made you see beyond what was right in front of your eyes. But if he brought it up every day, if that's all he focused on, if that's how he defined himself, then how would you define him? He understood that. We would often talk about race, and you could really be honest. They were just a fabulous group of people. Best place I've ever worked, hands down. Especially for the honesty and decency.

THE IMPACT OF THOMAS SOWELL
"CLARENCE, THERE'S ANOTHER BLACK GUY WHO THINKS LIKE YOU"

MP: How did you first hear about Thomas Sowell?
CT: I get this call from Richard one day, and he says, "Clarence, there's another black guy who thinks like you. His name is Thomas Sowell. And there's a review of his book in the *Wall Street Journal*." I'd seen a book by him before when I was at Yale, *Black Education: Myths and Tragedies*, and at that time, I threw it out and said, "I don't see how any black man could think this way."[2] And now, there was something salvific about receiving a copy of this. And I sought out the book [*Race and Economics*], read it voraciously, and this really had a tremendous impact on my life.[3]

MP: How would you describe that impact?
CT: Thomas Sowell is incapable of deception, and he is absolutely brilliant. His work is insightful. He grew up in Harlem, dropped out,

tested into one of the elite public schools in New York. He had to drop out to work. He went into the Marine Corps and, I think, that's where he got his GED. He's an avid photographer, phenomenal photographer. He learned that in the Marine Corps. As he said, he was "always one step ahead of court martial." I kind of like that. He left the Marine Corps. He went to Howard University at night and worked later in the Labor Department. Someone told him he should be at Harvard. He tested into Harvard, graduated *magna cum laude* in economics, and then got a masters from Columbia in economics, and then a Ph.D. in economics from Chicago, where he was, he told me, a Marxist, and made that same move to the right, to a more of a free market view.

Everything has to make sense, and if it doesn't make sense, he'll try to figure out what makes sense. What are the reasons for things? He didn't just spout these mantras that are so popular. And that's what was intriguing to me about him.

If you read his book *A Conflict of Visions*, he tries to sort out the group of people who are the anointed, who feel that they're in charge of all of us, and the benighted, who are people just trying to get through life.[4] You read his book *Knowledge and Decisions*, it is fascinating because it's not always the people who make the decisions who have the knowledge.[5] And it's not always the case that people who have the knowledge, get to make the decision.

MP: When did you first meet Thomas Sowell?
CT: The first time I saw Tom Sowell was in 1978. He was on the program debating Professor Ruth Bader Ginsburg at Washington University in St. Louis, and a friend saw the flyer, and I went there to see it. And, of course, took my book, *Race and Economics,* to have him sign it. I was a total groupie. Coincidentally, on that same program, but not at that event, was Professor Antonin Scalia. Who would have known that three future members of the Court, colleagues, would be there the same day?

A New Side to His Grandfather
"My grandfather raised me in a way that I could raise Jamal the right way"

MP: During this time, when you went back home, what were your relations like with your grandfather?
CT: It wasn't strained. I would come back and drop off my son, his great-grandson. And my grandfather loved that. When Jamal came, or any of his great grandkids visited, he just lit up. He just absolutely loved it. I sent Jamal to stay with him, so that Jamal could see the hard life: how we were raised, the discipline of my grandfather, so he can have a perspective in that continuity.

I would go down every summer, Jamal's there six weeks or so. Then I also want him to stay with my sister and her kids as they were growing up so he would always be familiar with his family. I'd go back to pick up Jamal, and Jamal's got all these different cereals. We were only allowed one cereal to be opened, Kellogg's Corn Flakes. He would have Fruit Loops, or something, Frosted Flakes; just every sweet kind you can think of. And they're all opened, five boxes open at once.

And so I asked my grandfather about this injustice. And he said that they were all open because Jamal wanted the prizes inside. And I said, "But you forbade us to do anything like that." And he said, "Jamal was going to get ice cream whenever he wanted to." He was watching cartoons with Jamal, something he never did with us. If you were watching cartoons, he would come up and turn the TV off. So I said, "I sent Jamal here to get the discipline. Why are you doing this?" And he says, "Jamal is not my responsibility. I'm going to enjoy my great-grand." And then I saw a side of him that was quite different. We didn't argue, and it was not where we had patched over differences or dealt with them, we just didn't fuss about that.

MP: Did you feel like you would have wanted some of that when you were growing up?

CT: Oh God yeah. Who wouldn't? And maybe it just showed you what he was capable of and what you missed out on. He would be lying on the floor, and Jamal crawling all over him, and suddenly Jamal suggests, "Let's go get ice cream in the truck." I mean it was all about Jamal; sun rose and set on Jamal. So yeah, I would have loved it. My grandfather also admitted later in life that he thought that he probably was a little too hard on us.

My grandfather figured a lot of things out. He was very concerned about what happened to little kids. And he always said that he was a motherless child who had been handed from pillar to post, and that he didn't think that kids should grow up like that. I thought he and my grandmother were the most compassionate people I'd ever met, because they always told us the truth. Think of the compassion he has, assuming that inside is this warm and fuzzy guy, too. And that because of his hard life, he would want us to have a softer life. But he looks out through life, and he sees how hard it's going to be. What's the most compassionate thing to do? To prepare us for that hard life, not indulge himself with a relationship with us that was fun for him, but in the long term destructive of us. My grandfather raised me in a way that I could raise Jamal the right way.

WORKING FOR MONSANTO
"I COULD FEEL THE GOLDEN HANDCUFFS CLOSING"

MP: At some point, you left Senator Danforth's office and went to work for Monsanto. How did that happen?

CT: Jack Danforth got elected to the Senate. I had already been there two and a half years, and I really wanted to move more toward business. I had better options now. I went to Monsanto. It was a fine job, but it was not enough work for me. I had too much energy, and they spoon-fed the work, and they parceled it out, and I was used to the work pouring in. Remember at any one time, when I was doing tax cases, I had six hundred or so open tax cases. I had a lot going on, and suddenly, now I'm in a job—it'd be like going from a hundred miles an hour to about fifteen miles an hour. You're still moving, but boy, that's a snail's pace.

I was underemployed. I had lots of time, and I read books. John Bolton, who would become Ambassador Bolton, was my classmate at Yale. I called him up, and I think he was at a local firm here in D.C. and asked him if he would send me an intellectual care package. So he sent me all these reports from AEI, the American Enterprise Institute, and articles. I would read those in my free time, in my windowless office. And I would read *The Economist, Business Week,* every business magazine, or paper. It was good in a lot of ways. I got to think about a lot of things.

MP: Did you go speak with the affirmative action manager about problems you had identified?
CT: Well, actually, I rarely saw the affirmative action EEO guy. I became very agitated because I met some of the black employees, and I knew some of the actual things that were happening to them. I was very interested in what was happening to the other black executives.

I confronted him about it, and he pulls out this EEO report, with the numbers on it—it was one of these computer printouts—as though these are people. You know, he is not talking about who's getting training, who's got mentors, what assignments they have, who's getting promoted. He's got his report that he shows to the Labor Department, and that is these statistics. That's what I was talking about. And

I would just go sit outside his office. I'm sure the poor guy started calling and finding out, "Is he there?"

MP: Wasn't the affirmative action manager African-American?
CT: Yes.

MP: He wasn't sympathetic?
CT: He was doing his job and his reports were okay.

MP: He didn't care that these other black managers were stalled?
CT: Well, I don't know if he cared. He was doing his job, and the reports were okay. That's the most I got. But I just thought that we were kidding ourselves. We're looking at numbers and the numbers prove everything. And human beings are having a lot of difficulties.

MP: On your thirty-first birthday, you went to the law library of the St. Louis Bar Association to think things through.
CT: I had a long history of self-improvement projects. Remember that list of magazines in college and in law school? I started subscribing to *Success* magazine. You'd get a small magazine, a little bigger than pocket size. It would have all these tips in it, all this positive thinking. And remember now, I'm cynical, I was negative, and I'm trying to get out of it. It's like cleaning up your act. One of the things I did, and it's as simple as this: I made a chart with a plus sign and the minus sign. The idea is: increase the pluses, reduce the minuses. These are all things, I guess, self-help programs out of the *Success* magazine. You had to think in these increments, five years from now, ten years from now. I went through all these exercises, and I realized that there was no successful person there [at Monsanto] that I wanted to be like. Which tells you: I don't want to be here. I would go through all these self-help things, and I did that for years. I did that on my thirty-first

birthday—at the St. Louis County Bar Association Law Library. I think it was in Clayton, Missouri. And I just took a legal pad and a pen, and I stayed there all day, leaving only to go to lunch. And then the next day, I walked in and quit my job.

MP: You have spoken about resisting the "golden handcuffs," of not wanting to get too comfortable in a corporate job.
CT: I was on my way home, we had just got in this house, and there was a three way stop there, because there was a golf course across the street. And I stopped, looked at my house. Nice-looking place, nice street, nice environment. I was young, I just turned thirty-one. I could feel the golden handcuffs closing, that "it's going to get comfortable now." My boss wanted to know what was wrong. What could he do? And I said, "It's not you." Then he said he worked out a way for me to get a pay increase, to get a bonus. He had all these things to keep me, and I said, "It's not you."

I had a great boss in the company, Wayne Wethers. He became my friend. He was thoughtful. He was a good mentor. When I was at Monsanto, I was not in the right job. It wasn't the company. I was in the wrong place. So I just went in and quit, as opposed to staying around and grousing about it.

Shortly after that I get a call from Senator Danforth to see if I would be interested in working for him.

I told him I'd do it as long as I didn't have to do civil rights or race issues. And there was a reason for that. I didn't want to get in the eye of the storm because I had decidedly different views by now. And anybody who offered those views was going to get killed. And I didn't want to be in that position. And I also think that there's this tendency to put blacks in civil rights jobs. That said, he said he would offer me a job working on energy, environment, and public works issues. That was when President Carter had declared war on the energy crisis. And I just thought that would be fabulous. I thought that the future, coming from Monsanto, was going to include: How do you dispose of the waste that we create? I thought the energy issue was going to get to be complicated with the environmental issue—this is going to be fascinating. And it was on those terms that I came to Washington. It was a cut in total compensation, and quite a significant one; the cost of living was drastically different from the cost of living in St. Louis.

MP: Let me ask you about a couple of other things happening at the time. Blaxploitation films were popular then. What was your attitude towards them?
CT: I think I may have seen one, I may have seen *Shaft*. *Superfly* and all, I thought they were horrible.[6] Not because I didn't want these guys working as actors. I didn't like the image. My image of the black man, and blacks in general, was more of what you would see in this most recent movie on NASA [*Hidden Figures*], or *Akeelah and the Bee*, or *Something the Lord Made*.[7] It wasn't this slick guy, in an outlandish outfit wearing the fur hat and the platform shoes, that kind of stuff. That wasn't like the world I grew up in. That wasn't the barbershop that I went to on Saturday morning. That wasn't Mr. Miller next door, Mr. Honchild, that wasn't Mr. Coin, or Mr. Joe, or my grandfather, or Cousin Robert, or Mr. Dallas. These were working people. All of a sudden, I'm looking at this slick guy. Those are the guys that my grandfather used to ridicule. He believed you should only have a brown suit and a blue suit, and a black suit for funerals. That was it. You should be frugal, and you should work hard. Now you get the blaxploitation movies exalting drugs, pimping, and lawbreaking, and I'm not saying that doesn't happen. I'm not saying it isn't just fiction, but I was against the image because it was a cool, and attractive, and

an empowering—to some—image. And I just thought it was wrong. That was my view and I expressed it.

ATTACKS ON BOOKER T. WASHINGTON
"YOU DENIGRATE. YOU DEFAME"

MP: You've said that your thinking is more aligned with Booker T. Washington than with W. E. B. Du Bois.
CT: W. E. B. Du Bois was a self-described socialist. We all admired him and appreciated all the work he did with the NAACP. We revered W. E. B., but Booker T. was a legend. In fact, most blacks I knew, especially like my grandfather, they wouldn't even say, "Booker T. Washington." They just say, "Booker T." And then it was a very popular name, too, for black youth. He used to give the Sunday evening talks, chapel talks, at Tuskegee, and I think I've gone back and read just about all of them. They're basic things, things I heard growing up, about hygiene, and frugality, and hard work, and learning the basics, and getting things right. I have been a fan of Booker T. and Frederick Douglass for quite some time. They're both freed slaves, one a runaway slave and one a freed slave.

MP: Why do you think that in the black pantheon, W. E. B. Du Bois is at the top, and Booker T. has been somewhat devalued at the moment?
CT: Well, who writes the books? My grandfather doesn't write the books. Who creates the literature? It's not my grandfather. But that's true in society. If you're more conservative, even a member of the Court, you're not going to be treated that way in the literature. The liberals are writing the books. That's just the way it works.

MP: Some of the criticism of Booker T. must sound familiar. He is often called an Uncle Tom.

CT: Yeah, that's what you do: defamation. You denigrate, you defame, you engage in all sorts of calumnies. That's just the way it is. I understood that in a limited way, before I was sort of thrown into it in my early thirties, in the government. That's one of the reasons I didn't want to serve in government, because you realize you're going to get killed. That's what they do. The very people who were so "tolerant" are the ones who use defamation. I just found it fascinating, to have gone to all-black schools, all-white schools, in the South, and at no time being subjected to the kind of things that happened in the Northeast, and among the elite. Never, not once crossing the race line to go to the public library, not once even when I could finally walk across parks that I had been prevented from going across, not once was I accosted. Not once, walking through white neighborhoods was I accosted. I remember going into a Big Boy restaurant before it was integrated, with my white schoolmates, and being stared at but never really defamed, and then not being defamed by my white classmates from the South. Defamation would come from people who were self-proclaimed "tolerant" people.

MP: I think you've described going to restaurants with your white classmates at Immaculate Conception and having that kind of experience.

CT: I went with some classmates, first when I was in the seminary, and some of them didn't do anything, a few of them crossed the street because it was still anathema to be seen with me. That's the most that happened. Then, when I was in Immaculate Conception, my first year of college, we were at a Shakey's Pizza Place, and we were having way too much fun, and I got booted out. So all my schoolmates left with me. I really liked that. I don't, in retrospect, care for my conduct that got us kicked out. But I do like the fact that my schoolmates went with me.

CHAPTER FIVE

ENTERING THE ARENA

*"You're not really black because you're not doing
what you expect black people to do"*

MP: When you first came to Washington in 1979, you have described
how you loved seeing the monuments, and it was a little like the movie
Mr. Smith Goes to Washington.[1]

CT: Oh God, I loved it. I got goosebumps. I took the bus in every day,
it would come by the White House in those days. Pennsylvania Avenue
was open, and I would literally get goosebumps every time I went by.
It didn't matter. I mean, "Wow." My grandfather, if he could just see
me going in front of the White House. I admit I was a bit of a hick. I
don't know about you, but when I see the monuments, they symbolize
something important. This is the seat of our government, the symbols
of what we believe, whether we live up to it or not.

MP: By 1980, you had changed your registration to become a Republican. What made you make that shift?

CT: Virtually everyone in the South was a Democrat. My grandfather was a Democrat. No one explained why, but it was almost

reflexive. I think it has a lot to do with the Roosevelt administration, but also we were Catholics. The nuns were very much JFK proponents. I started voting at eighteen. My first vote was for Hubert Humphrey for president, then I voted for George McGovern in 1972. Those were more reflexive votes. I really did not think that deeply about it, other than I thought both of them were a little bit conservative for my taste. And by the time I got to Washington, I had thought a lot more about things. I had registered in Missouri as an independent. I was not a Democrat when I came to town, but I was not a Republican, and I registered as a Republican to vote for Reagan in Maryland.

MP: Shortly after the election of Ronald Reagan, you were invited by Thomas Sowell to the Fairmont Conference in December 1980.
CT: I had met Tom Sowell in 1978 at the Washington University Law School. When I came to the Hill, he had made several trips and made presentations to some of the staffers, and they gave him a bit of a hard time. I was the only one who had read his books and defended him. We became acquaintances, and as a result of that, Tom Sowell invited me to this conference. And it would be named the Fairmont Conference because it was held at the Fairmont Hotel in San Francisco. It was about race and how we rethink the policies toward blacks in this country in a new administration.[2]

MP: You met the *Washington Post* reporter Juan Williams at lunch?
CT: I sat at this table, and there was a young black reporter [Williams] there. And I knew nothing about the press. We talked candidly, and, of course, I was very enthusiastic about a lot of things. One question he asked me was, "Why was I so interested in all these social issues?" And I explained to him, it was because of the

destruction I saw it doing at home in Savannah. And as an example of that, I used my sister and her kids being objects of these programs. Little did I know, he would write an article about this and would turn it into an op-ed, which would be the source of a great deal of criticism.

MP: That was your first time being in the news?
CT: This was the first time I was the focal point of a news article, December 16, 1980.[3] I have never forgotten. The first I knew Juan Williams was doing this story, our press person in the office for Senator Danforth, Janet Brown, comes by and says, "The *Washington Post* wants to take a photo of you." They sent a photographer, and my heart sank. So that was the first I knew this was about to happen, and, of course, I panicked.

MP: When the article hit the stands and people read it, what was the response?
CT: It wasn't positive. I was horrified to suddenly see my views sitting out there. We all have views, but the last thing you expect is for them to be on full display for the whole world to react to. It's an interesting world we're in, where people claim to be tolerant, but they really aren't. For minorities, or if they put you in one of their designated groups, you're not supposed to have certain thoughts. There were these set opinions that were supposed to be universal among certain groups, and to criticize these policies, particularly their effects, you were a bad person.

Then license is given to others to attack you in whatever way they want to. You're not really black because you're not doing what you expect black people to do. You weren't supposed to oppose busing; you weren't supposed to oppose welfare.

MP: Maybe the *Washington Post* story, which was the first time you personally were out front, was a Rubicon moment for you. Perhaps it marked a course for you, Justice Thomas?

CT: Oh, I don't know if it marked a course, but there was no going back. The only way you could go back, and I'm not going to name names, but there are some people who would apologize for having said it. That would be the next step, "*Mea culpa, mea culpa. Mea maxima culpa.*" You say, "Even though that was truth, I was wrong. I shouldn't have said it. I was insensitive." So in other words, you keep moving back from what you said. Or they wanted me to say that I shouldn't have mentioned my sister.

I didn't want to mention my sister—I would not have done that if I had known what I was doing exactly—because I thought it was a private conversation. But let's just say for example, if I had been asked, "Oh, why are you so concerned about breast cancer? Why are you wearing pink?" "Oh, because my sister had breast cancer." I mean she didn't, but what if that was the example? People would say, "Oh isn't he concerned about his sister? His sister's been a victim of breast cancer; she's a survivor. He's concerned about it." That makes sense. But if his sister is a victim of social policies and it's causing permanent damage to her and her offspring, then you're not supposed to mention that. I understand that now, but I didn't back then.

There was some significant vitriol toward me. If you walk down the street, people glared at you. One letter said that I had "a watermelon-eating grin on my face." I've never forgotten that. Well, I don't know what that means, but it was not a compliment.

MP: It's interesting that people are undeterred from using racial stereotypes like that one.

CT: Racial stereotypes are fully available when you attack someone who was not reading from the sheet of music he should be. Years later,

Hodding Carter, who was in the Carter administration, in criticizing me, said that I reminded him of "a chicken-eating preacher," and there was absolutely zero reaction. So if you are the person they expect you to be, and you do what you're supposed to do, and these things happen, then there will be this hypersensitivity about racial comments. I would be defended. But if you are not, if you leave the plantation, then you are going to be on your own.

MP: It's particularly shocking that Hodding Carter, a white man from the South, would say this.
CT: It's not shocking to me. None of this was shocking. One of my fears when I was at Monsanto and thinking through the possibility of my views being public, you knew you'd be thrown to the wolves. That it's okay to have a view privately, but God forbid that it be made public, or that you're in public life. There are any number of times there were blacks who would come up to me and whisper, "Oh, I agree with you, but I'm not saying that." I understand that, you don't want to take the heat, you want to hang in the shadows. And so the criticism, as a result, has its effect. It creates a fear of being honest. You know, there was that great line in *Invisible Man* where Ralph Ellison says that the worst he was ever treated is when he told the truth. So you're not supposed to tell the truth. The black kid [in *Invisible Man*] tells the white benefactor at the college the truth. He shows him these places that he shouldn't be showing him, and the head of the school says, "Don't you know we're supposed to lie to these people." That's a part of it, I understand. But I didn't want to go through the torment of that.

MP: On the personal side, your marriage was strained at this point?
CT: It is one of those things and I just—I didn't think it was going to work. I think many people go through that.

MP: Of course, many do. But what do you think was the reason in this case?

CT: You know, I really don't know. It just wasn't there, and I think that you have to be honest with yourself, and not wait until it deteriorates, or you do harm to somebody who did you no harm.

MP: I can imagine how difficult it must have been, for all three of you.

CT: Yeah, it was... You know, you live with it. Jamal came to live with me. His mother thought it would be best for me to have primary responsibility. Being with him was my happy place, being at home with him.

MP: The difficulty in your marriage was one of the things that led you to the process of going back to the Church.

CT: I think it was Paul who said, "We are at our strongest when we are at our weakest." It was a difficult time. It was challenging, and it was very confusing. And there were very few people I knew could give me advice and counsel. So I went where I had gone for most of my youth, and that's before the Blessed Sacrament over at St. Joseph's [Church], behind the Senate. It was just a short walk. I would just go over and make visitations during the day.

MP: Since you had left the Church for a while, did you have to think through the things that you had rejected and look at them differently?

CT: My grandfather used to say something that I have never forgotten. He would say, "Hard times make monkey eat cayenne pepper." And sometimes we realize that we have no other place to go; you run out of options. So I didn't think my way back; life drove me back.

MP: After all these hard times and political changes and life changes, was your faith different this time, in some way, than when you were a seminary student?
CT: Actually, I don't know how different it was. I was older. I had been away from the Church, and I still didn't go back to the Church. It would be years before I went back to the Church. It would be an on again, off again sort of thing. But that's like—everything in life is not necessarily a straight line.

MP: You still had your doubts?
CT: Oh yeah. I was not going to Mass. I went and did visit it, and I continued that practice throughout the eighties, that I would make almost daily visitations to the Blessed Sacrament. This is a rough town. Washington is a hard place. And the things that happened, didn't make sense to me—that someone could watch you doing "A" but then they would say you were doing "B." The games that people play in this town made no sense to me.

I come from an environment where you had to be honest with yourself. You either planted the corn, or you didn't. You either fed the hogs, or you didn't. You either stripped the fodder, or you didn't. You shucked the corn, or you didn't. And when the either doing or not doing would have a lot to do with your survival, you were always pretty straightforward.

Now suddenly you're in a world where one reporter would say to me sometime later, "We're here not to report the news, but to shape the news." What does that mean? Where did we get the authority? Where do we get the right to shape the news, rather than say exactly what happened? So where do we get the right to shape the reality of planting corn? To shape the reality of feeding the hogs? This town would drive you to your knees.

JOINING THE REAGAN ADMINISTRATION
"PUT UP OR SHUT UP"

MP: In 1981, you received a call from the Reagan administration's Office of Presidential Personnel about possibly joining the administration and working in the civil rights area.
CT: I was asked would I be interested in interviewing for a job over at the Department of Education. I wasn't interested in getting into civil rights stuff. I had a general idea of what my views were, and they were not consistent with the popular views. And I would get more of the harangue, more of the criticism and animosity. But I talked to Senator Danforth, and I talked to others on his staff. It still wasn't persuasive to me. I talked to one of my mentors who has since passed away, Jay Parker, and he basically said in a nice way, "Put up or shut up"—either go do it or don't talk about these issues anymore. Well, that was a tough one to swallow. Jay was very direct and very honest, unlike much of the city; what he said he meant. He was really a good man. I interviewed with then–Secretary of Education Terrel Bell, and it would be shortly after that he offered me the job [of assistant secretary for Civil Rights], and within a week or two, I was over there in an acting [assistant secretary] position, at the ripe old age of thirty-two.

MP: At the Department of Education, you've mentioned that you asked to see studies of the performance of blacks in integrated schools compared to segregated schools.
CT: Things that don't make sense make me uncomfortable. I remember the summer I taught myself algebra. You get an equation. It's supposed to balance out. Once you figure that out, then the whole process is how to balance out equations. "X" equals what? "Y" equals what?

One of the arguments for school busing and integration, not desegregation, was that it would improve the education of black kids. I'm at the Department of Education now, and I had a lot of energy. What actually happened with the improvement of education because of busing? That's a simple question: If you argued that if you did this, then what is the evidence of it now that you've been doing it for quite some time? I agitated for this and kept asking, and eventually one of the senior people said to me, "There are no such studies. We were never interested in the education; we were interested in some other things." And then he explained to me that their theory was that if you required kids to be bused across these metropolitan areas, from the black neighborhood to the white neighborhood, and from the white neighborhood to the black neighborhood, then eventually the parents would move to the neighborhood where the kids were going to school, and it would integrate the neighborhoods.

"You've got to be kidding me, right? Have we lost our minds?" I said, "Well, that would be news to these black parents, because they didn't want to put their kids on those buses, but they were told their kids would get a better education, so they were willing to go through that for something that was good. And now you're saying that it had nothing to do with that." I was told that more than once, by totally different people, that it was never about education—it was about using that model to integrate neighborhoods.

MP: You were also involved with resisting some efforts to abolish historically black colleges by civil rights groups, such as the NAACP?
CT: There was an effort by some, not necessarily in the Department of Education, to eliminate the black colleges. I thought that was absurd. And I remember having countless meetings with a group called NAFEO [National Association for Equal Opportunity in Higher Education] and with black college presidents. My office had

a conference room, and there was a back way to get into the conference room, and I would let them in and out, as some of them didn't want to be seen with officials in the Reagan administration.

One of the things they we were concerned about was this effort to eliminate schools that had been very helpful to blacks and had educated generations of blacks. And that's fine if the school goes out of business. But if a school was serving a function, why get rid of it? Why would you close a North Carolina A&T [Agricultural & Technical State College] when it can be an engineering school, it can do computer science in the future?

What we were told is they have no right to exist. This is by people who claim to be for minorities, and I thought it was absurd. But it was the same sort of carelessness or recklessness toward blacks. You get rid of it, now what do you do? You move these black kids around in these metropolitan areas, and it has unintended consequences like the de-population of the inner city. Now what do you do? Well, you go on to another project. To me, that is reckless, and you destroy human beings.

MP: Was the NAACP against historically black colleges because those colleges had a greater proportion of black students, and under the NAACP's theories, that suggested a problem?

CT: It never made a lot of sense to me. There was some premise that in order for us blacks to perform well, we had to sit next to a certain number of whites. And I had been fortunate. I had gone for the first ten years of my education to all-black schools. Then I went the next ten years to all-white schools, or virtually all-white schools. In the black schools, the students there were excellent. In the white schools, the students were excellent. But math was math in both schools. Physics was physics. Blacks could learn physics in a room full of blacks with a black professor.

I thought this argument was absurd. Now is segregation wrong? Is it morally wrong? Is it constitutionally wrong? Yes. But you don't have to denigrate the education, you don't have to denigrate the way people live, in order to say that. I don't know what the theory was exactly. When you're perplexed, you ask someone, "Tell me again, why you're doing this? Because I don't understand."

I've had the experience of segregation and integration, and I'm the one who would say, without one bit of hesitation, segregation is repulsive and wrong, and unconstitutional. But when you have these policies in the name of getting rid of that, where you are imposing another brand of coercion, shouldn't you at least think twice about it? Shouldn't you think of the consequences? Because you can't hand in a human being after you've harmed that human being. There's no exchange window. The very people that you are using in these kinds of social experiments are the most vulnerable in your society.

Years later I would ask a guy (he was white) whether he would do to his daughters what he did to black kids, and he said, "No." I said, "Do you see the similarity between that and Dr. Frankenstein? How ghoulish you are? That you would do this to somebody else's child, something you would never do to your own child? You would never bus your child all over God's creation for a worse education, ever. Not in a hundred years, and yet you would do it to somebody else's."

HIRING ANITA HILL AT THE DEPARTMENT OF EDUCATION
"WOULD YOU HELP A SISTER OUT?"

MP: When you were there at the Department of Education, how did you come to hire Anita Hill?

CT: Gil Hardy [Thomas's college and law school classmate and the best man at his first wedding] called to ask me, "Would you help a sister out?" That's quintessentially Gil; he would help everybody. I asked, "Was she a Reagan supporter, or a Republican?" and he said he did not think so. I thought it was going to be very difficult, if not impossible, to hire her as a political appointee. When I finally interviewed her, I asked her, "What do you think of Reagan?" She said, and I have never forgotten this, "I detest him." That's not going to help get you hired as a political appointee, but we figured out a way to hire her as a career employee.

Gil and Anita worked together at the law firm Wald, Harkrader, and Ross. According to Gil, she had been asked to leave her law firm after less than a year there. You don't leave a major firm and take a career job in a place like the Department of Education unless something had happened.

MP: Wasn't that a red flag?
CT: Well yeah, it was to me. But Gil is my buddy. When you have not been able to get a job, and recall that I had only one job offer, then you try to look out for people who are struggling—that there is some injustice, and you are obligated to help. With Gil, we were always that way. If he had to move, you helped him move. If I had to move, he would help me move. If you were down, he would come over. That was Gil. And it was the way we treated each other, that you would show up. Gil had a good heart, and he would help anybody. If he saw a dog sick on the side of a road, he'd stop and take it to the vet or to a shelter. If he saw you broken down, he'd stop and help. I would hire other people that others have asked me to hire. If someone calls you up, says "This person is down on their luck, they're a really good person, I can vouch for him," you hire them, if you could. You help.

She needed a job. It was as simple as that. Why did I go to Jeff City? It wasn't my goal to work for a Republican. It wasn't my goal to go to Jeff City. I needed a job. Why did we do what we do? I mean why do we wash dishes if we have a Ph.D.? We need a job.

EEOC—FIXING A BROKEN AGENCY
"I JUST WANT YOU TO KNOW THAT NOTHING THAT YOU DO THAT IS POSITIVE HERE IS NEWSWORTHY"

MP: How did your next job offer come about?
CT: The Reagan administration was running into the storm. Everything the president did, he was called a racist. That was from the very beginning. The man hadn't even arrived in town yet, and they were calling him a racist. One of the cabinet secretaries in the Carter administration [Patricia Harris], who was black, said some things about Ronald Reagan. Thomas Sowell wrote a couple of op-eds: One was "Blacker Than Thou."[4] And then the second was, "Blacker Than Thou 2," when [Secretary Harris] responded.[5] It was that atmosphere, one where we were constantly attacked for being in the Reagan administration. Years later Senator [Edward M.] Kennedy and the senator from Connecticut [Lowell Weicker] would ask me, "How can any self-respecting black person be in the Reagan administration?" That's the kind of attitude you had.

They had difficulties filling civil rights slots. And the administration had nominated this black [businessman William Bell], I think from Michigan, to be chairman of the EEOC, and he could not get through. The civil rights groups ganged up on him, and at some point the [Reagan administration] realized he was un-confirmable. They started looking around for, "Who can we make do this job?" And Pendleton James [assistant to the president and director of the Office of Presidential Personnel] called me up and asked me to come talk to him about various things, including what they could do with that job. He asked me at the end would I be interested in the job. I said, "I've got my own problems, and in fact, I'm thinking of bailing out of here myself. I've had enough of this. This is horrible."

He asked me on what conditions would I do it. And I said, "Well, speaking theoretically, I would take it if I'd get to choose my own people and not be told what to do. Total independence." A little while later, he called up and said, "I've just come from the Oval Office and the president wants you to be chairman of the EEOC. Would you do it?" And I pause a second, what am I doing jumping out of the frying pan into the fire? You're locked in. I'm going to get killed. I was under constant attack. Oh my gosh. And I was thirty-three years old now. So I went. That was how it happened.

Pendleton James was a man of his word. He never forced me to hire any political appointees. No one ever interfered. No one ever told me what to do. There were some lower-level people who tried but good luck with that. My view was, "I am going to get killed out here, and if I'm going to get killed, it's going to be for what I do, not me doing what you want me to do."

MP: When you arrived at EEOC in May 1981, you found lots of problems.
CT: Well, there were more than lots of problems. They had about $140 million budget at the time. The books hadn't been balanced in over a decade. The computer system was antiquated. They were housed in a sick building, with fleas in the carpet, all kinds of mold and stuff in the vents and in the windows. It was very, very difficult. And I knew whatever happened, I would be blamed for it, because my predecessor, Eleanor Holmes Norton, was an icon. And icons

don't get blamed for these sorts of things. And I just knew it would fall on me, so I was more focused on those management things.

When I went through confirmation, Senator [Orrin] Hatch, who was on the [Senate Education and Labor] Committee, made it very clear that he wanted these management issues cleared up—the lack of systems, the lack of expense reports, millions of dollars unaccounted for. That's what I was focused on. The EEOC had fifty offices around the country. I have to somehow get a handle on all these managers, and all these problems.

The media wasn't interested in management issues. They were interested in the salacious, the exotic, and then the issues that they had created. When I got to the EEOC, a reporter told me early on, "I just want you to know that nothing that you do that is positive here is newsworthy."

The first extensive piece written about me was an interview by a guy named Ernie Holsendolph in the *New York Times*, on July 3, 1982.[6] Mr. Al Sweeney, who was our press person, was a black gentleman and good man, and he knew this Ernie Holsendolph, who was also black. Al asked me to talk to him, so I did. And suddenly I've got this profile piece on July 3 that is really not a profile. It's just more about peoples' criticism. I hadn't done anything; I'd just gotten there in May, just arrived. So it's starting this sort of chumming the waters, so that I can be attacked.

One focus was on this issue of the number of cases that are closed out versus the number that had a full investigation. The agency was processing around seventy thousand cases a year. In other words, opening a file on an investigation, and then closing it. We didn't have the capacity to do that many cases. Something wasn't right. People hadn't been trained. They hadn't been doing full investigations. You can't do that many cases with no systems, that fast. I'm trying to figure out what happened. There were no routine reporting systems to figure out what was going on.

You're getting a handle on all those things. So the first thing you want to do is get people to be candid with you about the volume of cases. As one manager told me, "We would actually just throw them in the trash." Or they were being settled for hundreds of dollars, whether they had merit or didn't have merit. And I thought our job was to differentiate between the meritorious, and the non-meritorious, first, and then make sure that the meritorious receive full benefit, not just sort of a routine hundred or two hundred dollar payout.

At the EEOC, we were looking at the cases. How were they actually decided? Did somebody just write down an answer? Did someone just dismiss it? There's a process for doing it, and to give people the full benefit of the law. And it isn't just in the ultimate numbers. It is in how you got to those numbers.

CLASHING WITH CIVIL RIGHTS LEADERS
"ALL THEY DO IS BITCH, BITCH, BITCH, MOAN AND MOAN, WHINE AND WHINE"

MP: You also clashed with some prominent civil rights figures. Do you remember the Juan Williams *Washington Post* October 1984 article where you criticized civil rights leaders?[7] You said, "All they do is bitch, bitch, bitch, moan and moan, whine and whine."
CT: I've been criticized now since 1980, so this has become a way of life. We were nothing; we were irrelevant. We were, maybe, a nuisance to them, but we got treated pretty shabbily.

I'd gotten one of these "come up" calls from Vernon Jordan [a civil rights leader], where he asked me if I had said that, and I assured him that I had. And he told me that if he were still out there as a black leader, he would use me as cannon fodder. And then he said, after I was done with this job, I would need a constituency if I wanted to do as well as he did. And I just told him that I didn't really trade in the misery of black people and that I didn't want to do what he did.

MP: How did he respond to that?
CT: He was very firm that I was creating problems for myself if I wanted to do well. And to his credit, when I was nominated to this Court, I would not say he was supportive, but he was not vitriolic. I think there was some ambivalence. Same thing with Ben Hooks, head of the NAACP. The thing that amazed me was we could have done a lot of good quietly, if we had agreed to disagree, like I had done with some of the black college presidents. Look, I'm not going to agree with you on policies "A," "B," and "C," but on the rest of the alphabet, we agree. For example, you shouldn't just wipe out black colleges. You shouldn't have policies that don't work, you shouldn't mindlessly build high-rise housing projects, shouldn't do that. You should think these things through, and I think we could have done a lot. But that wasn't the case. It was sort of like the old Westerns: somebody has to wear the black hat, someone has to be the antagonist, and someone has to be the protagonist. That's just the way it is, and I was the antagonist in this production.

MP: What was the exact line that got Jordan upset?
CT: I think it was, "Bitch, bitch, bitch, moan and moan, and whine and whine." I did say it. I'm not going to deny it. Juan [Williams] called me up, and Juan and I had known each other. Juan and I didn't agree on any number of things, but to his credit, he was always very honest. And he was saying what did I think about these attacks on Ronald Reagan. And I found them unhelpful. My question is: How do you work with him, if you just call him everything but a child of

God? You just call him all these names—he's a racist, he's this, he's that, and now you expect to go work with him. I mean you still have a country, you still have the leader. And I think my point was you wouldn't do it with a judge, you wouldn't do it with someone whose opinion or decision that mattered in your life. You wouldn't go to your eye surgeon—let's say someone has cataracts, and they happen to have a cataract removal procedure. They wouldn't go to the doctor who is about to perform that and call him a jackass. You might call him that months later, but not before the surgery. I said that instead of being helpful, "They bitch, bitch, bitch, and moan and moan, whine and whine." It was all this negativity. You're grousing, but you're putting nothing that's usable on the table. That's all. I think I went on to say some other things. But the point wasn't to insult them in the way they have insulted me, but it was to say in a less than elegant way that grousing was inadequate.

Conflicts within the Reagan Administration
"There are only two things in life I have to do: stay black and die"

MP: During your time at EEOC, you had some disagreements with others in the Reagan administration, particularly the Department of Justice.
CT: What we had were conflicting approaches and attitudes. They tended to want to undo a bunch of the consent decrees that had race-conscious remedies and quotas in them. I didn't disagree with them in principle, but I didn't think that should be the focal point. That's not our first thing; I thought we should have had a much more positive approach: Here's what we're going to do positively

to enforce civil rights laws. And then once you have that, then you say, "That does not include counting by race," which I do agree with.

There were people who didn't quite understand the impact of what they were doing. It was just a judgment call. It was a tone. It was an attitude. It didn't mean that they were necessarily bad people. It meant that they were full steam ahead, and they were stepping on some toes. And I just thought it was the wrong approach.

I've thought about these things over the years. I'm in my thirties, and I'm rambunctious. You're in the middle of a lot of battles, and it was really irritating. I've got an agency to keep going, and you read in the newspaper that the Justice Department has done something that's going to make your day even worse. And because I would not openly criticize any of these guys, or break ranks, they would say that I was a nonentity. I love it. Even in this job, I go from being really, really profoundly stupid to the evil genius.

They called me to a meeting at the White House Mess [a restaurant for staff in the West Wing of the White House] to read me the riot act. And they started out by saying something like, "Well, Clarence, you have to—" And I stopped them and I said, "There are only two things in life I have to do: stay black and die. I don't have to do anything else. It's all optional."

MP: How did President Reagan treat you?
CT: President Reagan was always very supportive. In fact, he called me up when things started looking bad, to give me a pep talk, and it turned out I had to give him a pep talk.

MP: What did he say?
CT: Oh, he was bemoaning the fact that he was being called a racist, and it was very upsetting to him.

ANITA HILL AT THE EEOC
"YOU'RE A RISING STAR AND I WANT TO GO WITH YOU"

MP: What was Anita Hill's response to your announcement that you were leaving the Department of Education to go to EEOC?
CT: I was very interested in black colleges' not being integrated out of existence. I prevailed upon a friend of mine, Harry Singleton, who had been at Yale with me, and who was my son's godfather, and I asked him to come over [to the Department of Education] and save the black colleges and he agreed to do it. Among the other things, he agreed to keep my staff. So there would be no change, and there would be no change in policies, just a new head of the office. The only thing that I remember [Anita] saying was that I was a rising star and she wanted to go to EEOC with me. Not, "I agree with Reagan," or anything like that. "You're a rising star, and I want to go with you." And she would tell Harry the same thing.

MP: When Ms. Hill went over to the EEOC, an issue arose with her interim performance review.
CT: I had nothing to do with that. I had a chief of staff who was a new addition, Chris Roggerson. Chris was an older black gentleman who had been at the EEOC and been in government for many years. He offered to come and help me get started. Chris was interested in moving to the West Coast, and I had moved the manager out of the San Francisco office and would eventually move Chris there. Chris had come in, and sat with me, and he was a pretty low-key guy, and he went over the personal staff review. I had a fairly substantial personal staff, and I was a little surprised that he gave Anita Hill a mediocre rating. He gave Allyson Duncan, and some of the other employees, high ratings. And they were all career lawyers who were on my staff.

There was an attitude issue [with Anita Hill], he pointed out, and I again attributed that to her being naive, or being young, that sort of thing. You're always looking for the best light: give people a warning, maybe they'll straighten up and do better. At any rate, Chris left, and he took the job in San Francisco. Now I needed someone to be the top person on my personal staff. And I chose Allyson Duncan. Allyson was a career person; her work was methodical. She was a good worker, and very bright, very conscientious, and easy to get along with. And when I did that, Anita Hill stormed into my office, and she said that I only chose Allyson because I like light-skinned women. And at the time I was dating a light-skinned black woman, and I said, "That's absurd." And the next thing I mentioned was the performance ratings, and she said, "I'm better than her, because I went to Yale, and she went to Duke." That was it.

I talked to Gil about it because she's his person, and he attributed it to her being upset, so you try to forget about it. Then, she said she wanted to leave, and we worked that out, and I helped her get a job that following summer at Oral Roberts Law School.

MP: You also mentioned that during this period before she left, she was always asking about your activities and your social life.
CT: That's not unusual. You have young people who think that you're doing important stuff and want to be with the rising star. So they are interested in that, and she was particularly interested. There's a certain degree of ambition. I don't know. I'm not a party type of person. I wasn't an "about-town" kind of guy.

MP: It's seems odd that she wanted to go to Oral Roberts University, given her liberalism.
CT: She's from Oklahoma. And you don't have a lot of options when you've been asked to leave the law firm. You worked in the Department

of Education. You worked at EEOC. It's not like law schools are clam-oring, and she was happy with Oral Roberts.

Dean [Charles] Kothe, who I had gotten to know at Oral Roberts, liked her, and he asked me about her. I told him that perhaps she was a little bit immature, and had had some difficulties, but I attributed that to age. He liked her. I had sent her to do a program that he had, and he took a liking to her, and it worked out. And then she did fine there, I guess.

Dean Kothe's a good man, too. And I remember, I would stay at his house in Tulsa, and then he would drive me back to the airport. It was part of the routine. And this one time I was there, [Anita] insisted on coming over. She called, invited herself over to breakfast, and then insisted on driving me to the airport herself. Because she had a new car, and I was happy for her.

MP: What was your relationship with her at this time—were you her friend, her mentor?
CT: I wouldn't call it that. I was friends with virtually everybody. Not everybody had a great experience at the EEOC, but I mean she would call from time to time, ask for favors. And mostly she was wonderful. And I had a wonderful secretary named Diane. And she would talk to Diane, and Diane would log the calls. But again, you have to remember: I'm running an agency. I don't have a lot of chit-chat time, and a lot of people would start calling, including her, calling me at home. So I changed my phone number because I was having difficulty sleeping. Remember now, in these years I had over sixty oversight hearings. I was investigated by GAO [Government Accountability Office]. I was always getting beat up in the newspaper, criticized by civil rights groups. I was not focused on all these people. I tried to be helpful to everybody, even the people that I didn't necessarily think were the best.

MP: How was Anita Hill regarded at the agency?
CT: She was not liked. I mean, that's just it, I'm sorry. One of the things I used to like to have is these coffee klatches in the mornings. I got in early, and would have them around 8:00 or so, and everybody sat around, and we would talk about just whatever's in the news. She got really angry with someone one morning and stopped coming—that sort of attitude. And many of the staff had strong negative feelings toward her. I didn't. But there were a number who did not care for her.

MP: But the bigger picture, as you say, is that this was a difficult time for you.
CT: This really encapsulates what has happened to our society. This was almost a nothing. This was not something that was even relevant to my day-to-day stuff. I was busy. I had a lot going on. You had a staffer who was a bit of an annoyance, who you were trying to help. You've tried every way you could. You try to be positive, but you got a lot going on, and that is not a center of anything. It was not a center of my work. It was not a focal point of my energies, my emotional energies were drained. I was going through divorce. I was sleeping on the floor in a little apartment. My grandparents died. I was working out a lot of things, and this was not a big deal.

LOSING HIS GRANDPARENTS
"SOMEBODY OPENED THE TRAP DOOR, AND YOU
FELL THROUGH. THERE WAS NO FOUNDATION"

MP: Your grandfather's sayings, like, "You can give out, but you can't give up." What was your focus at the time?
CT: Well, I mean, you think about it. There wasn't a whole lot of positives going on. Things were not going well, and in fact, things

were going quite negatively. And there were some people who were actually telling me that I should stay at the EEOC a few years, and then bail out and sort of re-invent myself to get the stench of the negative criticism off of me. But there were also people who thought that I was forever done in this town, and they would counsel me to do things like, "Just trim your sails. Change your views, soften your tone." So I heard all of that.

Those were things that consumed a lot of my time, and it was bad. It'll make you careful about history, and people who write about history. The things that people have focused on, after the fact, had almost nothing to do with what we focused on at the time. My time was consumed with running an agency. It was extremely, extremely difficult.

I didn't have any money. And I was still, again, in this one-room apartment, my mattress on the floor, and I had to borrow and run up this one credit card that I had to keep going back to Savannah. Then I even lost that credit card, and then I remember having to go take out a loan at Household Finance. You remember them? They had a very high-interest consumer loan; that wasn't good. So things weren't quite going well, and then I was getting beat up. That was when you begin to, as I said, rely a bit more on your faith, because there's nothing else. I mean, it's not like I had a lot of places to turn.

MP: What was the one credit card you had and how did you lose it?
CT: Well, I had a Sears credit card, and that was it. And the good thing about Sears was, Sears owned Budget car rental. So that meant when I traveled, I could at least get a rental car. I was on the board of trustees of Holy Cross College, another thing that they brought up and criticized me for when I was nominated. In order to save time, one of the things I would do was if I had to go to a board meeting at Holy Cross, I would go and work in the Boston office, and it would

be a full day that way. Basically, kill two birds with one stone, and I wouldn't have to make the trip to the Boston area again, because I've been there. And now I can go to the board meetings at Holy Cross, which were on Saturday. I would fly in, I would rent a car, and then drive to Holy Cross. So I go to the airport this time, with my little Sears card, and the guy says, "I have been instructed to cut your card." And he was nice enough to rent me a car anyway. But that was it. I remember, that was one of the low points, you know, that things aren't going exactly real great. Because I didn't have a credit card, I could only go to hotels that took cash, which limits your choices.

MP: How did you first hear that your grandfather had died?
CT: I don't know how we get so busy in D.C. I totally regret not going home more, I just regret it. I was working long hours in the EEOC. I was traveling, and going to the various EEOC offices, having meetings, trying to get the ship right. I was headed to Chicago to be beat up on by some group, Women Employed, and God, they were really upset. And they came in with their briefcases, to be angry at me, as if this is new. But at the end of that, I was with my brother, and he told me my grandfather had died. And that was like, I think from then on, I was in a bit of a fog. It was really horrible. It was March 30, 1983.

MP: Did you go down for the funeral?
CT: Oh yeah, I flew down to Savannah, and it was only when I saw him at the funeral home that I realized that he was truly dead. I saw him in the coffin. It was horrible.

You think about what you did, and you didn't do, and things that you said, and didn't say, and that you should have said. There's a finality to it.

MP: When was the last time you saw him alive?

CT: My grandmother was in the hospital, and he and I were in the waiting room. We were talking, and he said, "You know, we're alike." That was the only time that we'd ever embraced, it was sort of brief, and it was like the opening when you say, "Well, this is going to be better," or, "It's going to be okay." And that was, I think, in February.

MP: Your grandfather died shortly thereafter.

My grandfather died on March 30. I went down shortly after that, and my grandmother was not doing well, and she was frail and had lost a lot of weight and looked nothing like the woman who raised me. And so I was there on a visit. Shortly after my grandfather's death, my grandmother had a stroke while lying in bed. It was the middle of the night, we were out in the country, and I remember lifting her little, light body up off the bed. I mean, just sad, I had put her in this rental car that I had and drove all the way to Savannah and put her in the hospital. I told my brother he needed to get there.

And so once again I went back to work because there were things I had to do. My grandmother died the following weekend. My brother was there. It was as though she waited for him to show up. And once he showed up, and she saw him, within an hour or so, she was dead. So that was May 1, 1983.

It was like a trap door, somebody opened the trap door, and you fell through. There was no foundation. You take it for granted that they exist, that there's a permanence to their existence. And then you realize they're gone. And then it was like, why am I even doing these jobs? It's like you want to go back home. People were beating me up. I had all these hearings. I think I had a hearing before Representatives Mary Rose Oakar and Pat Schroeder, and the congresswoman who ran for vice president back then [Geraldine Ferraro]. And they yelled at me and called me all sorts of things. Again, remember that once

you isolate yourself, you're the black guy over here, you're unprotected. You're the calf that's roaming around away from the herd.
And in the end, you can be now attacked by the predator, by the
critic, by the person with bad intent. And that's what happened. I
was isolated and unprotected. Anything they said or did would be
countenanced. There were a lot of other things going on, so yeah, I
felt like a bottom fell out. And you start wondering why the hell
you're even doing this stuff.

CHAPTER SIX

BIRTH OF AN ORIGINALIST

*"I decided that the principles on which I was raised,
my grandparents', the principles of this country,
were worth dying for"*

MP: When you returned to D.C., what did you do next?
CT: And by the time I got to Washington, I had thought a lot more about things.

So, I'm asking myself why am I doing this? I have no money. Don't even have a car. I'm walking every place, and I'm getting the heck beat out of me. As someone said, "Clarence, nobody likes you." So that was the way it was. So I'm asking myself, "Why am I doing this?" I mean, it's a real question. It's just not metaphysical, it's not theoretical. This is, "Why the hell are you even here?" And there's nothing positive going on.

I had to flip it around a little bit. For what will you die? Is there something in life that you will die for? Because I think if you can say that, then you can figure out for what you live. Will you die for your children? Yes. So you live for them. Will you die for your country? Yes. So will you live for it? So what about your principles? That was the question.

I decided that the principles on which I was raised, my grandparents', the principles of this country, were worth dying for. In my own view, if I wasn't physically killed, I was going to be killed reputationally. It's over for me. So at this point, it isn't that you get over the problem, it's that you accept it. You're willing to accept the inevitability of your destruction for doing what you think you are required to do.

So what are these principles? I was interested in: Why this government? Why not a parliamentary system? Why not a dictatorship?

Founding Principles and Natural Law
"I was looking for a way of thinking, a set of ideals that fundamentally, at its core, said slavery is wrong"

MP: You are looking at these questions when you were chairman of the EEOC?
CT: Yes, think about it. I had an agency that was imploding, an agency that hadn't balanced its books. So we've got all the financial systems in place. We were beginning to automate the agency. We had gotten personnel records. We didn't even have personnel records. When I got there, we were still paying some dead people. We found that there were some things that were not really accurate. So we got these things in order. I had moved some people out who were in the way of getting work done. We finally were beginning the long march to getting stuff organized. Well, I had been basically chairman and CEO from '82 until about '86 or so after I was reappointed in 1986.

And I said there's a lot of work that I need to think through. This city, with all these issues and all these attacks, these episodic things that are unconnected, all these hearings that I've had. Congressman

Gus Hawkins, who's the chairman on the House side, dragged me up to these hearings, and the hearings made no sense. They were just different ways of tormenting me, of beating me, and then I'd go back to my office to do exactly what I was doing when I left. I'll take the beatings, but I'm going to go back and do what I think is right.

And I think they expected me, at some point, to change. But I decided to go outside of the agency and hire a chief of staff, Pamela Talkin, who is now the marshal at the Supreme Court.[1] Pam did not share my views ideologically. She's more liberal, which wasn't why I was hiring her. I wanted someone who had the ability and the backbone, the honesty, to be my chief of staff, and she did. She came in, she was fabulous, absolutely fabulous. So that freed me up, because now she had the day-to-day stuff that I had been doing,

I had these slots for speechwriters. I didn't need speechwriters, it's useless; I could write my own speeches. Ken Masugi was a Straussian from Claremont [Institute] with a Ph.D. in political theory. And John Marini was also from Claremont, and a Ph.D., and they came on my staff. We would literally spend hours discussing the Founding. And then they would give me reading materials, and we would write articles, and we would go off to American Political Science Association events and argue with positivists, and libertarians. Oh, gosh. Now that was a lot of fun, in the sea of all this stuff.

They were upset with me because I was too much of a libertarian for them. We would go over to [the] Cato [Institute] and argue over it. We'd go argue with the lawyers at the Justice Department, those positivists.

I was looking for a way of thinking, a set of ideals that fundamentally, at its core, said slavery is wrong, at its core—which natural law, of course, does. The second thing was: What would be a coherent and cohesive policy, or a set of ideals, that pull these disparate groups in our country together? You never hear "*E pluribus unum*" anymore.

But what was the *"unum"*? What was it that we all believed in? We can all have different opinions on different policies, but what, at the core, do we all believe in? That's what I was looking for.

MP: How did this shape your views on natural law and the Declaration of Independence?
CT: The thing that was important to me was what the Founders thought. So where do our rights come from? They had to set up a government, right? If you start with the Magna Carta, and you say okay, kings have all this power, and the barons seized some of it back, and just looked at it as a practical document. These are limitations on the authority of the king. Now the Framers started a different way. They didn't start with the absolute power of the king. They start with the rights of the individual, and where do those rights come from? They come from God, they're transcendent. And you give up some of those rights in order to govern; they're inalienable rights. Okay? And now you give up only so many as necessary to be governed by your consent. Hence, limited government, enumerated powers, separation of powers, federalism, and the judicial review. It all makes sense. And the unit they're trying to protect is the individual.

MP: "All men are created equal." The idea is that it's in the nature of man.
CT: Exactly. We did a lot of Lincoln, and that got me into the Civil War. That "A" can't own "B."[2] How do you own property? How do you own another person? That's what came up in a meeting during the confirmation with [Senator Howard] Metzenbaum. He asked, "Why do you believe in natural law?" Well, okay, let's go have a human being sandwich. Obviously, you're repulsed by it. Why? Is it natural? Where does it come from? You're naturally repulsed. All

these things that seem to offend people in society. Where did they come from?

MP: As you know, I was president of the Claremont Institute. Not only is it striking that you brought these "Claremonsters" into the EEOC, but it is just amazing to me that you brought in professors to try to learn something. Mostly in Washington, heads of agencies think they know everything.

CT: Think of when you run an agency. You are swamped. The sort of nonsense that they attack me with are things I can't remember half the time. When you were focused on budgets, testimony, investigations, personnel matters, that's your day. It went from meeting to meeting, day after day, and crisis to crisis. And we had a lot of problems. And I was traveling a lot, all over the country, trying to keep the troops going, trying to build a computer system, internal systems. And then I had all these hearings, and they were talking about things, they were talking about quotas, and goals and timetables, and blah, blah, blah, blah. And so you had all these disjointed things.

My mind needs a coherent principle, and then you can put little pieces on it. You give me a tree and I can put leaves on it. But I can't have all the leaves blowing in the wind and no tree. If you remember back in the eighties, people would say, "I have the book *Modern Times* [by Paul Johnson]."[3] But see, I would read it. Then I'd read Louis l'Amour. You know, that'd be my reward. Remember *Closing of the American Mind* by Allan Bloom?[4] A lot of people had it; few people read it. Great book. So Ken and John fit right within that.

I had the energy, I slept two to three hours a night. I was always up. I was always on planes, always had time to read. And we would go to places and we would say, "Let's go debate the sixties socialists," and we would go right there. Oh gosh, we got in more trouble. But it was great. I mean, it was just a wonderful group. And then I flew out

to Claremont [Institute in California]. I met Larry Arnn [the president
of the Claremont Institute], Harry Jaffa [the Lincoln scholar and
political philosopher] on a number of occasions. There were others.
Ed Erler. Charles Kesler. We'd go over to Charles Kesler's apartment
and listen to country music. I think he liked [country singer] George
Jones, and I liked George Jones. It was great. I consider it not only
one of the seminal periods of my time at the EEOC, but also one of
the most formative intellectually of my tenure in D.C.

THE FOUNTAINHEAD AND LIBERTARIANISM
"WHY DON'T YOU GET TO THINK THOUGHTS THAT THEY SAY ARE CLOSED TO YOU?"

MP: Well on the more libertarian side, you also watched *The Fountainhead*, the movie based on Ayn Rand's book of the same name, right?
CT: Oh, I still do. I still watch it a lot. I like *The Fountainhead*. I like
the individual. I mean, think about it, I'm in Savannah, Georgia. What's
going on in Savannah, Georgia, during my youth? All these things the
government tells me I can't do: I can't walk across the park, have to
walk around; I can't drink out of this water fountain because the colored one is over here; I can't go to Georgia Tech. There are all these
limitations. If you drive down here, you don't have any rights, if you go
over there, you don't have any rights. On, and on, and on, and on.

When I read *Fountainhead* and *Atlas Shrugged*, I'm not going to
tell you I understood objectivism, but it emphasized the individual.[5]
I'm free to do what I want to do. That's in the individual. Then I read
later on, after *Black Boy* and *Native Son* by Richard Wright, I read
Ralph Ellison's *Invisible Man*. Again, where is the Invisible Man?
Underground. You get to think for yourself. You get to be who you
are, despite what society says. So if you have stood against segregation,

you've had to go in doors that they said should be closed, right? Then why don't you get to think thoughts that they say are closed to you? Even if your own people are saying it?

So, let's just take an example. We agree that it was wrong for me to be prevented from going to the Savannah Public Library. Okay. People agree. That's just against society. So then, okay, what if they let me go in the library, but they said, "There's a certain part of the library, or certain stacks in there, that are off limits to blacks?" Oh, that would also be wrong. Oh, okay. What if they say, "There are certain books that are marked, 'No coloreds allowed'"? Would that be right? No, that would be wrong. If all those things are wrong—it's wrong for them to prevent me from being in the library, it's wrong for them to prevent me from going to certain parts of the library, it's wrong for them to prevent me from going to certain books in the library—why is it right for them to tell me I can't have certain thoughts that are in the books in the library? Obviously, there's no answer. It's absurd.

MP: To this day, you show *The Fountainhead* to your clerks, right?[6]
CT: Oh yeah.

MP: And this is the movie with Gary Cooper?
CT: It is a great movie. People laugh at me because I pretty much got it memorized by now. They laugh at me because they said it's over-acted. It's great. Oh God, it's sort of like *The Magnificent Seven*, you know.[7] There are certain classics that we have to watch.

MP: What are the lines that you like from the movie?
CT: "Will you fight against the whole world? Yes." I love those lines. Or Dominique Francon says, "We both have strength, but not courage." Think of all the people you know with all the talent in the world, who have strength, not courage. And I just love that. We all

have these human weaknesses. People are willing to make the choice of selling their souls in these Faustian bargains. I'll sell my soul for a career, for a promotion. But what about the principles? Go back to 1983. I have to decide for what will you die? Is it worth it? Yeah. Are you fighting for principles, or something? Those are lines in there. Yes.

It's like my grandfather when I asked him, "Daddy what should I do? These people are beating me up." He said, "Boy, you have to stand up for what you believe in." That's very clear. I mean, we confuse it because we don't want to do it, because it's hard. Just because it's hard doesn't mean it's wrong. A principle is a principle. I think one of the reasons segregation lasted so long is because there were people who knew better, but who were afraid. They didn't want to take the risk: "Oh, I don't want to be the one. I'm not going to rock the boat. It doesn't make sense to me, but not me. I'm not getting up front." Why can't we say that it is wrong? You will fight for principle. You will give up your job for principle. You will stand against the whole world for principle.

FINDING HIS SOULMATE
"SHE WAS A GIFT FROM GOD THAT I HAD PRAYED FOR"

MP: Was it tough being a single parent in Washington, D.C., when you were still in your thirties?
CT: Life is tough. Jamal was a joy to be around. Being with him was my happy place, being at home with him. We didn't have much. The apartment was empty. I took in a couple of kids at different times, including my own nephew. It was great, but then they left. Jamal and I enjoyed our time together. I remember when he and I went in 1986 and bought our first TV and VCR, which was a little thirteen-inch color TV. We got it from Montgomery Ward. And it was a huge investment for us, but it

allowed us to play video games. Remember there was a little tennis game, you hit the little bob, a little dot that went across the screen, and he would, oh gosh, he would beat me on that. We'd get our KFC, or something, and watch movies on Friday night on that little TV. His wife says sometimes, even now, "You all spend way too much time together." But, you know, we have the same jokes. He was a Redskins fan, I was a Cowboys fan. It had its challenges. I cannot say any negative things about raising Jamal. Jamal was a really good kid and a lot of fun to be around.

MP: How did you come to meet Ginni?
CT: I was scheduled to go up to New York to a meeting only because my chief of staff, Jeff Zuckerman, was trying to be general counsel of the EEOC and needed to meet a senator who wouldn't change the meeting. And he had scheduled to go to this event in New York, and he said the only person the conference would take in exchange for him, if he cancelled, was me. So I went up to New York, and she happened to be there. And we shared a cab to the airport. You always make this promise: Let's do lunch. How many times have you lived up to that one? Almost never. And so I didn't.

This was 1986, and Dean Kothe set up a luncheon to have some people meet about my reappointment at EEOC. There was a torrential downpour of rain, and only two or three people showed up, and she was one of them, drenched. When I got back to my office, I told my secretary to schedule a lunch with her. We had lunch on May 29 at the Hunan Rose on K Street, and we got married on May 30, the following year. And we've been inseparable ever since.

She was a gift from God that I had prayed for. And then I was iffy, because I started questioning God's package. You know, like what are you doing?

You pray for God to send you someone, he sends you someone, and you say, "Oh, but she's white" or, "She's younger." He's sent you someone. What are you talking about? So that was the end of that, and she has been a fabulous gift from God.

We got married at St. Paul's Methodist Church in Omaha on May 30, 1987. We had a reception, with some of the professors and teachers who were very kind to her at Creighton [University]. It was wonderful. And her mother was just a delightful, wonderful human being. Her mother was from Atlantic, Iowa, her father from Emerson, Nebraska, both farm communities, and they met at the University of Nebraska. That's why I'm such a Nebraska fan now. Her mother, who is not a sports fan, was a huge Nebraska fan, and I am for anything Nebraska: volleyball, bowling, football, basketball, doesn't matter.

We've been married over thirty years. I've been married to her over half her life, and she's exactly the same person now as she was then. She believed in things. She was unspoiled by the city. She wasn't cynical. She had ideals, she had hopes and dreams. She's been as dear and close a human being as I could have ever imagined having in my life. She is absolutely the "sine qua non" of my life.

How many people do you know over the years in Washington, who've been around politics, and lobbying, and this environment, you can honestly say they are exactly the same? They are unspoiled by it all. There's just always that basic goodness.

D.C. CIRCUIT COURT OF APPEALS
"CLARENCE, IT'S NOT SLAVERY. YOU CAN LEAVE IF YOU DON'T LIKE IT"

MP: At EEOC, you were approached to be a judge on the D.C. Circuit?
CT: In 1988, I had written George [H. W.] Bush about some things I thought he should do in appointing minorities in his administration

to avoid some of the mistakes we made in the Reagan administration. He wrote me a note back saying that he would pass my recommendations on.

George Bush's transition team asked if I would be interested in becoming a federal judge. I got a call during the transition period from Mike Uhlmann, who was in domestic policy during the Reagan years. Mike was a good man, and he was asking me about the future of the administration. At the end, he asked me whether I had any interest in being a judge. "That's a job for old people," I said. "I'm forty. I can't see myself spending the rest of my life as a judge."

They asked me to talk to Larry Silberman who was a judge on the D.C. Circuit. I said, "I don't want a lifetime appointment." He said, "Clarence, it's not slavery. You can leave if you don't like it."

Mark Paoletta, who was a lawyer in the [White House] Office of Presidential Personnel, called me [in March 1989] and asked for all of my speeches and articles. And I sent them to him.

I talked to another judge, and he told me he thought that I should do it. And then I just postponed it. Virginia and I prayed about it. And I kind of weighed it: I don't think I want to do this. I don't want to go through this again, and I don't want to be in D.C.

Then I get this call to come and have breakfast with [Attorney General] Dick Thornburgh and the attorney general's top people, ostensibly, to give them advice on how to avoid problems. This is the beginning of the Bush administration, and at the end of that breakfast, they said, "Some people think you should be a judge on the D.C. Circuit; would you?" I said, "No, I haven't made up my mind. I'm really ambivalent about it. I don't think so." They said, "Well, would you at least fill out a form to get the process going?" I said, "Well, I'll do that." And they said, "Is it okay if we send it over this afternoon?" And that was it. And I told Virginia that I think God is sending a sign that this is what I need to do. And we prayed about it. But it's God's will and this is what we'll do, and that's what we did. And then they beat the heck out of me. That was life. It's just been—the beatings continue.

But once I got to the D.C. Circuit [in March 1990], I really enjoyed it. I enjoyed the work. I liked the people. Virginia worked across the street from me [as a political appointee at the U.S. Department of Labor]. So we commuted in every day and we really enjoyed our little house. We really enjoyed our projects. We enjoyed our anonymity, and our time together.

MP: What was your colleague Judge Larry Silberman's advice about judging?
CT: When I went on the D.C. Circuit in 1990, Larry Silberman came by the office and said, "I'm not going to tell you what to do. But I do want to give you a bit of advice on judging. What you should do in each case is ask yourself this question: What is my role in this case as a judge?" That's what I ask myself to this day. Our role is limited. He was another gift from God. He was solid as a rock.

MP: What are some of your memories of your time at the D.C Circuit?
CT: I wasn't there long enough to have a lot of memories. I met some really good people there. Jim Buckley and Dave Sentelle, who's still a really dear friend. He was there a few years ahead of me. Karen Henderson, who is still an active judge there, came on after I did, and Ray Randolph and all the people there. It was intellectually challenging. It was not the EEOC; I had no [Congressional oversight] hearings. I loved being with my law clerks, loved the ability to just sit and work on something, think about it, and craft an opinion.

I remember sitting the first time with Dave Sentelle, who's from North Carolina. Dave was either one or two in his class at University of North Carolina Law School. He's always telling you that he is this country lawyer, he's just a simple man from North Carolina. We came off the bench, early in my tenure, and I said, "Dave, you know there was an internal inconsistency in that lawyer's argument." And he turns to me, "Clarence, he met himself coming back." And that was the folksy way his brilliance would be wrapped up in these colloquialisms. I loved that. I was only there fifteen months before I was nominated [to the Supreme Court], which was too bad. I could have stayed on the D.C. Circuit. I would have been quite content.

CHAPTER SEVEN

SUPREME COURT NOMINATION

"Only in America"

MP: How did you come to be nominated for the Supreme Court?
CT: I have no idea why or how I got nominated. All I know is that Justice Marshall retired, and that was a shock.[1] My reaction was, "Oh no, this is going to be bad. People will go on a rumor that I'm one of the nominees."

I get a call from [White House Counsel C.] Boyden Gray the very afternoon Justice Marshall retired, saying, "Are you ready for another walk around the park?" He and I had taken a long walk at one of these Race for the Cure events earlier that spring. And that's the reference, "another walk around the park." He sent Mark Paoletta over to take me to the situation room at the Justice Department, and Mark parked across the street from the D.C. Circuit, across from where my wife worked, at the Labor Department. And we drove to the Justice Department. And that's where it started.

MP: What happened in that meeting at the DOJ?

CT: They wanted to know who I thought my views and approach were closest to on the Court. And I said, "Justice Scalia" and that was mostly because of his opinion in the *Olson* case.[2] I didn't know Justice Scalia. The second thing they asked me was whether or not I've had any difficulties about being in an interracial marriage. And I said only from liberals and bigots, and that's pretty much it. They asked a few other questions about EEOC, I think, and then I went back to work, and Virginia and I went home.

The next morning, they took me to the White House, where I sat for most of the morning, and they didn't decide anything. And I was told that if they didn't decide by before the weekend, it wouldn't be me. That's what I thought, but I may have misheard that. Saturday morning came, I wasn't nominated and I said, "Free at last." I had a new Corvette, and Virginia and I drove to Annapolis and celebrated not being nominated.

So I went to work on Sunday, and one of my law clerks was all up in arms. He says, "Kennebunkport is on the line." It was the president telling me to come up on Monday, to have lunch to discuss "this Supreme Court thing."

And then I went up on Monday to Kennebunkport. And I looked around on this airplane, and I noticed that Boyden was on it and some other senior people, and I said if they're here with me, who's riding with the other people? And I started getting a little suspicious.

Earlier that morning, my wife said, "What if they nominate you? What are you going to say? You can't say, 'Oh, I thank my dog, and I thank my mother, and I thank my third-grade teacher.' You got to have something to say." She made me sit down and write a short statement. I wrote it on a legal pad. And then she said, "I want you to say, 'Only in America.'" And so I added that. I put that in my pocket knowing I would never use it.

We made it up there, and it was bad. They put me in one of these black SUVs and drove a hundred miles an hour to Kennebunkport. That was scary. Then we got in, and they went in some back way, so the media wouldn't see me, and then they made you do that thing that they do with the criminals: you put a newspaper in front of your face.

MP: When did you learn you would be nominated?
CT: We were walking along to the Bush's residence, and we ran into Mrs. Bush. And she said, "Congratulations," and then my heart sank. And she said, "Oh, I guess I let the cat out of the bag." And then I went up on the back deck, and the president introduced me to everyone, and took me into the kitchen, introduced me to the chef, and everybody in there, and then we went in the sitting area in their bedroom. I took off my jacket, and he and I sat and talked, and he asked me a couple of questions. He said, "If you get on the Supreme Court, can you call them as you see them?" I said, "That's the only way I know how to do it." The other was, "Can you and your family get through confirmation?" I said, "I've been through four, and I think I can get through one more." And then he said, "If you go on the Court, I will never publicly criticize any opinion of yours." And he repeated that, and then he said, "At two o'clock, I'm going to nominate you to the Supreme Court. Let's go have lunch."

We go back to lunch and he introduces me to members of his cabinet, and I think Brian Mulroney, the prime minister of Canada, was there. The people could not have been nicer. There were a lot of important people, but it was very informal. Then I called my wife; I called Senator Danforth.

We walked over to a small office, and I sat there and went over the statement, which I had written out, and talked to Mrs. Bush, who did everything she could to calm me down. She could not have been nicer. When I walked outside to the announcement, you could hear the reporters gasp, "Oh, Thomas." Then you started hearing the shutters from the cameras going off. The press conference was mostly not about me, but it was clear that I was going to be treated with some degree of unpleasantness.

MP: In your statement, you thanked your grandparents and the nuns.
CT: I thanked the people who meant everything to me, like my wife, my nuns, my grandparents—the people who mattered. When you reflect on your life, it comes down to the people who were there when you needed them the most. The Latin phrase is "sine qua non"—without which there would not be you.

I started thinking of what could have been—living on the west side of Savannah, in a tenement. I keep a picture of that on the wall in my office. It's not quite the same street, but it really is exactly like the street that I lived on in Savannah. It's a Walker Evans photo of the black neighborhood in Savannah, and I keep it there, because that meant there was an inevitability to your life there. It was going to go a certain way. Then you have these interventions, you have these things that break the chain. Then you start thinking of the people who were involved in that change. It's first my grandparents. Then they sent me to school with the nuns. Then there are people you meet along the way, who were really kind to you, who helped you. And then there are people in your life now, my wife would be central, that are wonderful people. Parts of your life, like my son. Those are the people I was thinking about.

GETTING READY FOR THE HEARINGS
"THEY ACCUSE YOU OF EVERYTHING BUT MURDER, I GUESS"

MP: Next, you began to prepare for the hearings. What was this time like?

CT: I mean the attacks started immediately. They accused you of having a Confederate flag on your desk. The things they accuse you of—they accuse you of everything but murder, I guess. They just kept coming up with things to discredit you. People distort your life. One reporter was going through records of mine trying to find my divorce records, because one of the accusations was that I was involved in domestic violence. That would be news to me. He was looking at my divorce records and found a tax lien, which nobody knew anything about. I suddenly became a tax cheat. I ask the IRS, "What is this?" Because when you go through confirmation, before you're nominated, the IRS has to assure that you have no taxes due. When I asked about this lien, the IRS said they had no idea what it was there for, and of course, immediately withdrew it. But it was that sort of thing, and it never stopped, every day. I think most people never saw it, because most of the kind of things they accuse you of went away, but they were just efforts to churn the waters. The point was that they kept trying different things and that started immediately.

MP: You mentioned to me you read some books about the Bork confirmation hearings.[3]
CT: I had read Bork's book when I was nominated to the D.C. Circuit. It was new at the time. *[The] Tempting of America* is excellent.[4] And I'd also read another account of his nomination, *People Rising* by Michael Pertschuk, which basically set out what the opponents did and how well organized they were and persistent.[5]

I read *The Trial* by Kafka because I had a sense that, it's one thing having to deal with things that you did, that you know about.[6] Someone says, "Well did you have a banana for breakfast?" You did, and you defend that. What if someone said, "You had a breakfast of bacon, eggs, sausage, and grits." You can say, "But I didn't have that."

But, they can still continue to accuse you of that, effectively, if they have the ear of the audience, or if they're effective at messaging, or propaganda, or misinformation.

Josef K. [the protagonist in *The Trial*] gets arrested one morning. You never know what he's arrested for, and then the whole rest of the novel is how he reacts to that and ultimately how it leads to his demise. It's really interesting to think about someone being arrested, and not knowing what they're arrested for. That's why I basically read it at that time. I reread it recently for a Law and Literature course. These things fascinate me. But I think that that is more akin to what happens in Washington, and certainly what happened during my confirmation, than anything else.

MP: Josef K. is up against a faceless bureaucracy and nameless charges.
CT: Bureaucracy is a faceless world against you. And what they create in your mind with these accusations is you must have done something, he's acting guilty. "He didn't really truly deny it." So you get those things. He could have been as innocent as could be. But the mere fact the accusation starts you down this path, and so the most you could say from what you observe, is maybe he reacted badly to having been accused. But then you asked someone: "What would you do, if one fine morning you were arrested and you had no idea why? And they didn't tell you why."

So my point is simply that it starts you down a road that is almost by definition illegitimate, and however you react, however imperfect you are, it's still an illegitimate trial. Look at Joseph K., he should have been more serious about the accusation, but there was nothing he had done, either. Well, why *shouldn't* it have gotten under his skin, and driven him to madness or to do the things that he did? Or maybe he shouldn't have gotten distracted. But does that make the initial accusation legitimate?

MP: Bork's strategy, during his unsuccessful Senate confirmation hearing for the Supreme Court in 1987, was to argue and to talk constitutional law. Did you think that this was not a strategy that worked?
CT: Remember now, I've had a lot of hearings. There's a silver lining in bad things that happen to you in life. And I think I was very fortunate to have made a lot of unpleasant trips to [Capitol] Hill. I don't know how many hearings I had, but scores, way too many. And you realize that it isn't normally about information. This is not a great debate. This is not a seminar. They are trying to score points against you, and if you've been in enough hearings, you realize that even when you answer, the person who asks you the question is onto their next question, and not listening to what you're saying. Some do, but for the most part, it's more histrionics than a debate or information exchange.

COORDINATED ATTACKS
"THEY HAVE TO MAKE YOU…INTO SOMETHING THAT IS REPULSIVE, REDUCED, SO THEY CAN'T SEE YOU AS A HUMAN"

MP: After you were nominated, did you meet with board members of the NAACP?
CT: Connie Newman [director of the Office of Personnel Management under President George H. W. Bush] set up a meeting with some of the board members. They were very nice, and they said they were

going to be noncommittal and were not going to oppose me. Well, shortly after that they opposed me. And what I was told by friends, who gave me a copy of the AFL–CIO's letter to [the NAACP] requiring them to oppose me, they needed cover for the women's groups to oppose me. They needed the NAACP out front early. That's what I was told, and that certainly is consistent with what happened.

MP: The theory is that if the NAACP opposes you, then the women's groups would then not be afraid to attack a black man?
CT: It goes to the ostracism and being cut from the herd. And this happened throughout my tenure in Washington. The people who are hypersensitive about every racial slight or criticism of the people they favor would never defend those of us who disagree with them from far worse slights and outright racialist treatment. And, so you're absolved, you're granted immunity, if they say, "We oppose this guy." So you give them cover. "It's okay to beat this particular guy."

MP: Why did the American Bar Association give you only a "quali-fied" rating, rather than its higher rating, "well-qualified"?[7]
CT: They did not give Bob Bork, who is probably the most qualified nominee in my lifetime, a [unanimous] well-qualified rating.[8] They gave him a mixed rating. So in a sense, they had disqualified them-selves. Any organization can be corrupted, or tainted, or misused. It depends on the people in the organization.

MP: You said at one point, "I couldn't be defeated without first being caricaturized and dehumanized."
CT: They have to make you into somebody who you're not. You have to be reduced to this little object. And I don't know whether the right word is reified, but it's just to be made into an object, and

made into something that is repulsive, reduced, so they can't see you as a human.

Early on when I was at the EEOC, the efforts started. The first article in the *New York Times* begins that.[9] The reporter [Ernie Holsendolph] said, "You're controversial." Who decided that I was controversial? When I was nominated to the D.C. Circuit, my mother called me and said, "A friend of yours came by and spent the day with me." I said, "What friend are you talking about?" "Oh, your friend from a newspaper." I said, "What is this?" And apparently a reporter from an Atlanta paper had read that I was from poverty in Pin Point and from Savannah and thought that couldn't be true.

So my mother gave the reporter my home number, and had him call me at home. He said that he had read this article, and he thought that it was false, and he went down to Savannah to prove it, and he found out that not only was it true, but it understated the truth. He wanted to print that, but he told me something along the lines that his editor thought I was controversial, and that that wasn't what he wanted. I just think they have reduced you to something that is easily disdained.

I went through confirmation in a Democrat Senate.[10] You had a number of Southern Democrats. And what I was told was that they had to be given cover to vote against me, and one way to do that was to caricature me that I was a nut case when it comes to natural law; that I was a bad person; that I was against civil rights; that I hated everybody; that I had abandoned my family; that I'd done this, and I'd done that. So I had to, somehow, assume the black hat.

MP: You've compared all these people buzzing around you spreading lies and misinformation to low-country gnats.
CT: If you have ever been down in the southeast U.S., and particularly in Georgia, you are consumed by little gnats, or sandflies. Some

people call them "No see'ems." But they swarm around you, they can be very distracting, and you have to learn when you're down there to work with these things around you. They sting a little bit, too. The only difference is that these gnats, the ones on [Capitol] Hill, are lethal. They are swarming like gnats, but they're lethal gnats, and that's the way you felt.

And now, how do you get your stuff done? How do you prepare? How do you read cases? How do you sit down and think when you're being surrounded by gnats? When I was picking beans, or peas, out in the field, being around gnats, and learning how to continue working, and not being distracted with these gnats, maybe it actually prepared me to deal with these people, because you learn how to sit and read. I mean, binder after binder after binder, on the Fourth Amendment, the First Amendment, law review articles, even while people are trying to destroy you. And that was the situation: we were swarmed by gnats, but still having to sit down, and think, and get your work done.

MP: On the other side, a group came up from Georgia, friends and relatives and supporters, around this time.
CT: It's so poignant that you bring that up. A number of people, like my cousin Jack Fuller, who was ninety-one at the time, came all the way up here. I don't even know if he'd ever been to D.C. before. Cousin Jack lived about a quarter of a mile or so from our house. We all farmed together. He and my grandfather grew up together. And Cousin Jack taught me a lot of things, about tying wire, fence wire, grinding sugar cane. We used his horse, Lizzie, to plow.

Cousin Jack was a good man. And my cousins weren't sophisticated, well-educated people; they were good people. They came up to reassert the reality, the context of my life, that was constantly being distorted by the so-called "tolerant" people. The irony has never escaped me. It's almost as though they were reclaiming facts, or reality. It was very encouraging to see them, to finally see comforting faces, to see truth. This is what my life was. It was one of the highlights during the worst part of the process. It meant so much that my cousin Jack, at age ninety-one, would come in at a time of difficulty to rescue me from the so-called "tolerant" people. In fact, to this day I keep a picture of me embracing Cousin Jack in my bedroom. To think that they would all come up here, to look out for me, it is still something that has an effect on me. It's just like we were reclaiming what's ours.

PREP WORK
"IN THE MIDDLE OF OUR SESSIONS, I MIGHT GET TEN PHONE CALLS, AND THEY'VE COME UP WITH SOME NEW WAY TO ATTACK ME"

MP: You mentioned reviewing these binders of material every day to prepare for the hearing.
CT: Lawyers from the [Department of Justice's] Office of Legal Counsel would come over in the mornings (almost every morning) and very quietly to the house, and invariably they would have one of those big black binders full of cases and law review articles, and they would ask me to read the materials, and they would come back, and we would discuss it.[11] Remember, I had been away from the law qua law for over a decade. I had done regulatory work at Monsanto, but that's in-house regulatory work and policies. I went to Monsanto in 1977, and now I'm looking at 1989. I had gone from Monsanto to the Hill and then I became a bureaucrat for the next decade. So I hadn't really sat down and written briefs, and thought of law as law, not as a basis for policy making, not as a basis for legislation, but law as a

law, for quite some time. I had to sort of re-acclimate myself to that world. So, I was sitting with [Office of Legal Counsel lawyer] John Harrison, with Mike Luttig, who was at that time [assistant attorney general] of OLC, to prepare me substantively, and to get me reacclimated to that world. It's one thing if I had months and months, and peace, and quiet. But, in the middle of our sessions, for example I might get ten phone calls, and they've come up with some new way to attack me. That went on for literally three and a half months.

But that aside, the way that we proceeded was that they would bring a binder over, and I would read it. I read all the material. Then we would discuss, I would have questions and there was only one area they would not discuss with me. They absolutely would not discuss *Roe v. Wade* with me.[12] They would not discuss abortion because they knew that I was going to be asked about it at some point. And they wanted me to be able to say that I did not discuss it with them. President Bush wouldn't discuss that with me. Boyden Gray wouldn't discuss that with me.

I would ask them questions. Let's say, one of the cases leading up to *Roe v. Wade*, was *Griswold v. Connecticut*.[13] And I would ask them about the reasoning in that. And I remember John Harrison would just look at me, and he would just say, "Mmhmm, mmhmm." They would give me articles to read on it, but they would never offer an opinion, or debate me back and forth about it, or engage me in any substantive discussion.

THE HEARINGS BEGIN
"ULTIMATELY, THE BIGGEST IMPEDIMENT WAS THE MODERN-DAY LIBERAL"

MP: After all these months of prep, it's September 10, 1991, the first day of the hearings, and you go to Danforth's office before the hearing starts.

CT: The whole process was awful. I went to Kennebunkport and was announced on July 1, and now we're in September. And virtually every minute of every day, between July 1 and September 10 had been full of torment and exhausting work. I get to Senator Danforth's office, and he's been a warrior and just fabulous. I could not imagine having had a better boss and a better person to meet in my life, particularly at that age, as a young man. He's a good man. I get to his office, and we sit, and we begin to discuss what's ahead. And he's just more comforting than anything else, and just before the hearings start, he had a very small private bathroom there. He said to Virginia, "You're going to think I'm really odd," but he invited us in his little bathroom and he had a portable tape recorder cassette player, and he played "Onward, Christian Soldiers" and we listened to that, and he exhorted me to let the Holy Ghost speak through me, and we went off to the hearings.

MP: He was a minister, in fact?
CT: He's an ordained Episcopal minister. And it's interesting because I saw him being more priestly during the confirmation than I had witnessed during the entire time I knew him. He kept that separate from the day-to-day work when I worked for him. We knew he was an Episcopal minister. He didn't wear a collar, and he didn't talk about it constantly, and he didn't proselytize. Piety was a private matter. So now I saw all sides of him, not just the senator, or the attorney general, but the man. And it was wonderful to behold. And certainly, he was wonderful to me.

MP: There were the opening statements from the senators and your opening statement and then the questioning begins.[14] It was really relentless, day after day. It must have been grueling. Even though you have been through congressional hearings before, this must have been extraordinary.

CT: I've had worse things in life. I've been blessed because I've seen worse. It was a lot worse to be hungry and not know when you got to eat, or be cold and not know when you're going to be warm again. These people who were doing the attacking had never known anything like that. They think that this is the worst that could ever happen. It was horrible, in every way, and I was worn down. I was exhausted. I was tired.

I felt as though in my life I had been looking at the wrong people who would be problematic toward me. We were told that, "Oh it's gonna be the bigot in the pickup truck. It's gonna be the Klansman. It's going to be the rural sheriff." And I'm not saying that there weren't some of those who were bad, but it turned out that through all of that, that ultimately, the biggest impediment was the modern day liberal. They were the ones who would discount all those things because they have one issue, or because they have the authority, the power to caricature you.

MP: Does this reflect your grandfather's distinction between rattlesnakes and water moccasins?
CT: I think he was right there. The moccasin doesn't give you a warning, and it strikes. A rattlesnake at least tells you. And I would really equate the outright bigot with a rattlesnake. You know they don't like you. Whereas the people who say, "Oh, we like you a lot," and then do you harm are more like water moccasins. There was a wonderful song by The Undisputed Truth, back in the seventies, called "Smiling Faces" and that basically makes that point. "They smile in your face," and then they stab you. So that was it. I beat up on myself for not realizing that more clearly.

MP: "Smiling Faces" begins with: "Smiling faces pretend to be your friend. Smiling faces shedding traces of the evil that lurks within."[15]

CT: Oh yeah, that's a great song. Look it up on YouTube. That became sort of a mantra, or at least a reference point, and that's what I was thinking sometimes during the hearings—the smiling faces, the people who say they like you and do you harm.

SENATOR BIDEN
"I HAD NO IDEA WHAT HE WAS TALKING ABOUT"

MP: How did Senator Biden treat you during the hearings?
CT: When I got nominated to the D.C Circuit, Joe Biden told me I would be confirmed—he was chairman of the committee—but that if I was nominated to the Supreme Court, basically all bets were off, that I would be treated differently.

MP: Didn't Biden promise to start the hearings with a softball question?
CT: Joe Biden promised a lot of things and said a lot of things. Before the beginning of the hearings, he took us to the hearing room, which was the Caucus Room in the Russell Senate Office Building. And he showed us around, and he explained that there would be a round of opening statements that would take some time, and then he would ask the first question, that it would be a softball question, and then he would just get me warmed up because it would be very difficult for me to get used to that setting.

   I don't recall exactly what the question was, but it had to do with the speech that I gave at the Pacific Legal Foundation.[16] And he misquoted it. I was perplexed because I didn't remember the speech. I've given lots of speeches, but it didn't sound right. It was not what I believed. And it seemed it was the opposite. You're flustered a little bit, because you're waiting for the softball, and it turns out to be a beanball.

MP: Senator Biden claimed you were praising Professor Stephen Macedo's views on property rights and that the Supreme Court should be activist in re-asserting property rights.
CT: I said that even if I agreed with Macedo you couldn't do that because either the law or the Constitution would actually be the determining factor; that the court shouldn't be activist. In the next sentence I disagreed with Macedo's point of view.[17]

MP: They did that a few times, taking your statement out of context. Eventually, it gets corrected, but they must feel they have gotten somewhere just by putting it on the table in a distorted manner.
CT: This is not an information exchange. People can say things. There could be insults, there can be slights, there can be innuendos. There could be an effort to unnerve you, to rattle you, to get you to look bad. So there are all these other things that are going on. There's a lot of this "gotcha," to get you to say something that leads to something else.

My view when I was at the EEOC is to just say what you think and to be consistent. And if people lay these traps, then so be it. But at least you have the comfort of knowing that what you said is what you believe. And if they have a problem with it, I think it's up to them to say explicitly and forthrightly what that problem is.

MP: Senator Biden was very focused on natural law.

From the documentary *Created Equal*

Senator Biden: Finding out what you mean when you say that you would apply the natural law philosophy to the Constitution is, in my view, the single most important task of this committee.... I just want to make sure we all know what we

are talking about here. That you and I know, at least, what
we are talking about here.

There is a fervent…and aggressive school of thought that
wishes to see natural law further inform the Constitution than
it does now. Argued against by the positivists, led by Judge
Bork. Now again, that may be lost on all the people, you know
and I know what we are talking about.… Someone may apply
it in a way, like Moore, who leads him in a direction that is,
quote, "liberal." You may apply it in a way that leads you in
a direction that is conservative, or you may, like many argue,
not apply it at all.

But it is a fundamental question that is going to be almost
impossible for non-lawyers to grasp in an exchange, but you
know and I know it is a big, big deal.

MP: How did you respond?
CT: Who knows. I have no idea what he was talking about.

MP: He was suggesting that natural law theory was an open sesame
for you to just use natural law arguments to impose your opinions
on issues like abortion.
CT: I have to be perfectly honest with you: You sit there, and you have
no idea what they are talking about. People may in the end, after the
fact, figure out what he was talking about at the time. I have no clue.
All I know is that he was asking me these questions about natural law.
I had looked at natural law. One, I was really interested in the
Founding, and you can't deny that natural law was an important part
of that. The Framers understood natural law and natural rights a
certain way, and it is the underpinning of our Declaration, which then
becomes the basis for the foundation for the Constitution.

The distinction that we made was the Constitution is the positive document. The Declaration may set out the architecture for it, the reasons for it, but here's the Constitution. The positivists say, "Ignore that and use this." But the Declaration informs the Constitution. It shines a light on the Constitution. It reaffirms why you have these things.

MP: Yes, Senator Biden seemed a bit confused about it all himself.
CT: One of the things you do in hearings is you have to sit there and look attentively at people you know have no idea what they're talking about. And it was fine. I understood what he was trying to do. I didn't really appreciate it, but I had no idea what he was talking about minute by minute. And I couldn't get caught up in that sort of confusion.

I think what Bob Bork's mistake was, he'd try to sort it out and make sense of it. My granddaddy had another saying; he said, "Boy, it don't make no damn sense, because it don't make no damn sense." And I'm not going to sit here and make sense out of something that doesn't make sense. So if he doesn't understand it, then I am not going to try to understand it. I know why I did what I did. Here's why I'm trying to do this: I had my reasons. I know what Ken [Masugi] and John [Marini] and I were working on. I know what I was thinking about. I know what I think. Now what *he* thinks I think is used to confuse me about what I think.

MP: I thought Senator Orrin Hatch had a good point about this in the hearings. He said that Bob Bork was attacked for not believing in natural law, and now the same people are attacking you for believing in natural law.
CT: Well, he was attacked for being a positivist. Just remember what the rule is: if people are for you, you can do no wrong. If they're

against you, you can do no right. That logic has nothing to do with it. Consistency isn't an order of the day. It's not a coin of the realm. You don't like this guy, here's what you can use against him, and whether or not it's logical or consistent has nothing to do with it.

MP: Another focus in the hearings was your views on affirmative action. What were the senators after on this issue?
CT: I have no idea what they were after.

MP: They wanted to imply that you were not—
CT: There is a view in society that blacks should think certain things. Years ago, all blacks had to believe in busing. All blacks have to believe in welfare. All blacks have to believe in quotas. All blacks have to believe—these were like tenets of being black, and they were assigned to you.

I was recently in D.C. going to lunch, and a young black meter-maid came up to me and said, "I've always been wanting to meet you." She was so excited, and she said, "You know the only thing I don't agree with you on is 'affirmative action.'" And I said, "What is it?" And she paused, and she said, "I don't even know what it is, and here I am saying I don't agree with you." And she went off muttering to herself, "I'm disagreeing with this man, and I don't even know what it is."

It becomes what people want it to be, from equal opportunity to quotas. Think of it as a weapon, a bludgeon: "Here's what blacks believe. He doesn't believe it: Therefore!" I mean, that may sound syllogistic, but that's just that. You assign it: "Here's what blacks believe. He doesn't believe it."

MP: They were focused on the "goals and timetables" issue, and whether they violated the Constitution.

CT: Yeah, that's a real hot button issue today. It's the same thing with these new sort of issues *du jour* that you're supposed to believe, if you're black. And if you don't, it's the same thing today. To be fashionable, there is an issue *du jour*. "We all agree with that, of course." And then tomorrow it's something else. I'm like my grandfather in that regard—principles have a much longer shelf life than these issues *du jour*.

ABORTION
"YOUR LIFE DIDN'T MATTER. WHAT MATTERED WAS WHAT THEY WANTED, AND WHAT THEY WANTED WAS THIS PARTICULAR ISSUE"

MP: The big driver for the Democrats opposing you was *Roe v. Wade*. They asked lots about that, and in many ways.

CT: I think it was central to a lot. It was certainly the key to the opposition from many of the women's groups. I just thought it was ironic that in my whole life, through all the years of preparation, and coming through Georgia, and all the challenges, that of all the things that they've reduced it to was something that wasn't even an issue in your life. Wasn't a matter you've thought about, but because that issue is so important to them, they will wash over your entire life. They will vandalize the little life that you've cobbled together because their stuff is so important.

What I realized, and should have realized more fully, is that you really didn't matter and your life didn't matter. What mattered was what they wanted, and what they wanted was this particular issue. And regardless of what I had done with my life, where I had been, where I had lived, it was all cancelled out, unless I agreed two plus two equals five. You have to say it. And that makes it true. Because they want it to be true.

MP: The Democrats spent a lot of time trying to get you to commit on how you would rule on abortion, and you did not want to commit.
CT: One, I didn't know. And two, I had just read all those cases again. I hadn't read those cases about privacy, and I hadn't thought much about substantive due process since law school. I had constitutional law in 1972; *Roe* was decided in 1973. I was more interested in the race issues. I was more interested in getting out of law school. I was more interested in passing the bar exam. My life was consumed by survival. I couldn't pay my rent. I couldn't repay my student loans. I had all these other things going on, that you were navigating, these worlds you're navigating.

They think we all should have been concerned about this one issue. I hadn't really thought about it. I thought about it generally but not in the sense that I had read *Roe* or re-read *Griswold*. This wasn't my issue. I have no idea why they thought it should be my issue, why I should think about it in the way they did.

MP: They refused to believe that you had not discussed it.
CT: Well, you know what? They refused to believe a lot of things. Isn't that fascinating? I had to have discussed it because they wanted me to discuss it. It goes back to their thinking on affirmative action. You have to believe in affirmative action because we think you ought to believe in affirmative action. Well, how is it different from slavery? How is that different from segregation? How is that different from being told, "You can't walk across that park"? "Oh, you can't think those thoughts." "Oh, you could not have done that." "You could not have used your time that way." How is that any different? You know

what? I'd prefer to be excluded from the park because I can live my life quite freely without having set foot in a park. But you can't live it freely without having your own thoughts. The idea that, "I have to do this," I found that more repulsive than the specific thing about which they thought I should think.

MP: Now, they might not have liked your views about affirmative action, but they knew them. In the *Roe* case, they thought they knew what you thought, even though you hadn't said it.
CT: They must have been in séances, or something, or are into reading chicken feet or something like that, because I had not discussed it. How would they know when my wife didn't know? How would they know when I didn't know? If I asked them a question: "What is your view on the new advances in quantum physics?" And you say, "I don't know." I could say, "I refuse to believe you don't know, I refuse to believe you hadn't thought about it because that's all I've been thinking about for the past five years." I make light of it, but the point is, not everybody thinks about what you think about. Not everybody reads the same books. I read the things I'm interested in. I'm interested in diesel motors and the difference between an 8v92 and a Series 60 Detroit Diesel. How many people are interested in that? Maybe two? That's all I'm interested in, and you should be interested in this. That's absurd.

The abortion issue is a much bigger issue, obviously, but the point is, I hadn't thought about it. I thought about it in the sense that maybe it would be hard—but constitutionally, ever read the cases? No. I was more in the race issues. I was more interested in black kids getting an education. I was more interested in the breakdown of the family. I was more interested in the social pathologies that were coming the way of blacks. Look at what I read, look at what I was interested in. Did Richard Wright or Ralph Ellison or Harper Lee have some long exposition or long discussion on abortion? No, that isn't what we were talking about. You're talking about race because that was a central part of *our* lives.

MP: They didn't want *Roe* to be overturned. And that was, as you say, the one thing that trumped everything else.
CT: Well, perhaps they wanted assurances, which is precisely what a judge shouldn't be doing.

MP: And one of the themes of the confirmation was how should judges decide, and what would your role be as a judge.
CT: I don't think they believe that a judge is to be impartial. I think they believe in legal realism. I think some people don't believe that law is to be neutral. They think that you bring a bias, and it's reflected in the way you judge.

MP: They didn't believe perhaps that you *could* judge impartially without simply going with your bias.
CT: Maybe that's because that's what they would do. There's a lot of projection here. They project their views on you, they project their attitudes, their outlook, the way they would do things on you. Well, that's not me. I've heard them say to me, "Well, if that happened to me, this is what I would have done." So that's what you would have done. Or they say, "Oh everybody does it." So you spread a certain approach or you make it universal.

MP: Right after the hearings, were there also written questions you had to respond to?
CT: We actually spent a lot of time responding to written questions. And it never ended because you had more people challenging what you said. Then the propaganda starts, that, "Oh you lied." They love

to call you a liar. That's the first thing they love to say, "Well, you say you didn't discuss *Roe*. Everybody discussed *Roe*. You're lying." So then the propaganda starts on that. Then they continued raising more questions, asking more questions. And then you had all the people who were testifying against you. I love people who show up and testify against you, whom you've never met. When you're nominated, you have people who show up that you barely know, who become experts on you, and these people testify against you, you don't know them from a hill of beans. And people say all sorts of things. You become this piñata, and you start attracting everybody who wants attention.

CHAPTER EIGHT

ANITA HILL

"That's when all heck broke loose"

MP: What did you do next?

CT: We were just exhausted. We went over just briefly, and it was out of season, to Cape May just to get away from the Washington area. We came back and that's when all heck broke loose. We had just gotten back, and I got a call from Lee Liberman, and she said, "The FBI is coming out."[1] She said it's something silly, she was laughing, and she said, "I've read it, it is just some illiterate statement with a lot of misspellings and typos, and it's not even an affidavit. It won't take much time, but we need the FBI to come out. It's best that I not tell you what it is because it'll just sort of taint things, but it's not a big deal." So the FBI comes out.

MP: What was that like when the FBI came to visit you?

CT: It was a black gentleman and a white female agent, and they show their identifications. And as soon as they stepped in, they said, "Do you know Anita Hill?" I said, "What?" And then they said, "Did you ever try to go out with her or did you ever discuss pornographic stuff with her?" "No, no way." And I said, "You've got to be kidding me." It's just like, you're deflated. You said, "This is where we're going now." And we sat down at the kitchen table in the little dining area, and the agent started reading the statement because he said, "We just got this."[2] And he started asking me about it. And he said, "This is odd because there are no facts in here." And then he said, "When did you first meet her?"

And, so I maybe, I felt more like Josef K. in *The Trial*, that suddenly you're minding your business, and you were arrested one morning. You're entering an unknown world. I have no facts, I have no idea what I was supposed to have done.

MP: And what did they say the next step for you would be?
CT: They said that agents were fanning out all over the country and investigating it. The committee wanted a report that afternoon, and they would get back to me in the afternoon and tell me what they were finding. In the meantime, a buddy of mine came in, very dear friend, he said he'd been a lawyer in this area, and he just happened to come in because they were attacking me so much. And he looked at it, and I told him what had just happened. He said, "Oh, this will go away. This doesn't amount to anything." And I said, "No, you don't understand, these guys do nothing that is frivolous. They've got more planned."

MP: Did the FBI get back to you that afternoon?
CT: The FBI called back that afternoon. They said, "This is uncorroborated. And what we're going to tell the committee is that it's uncorroborated. There are no facts. We don't think there's anything to it." He was very clear. He was almost apologetic that they had put me through this.

I ran into one of those agents about a year or two later, just happened to bump into him. And he basically said that he didn't realize how much they were after me. He was a nice man. They were all very nice. The FBI agents, the people who looked into this initially, could not have been more professional, and they were just very straightforward, very dignified about it.

MP: It is amazing that once they couldn't find corroborating evidence after fanning out through the country—
CT: I said it would never stop. It was never about evidence. It was about: "I have to be stopped," as one person said.

MP: When the FBI had concluded its investigation, it kind of ended the matter until Anita Hill's testimony was leaked. How did that happen?
CT: I get another call from Lee Liberman saying that it had been leaked to [NPR reporter] Nina Totenberg and Tim Phelps at *Newsday*.[3] I knew what the strategy was. I didn't know how they were going to use it, or what they were going to use. But this is where they were headed. The one thing that throughout your life you've tried to avoid is putting yourself in a situation. You read *To Kill a Mockingbird*. You've been watching your whole life, and you try to always be proper, and particularly in sexual areas, and suddenly they can just make these assertions. You know where they're going, they've got to knock me off. It was leaked. This was a crime. This was a criminal act that did this. But in any case, it was leaked, and that changed everything.

Before the Committee vote, I get a call from [Senator] Joe Biden, and he said, "Judge, I've got two speeches in front of me, one for you, and one against you."[4] That was kind of hard for me to believe, that he had two. But he said ultimately he was going to vote against me in committee, and I said he had to do what he had to do. But I really wanted to make sure I kept my good name, whether I was confirmed or not. He said, "Judge, don't worry about it. You'll keep your good name, nothing will happen to that. I know you don't believe me, but

I'll be your biggest defender." Well of course when it was leaked, he was no place to be found. A lot of people were no place to be found.

That really complicated the vote [of the entire Senate] that had been scheduled.[5] The day of the scheduled vote, we knew there was going to be a media circus because of the leak, so Virginia and I went over to Judge Larry Silberman and Ricky Silberman's house (she's since passed away) just to get away from that zoo. They didn't know where we were. I spent the day pacing around their little pool in their little backyard in Georgetown.

MP: It's never been determined who exactly leaked this to Nina—
CT: They had an investigation [conducted by special counsel Peter Fleming].[6] I don't know. I have not expressed great interest in finding out. It didn't matter to me who leaked it. I just find it incredible that it could ever even get going. And I blame that on people who should know better.

THE DEMOCRATS AND THE MEDIA RUN WITH IT
"IT JUST FELT LIKE THE MOB OUTSIDE OF THE JAIL IN TO KILL A MOCKINGBIRD"

MP: The media and Democrats certainly jumped on this leak. What was your reaction?
CT: This is the mob. That's what it felt like. It just felt like the mob outside of the jail in To Kill a Mockingbird.[7] They didn't have their little robes on, but boy, they were sanctimonious, and they had their torches, which were maybe computers and things. But no, this was the mob; wasn't any more a trial than Salem had trials.

MP: You mentioned the media circus, and we haven't talked much about that, but that had been ongoing?

CT: The media was always bad. They just pretend to be objective, but for the most part they were part of the mob from the beginning. But it just got worse. When you have media people calling up friends, and they ask, "Do you have any dirt on this guy?"[8] Not, "What is the story?" Just dirt. That pretty much should tell you all.

It goes back to when I was at the EEOC, that I was "controversial." I was brand new. How can I be controversial? That means I don't have the views that they've assigned to me. That's the only controversial thing. So I had then effectively been caricatured. The media was not trying to find out facts, they were clearly a part of one team versus the other. There were a few who weren't.

MP: The media also went out to Pin Point.
CT: Initially when the media were told I was from Pin Point, they said Pin Point didn't exist. And that was really funny. These guys know so much. They said, "You're a liar." Who would lie about where you're from? That's easy to prove, and who would lie about it? Every time you said something, and they didn't agree with you, you were a liar. One of the reporters went to Savannah and argued with my mother about the number of kids she had. How do you argue with a woman about the number of kids she had? I think she may have been there. She eventually had to tell them to leave.

MP: How could the reporter be arguing about the number of children she had?
CT: He said they can only find records for two kids. How can you be so arrogant to tell a woman how many kids she had? But I think that it is similarly arrogant to tell people what their views ought to be just because of their race. "I know what your views should be. I don't know you, but since you're black, your views should be this."

MP: Yes, I hear this still from your liberal critics. They say you are "a traitor to your race."

CT: Because you have views that you shouldn't have. You say what race? The human race? Which race? It is absurd. I love it when you are looking at a white person telling you that, and they just don't see how laughable that is.

MP: After it's leaked, then Anita Hill has a press conference.[9] Did you see that?

CT: Oh God, no.

MP: Did Ginni see it and tell you about it?

CT: She watched and told me it was slickly done, that it was smooth, and there were a lot of professionals there. But what she described was not the person who worked for me. As I recall, [Anita] was portrayed as conservative (not true), that she was quite religious (that'd be the first I'd ever heard of that), and that she was demure (no way). That's a nice image to paint, but that wasn't the person I knew. The person I knew was outspoken, could fly off the handle at people, get upset with people, a person who stormed into my office, could be pretty loud about things, and was quite liberal. She may have been religious, but never professed to be, that I knew of.

ANOTHER ROUND
"IT WAS HARD. I'M AT THE END OF MY LINE"

MP: Did you hear from Jack Danforth about the next stage for the hearings?

CT: I get a call when I was at Larry Silberman's house from Jack Danforth, Orrin Hatch, and Bob Dole. And they said that if [the full

Senate] voted then, they couldn't guarantee that I would be confirmed. Remember, we're dealing with a Democrat Senate, and that they thought we needed to address this matter and it was determined that they would have another hearing.[10]

MP: And how did you feel?
CT: Not good. It was hard. I'm at the end of my line. I don't know what they are going to do to me next. I still don't know what I'm accused of doing, so you're tormenting yourself. Did I say something? Did I make an offhand remark? Did I suggest something? And then you worry about what can they convince people that I have done. You got all these PR firms, and slick law firms, and interest groups. I'm just sitting there, I mean it's my wife and me. We're at home, and we have a couple of prayer partners who would come over, and we'd pray and listen to music. The phone kept ringing, and the news kept getting worse. Media was parked outside of our house, so you're literally under siege. Now you don't know what's going to happen. You don't know what they're going to say next about you. You weren't worried about what you've done. It's like what can they convince the world that you've done, because if they had made it this far with that, then they were going to go the whole way.

MP: After the leak, the media just camped out at your house?
CT: Yeah, they stayed, and then whenever we left, there would be a chase car, and there was a motorcycle behind us. President Bush invited us to see him for reassurance. Senator Danforth rode with us to the White House, and we were followed by the press the entire way. It was in every possible way disconcerting and awful. We'd never been through anything like this.

President Bush sat with me in the Oval Office. Virginia went for a walk with Mrs. Bush. The president apologized for getting me into this. I told him this wasn't his fault, that he didn't do anything to me. It should have been a great moment for a poor kid from the Deep South, and the elites have turned it into a nightmare because of something they want. Not because something I've done, or some crime I've committed: because of something they want that they don't think they'll get with me. He assured me he was not going to withdraw [my nomination], that he was going to be with me to the end if I could hang in there, and again apologized for getting me into it.

MP: Were there people pushing him the other way, to pull your nomination?
CT: I don't know. I wasn't there. You would need to get that from somebody else. I hear that there may have been people who thought he should pull the plug, but I'm not privy to that. I was too busy trying to survive.

MP: How did Virginia respond to this stuff?
CT: I mean, badly. She's my wife, we're close. We've only been married four years, and they had attacked us for being interracial, attacked her. They had attacked everything, until there was nothing left to attack. And this was just the one thing, that as I told her, the one thing that I have to let go: I did feel good after my years at EEOC, that I had this great reputation, and I had a great personal reputation. I didn't live a profligate life, that sort of thing. So, I felt good about it. I was very prideful of it. And suddenly now, that had to go.

MP: She, of course, didn't question anything after Anita Hill—
CT: I mean, just that question and the fact people make more of it than it actually was. I know my wife. My wife knows me. Someone flies in and says something, you don't suddenly doubt the person. And the mere fact that people ask that shows how effective the

propaganda campaign is: that you give it more credibility, give it more stature than it deserves. That's the part that's incredible to me, that in the context of your life, of all you do, of the way you live your life, suddenly someone throws a speck in, and you say, "Oh, that's important."

My wife asked me about Anita Hill. I told her who she was, and why I hired her, same story I've been telling anyone who wanted to know. And that was that. And same thing with Senator Danforth, when he came over that day, it was to ask me. And I said, "Jack, here's the story. Here's exactly what happened. Gil asked me to hire her." You've desecrated trying to help somebody. You desecrated a person who helped everybody. They have trampled everything, every good intention, every good idea, every good attitude, just to get their way.

MP: The committee then decides it's going to reconvene to hear testimony.
CT: They were going to reconvene to have a hearing, and Boyden Gray called me up, and asked me did I want to go first or second.[11] He'd suggested I go first, and then told me I have to write a statement. It was really exhausting. I hadn't slept in a few days, just a little bit, and so I got a quick nap, and drifted off. Then my wife woke me up, and I went downstairs and had some difficulty getting focused. She'd helped clear things away. Then I wrote my statement. She typed it, and we edited it till the wee hours of the morning, and read it to Senator Danforth around 6:30 a.m. He made us take out some polite statements about the committee. He said they didn't deserve it. Then we tried to lay down for some rest. Of course, I didn't sleep, and she didn't either. So we just sort of laid there, like, what is happening to us? Just this nightmare. And then we drove in, and I don't know what the committee expected, but I read my statement, and basically made it clear I wasn't going to withdraw. Then, that seemed to be upsetting

to them, and they shut the hearings down, and I went back home.[12] That was it.

MP: What was your state of mind during all that?
CT: Oh, not happy. I was exhausted. You don't know what's going on. You've been at this for an entire summer. You have basically played, throughout your life, by all the rules, and suddenly people can attack you. It certainly doesn't comport with anything you've ever heard of, except for the things that you were told to fear when you were a kid, and fear not from them, but from groups like the Klan, or from some guy driving a pickup truck in rural Georgia.

By the time I got there, I was pretty angry at the committee, at the process. I really never cared about being confirmed. I was angry that they could do what they did. Contrary to the first time I went to the hearing—you are this little person sitting there and this big important committee kind of looking down on you. And this time, they looked small, diminished, and it was that they diminished themselves, by demeaning themselves. I was not willing to put up with them.

They had pushed me back toward the attitude I had when I was in school: where you give no quarter, and you put aside politeness. What they were doing was just wrong. It was one thing in life not to have what other people had. You can live with that. That was my grandfather, who always said the Tenth Commandment, "Thou shalt not covet thy neighbors' goods," so you didn't resent them, or anything like that. But when people who have so much then attack the little you have, and attack you who have so little, and you've not done anything wrong to anyone, then it makes you really unhappy. And I was not willing to put up with it, at that point. And Jack Danforth was on board with that.

MP: So, then you left and went back home, and Ms. Hill testified.[13] Did you watch that?

CT: God, no. If someone said today is the thirteenth of December, and someone said that you are in Paris at the Eiffel Tower, and they testified that you were, what would it profit you to watch that when you're sitting here? I just didn't. I was tired of it. I'd been going through this all summer, with people making you into something you were not. As I said, I was tired of the lies against me.

MP: Did Virginia watch it?
CT: Oh yeah. She watches everything. I love that woman. If it was about her, I would watch it. If it's about me, she would watch it. Then she told me what they were saying, and I said, "Well, thank God. I know that didn't happen." Because I'd never known. So yeah, I was tormenting myself, trying to dig through my endless memories: Did I do something? Did I say something? Was it a joke? And when they said whatever it was, I said, "That didn't happen." So, it was the first relief I felt.

MP: At that point, you must have been at least thinking a little bit: Why did she do it?
CT: I really don't get into the psychoanalysis. She did it for whatever reason she did it. People are ambitious, people are self-interested, people are naïve, people can do all sorts of things. I don't understand it. I don't have the makeup to do other people harm. That's not my makeup. I can't put myself in Jack the Ripper's place. I can't put myself in a jewel thief's place because I don't have that makeup. I could not say that I'm a victim of somebody doing something to me when nothing happened. I wouldn't even say it if something did happen. But I don't understand it. I really don't. It's not profitable for me to do that. In my life, this isn't the big event. This is *their* big event. I'm more concerned about what my grandfather thought. Those are things that I spend my time on.

MP: What would your grandfather have thought about what was happening at this point?
CT: That these people created this. He dealt with reality. He could look through the fog of all this and see the reality. Like most people did.

GUNS BLAZING
"THIS IS THE WRONG BLACK MAN, HE HAS TO BE DESTROYED"

MP: What happened next?
CT: Senator Danforth called me at home, after that testimony, as I recall, and said that Senator Hatch wants to meet with you, and maybe Senator Dole. I went to his office. They wanted me to testify that night, to not let her testimony fill up the news cycle all evening. So I reluctantly agreed to come back at 8:00. I was tired of it. It wasn't really worth it to me.

What disappointed me most were the institutions. The institutions are designed never to let the mob get you, and yet in this case the institutions allowed it. My disappointment isn't with people who have axes to grind. It's with the sheriff who doesn't stand up, the senators who didn't stand up. That was my issue.

So, I get to Senator Danforth's office and we sit, and we begin to discuss what's ahead. I was exhausted, and I asked him to get rid of all the people because they were talking about getting confirmed, and I wasn't interested in that. I was really unhappy with them, with the system, with the Senate, with the people who let this happen. So Jack got rid of everybody. He and Virginia and I stayed. He turned off the lights. He sat there quietly, like a guardian angel. Virginia, always like a guardian angel. And I just laid down on the couch and closed my eyes.

One of the things that came to mind after I'd rested a little bit, I said, "Jack, this is a high-tech lynching," and he said, "If that's what you think, say it." And so, I wrote that on a legal pad, and went and laid down again. At the end of that, he prayed and said, "Let the Holy Ghost speak through you. Just say what you think." And he just exhorted me to go in the name of the Holy Ghost.

One of the encouraging things is during a lot of these hearings, there'd be these ladies, these wonderful people—I had no idea who they were—they would line the halls, and cheer us on, even in the darkest times. My wife designated them "angels."

That was it. I went to the hearings and said what I had to say.

MP: Did you write it out ahead of time?
CT: No, no. I had a couple of things written down.

MP: Were there any advisors trying to discourage you from saying what you wanted to say?
CT: Nobody was allowed to talk to me. I was done with it.

MP: So then you gave that remarkable speech, calling the process a "high-tech lynching." Everyone remembers it. What were you thinking as you were giving the speech?
CT: I wasn't thinking anything. I was tired of it. I was tired of these people. I was tired. This was a disappointment. Think about it: I mean, if you look at an entire life, you start with nothing, you asked for nothing, you did your best, you played by the rules. You never hurt anybody. You didn't try to get ahead by harming another person, and this is what they do, because they have issues. And the institutions that you counted on to prevent it, permitted it.

A portion of Judge Thomas's "high-tech lynching" statement is shown in the documentary *Created Equal*. This is the
full statement he made to the committee.

Senator Biden: Do you have anything you'd like to say?
Judge Thomas: Senator, I would like to start by saying unequivo-
cally, uncategorically, that I deny each and every single allegation
against me today that suggested in any way that I had conversations of a sexual nature or about pornographic material with
Anita Hill, that I ever attempted to date her, that I ever had any
personal sexual interest in her, or that I in any way ever harassed
her.

A second, and I think more important point. I think that
this today is a travesty. I think that it is disgusting. I think that
this hearing should never occur in America. This is a case in
which this sleaze, this dirt, was searched for by staffers of
members of this committee, was then leaked to the media, and
this committee and this body validated it and displayed it at
prime time over our entire nation. How would any member
on this committee, any person in this room, or any person in
this country, would like sleaze said about him or her in this
fashion? Or this dirt dredged up and this gossip and these lies
displayed in this manner? How would any person like it?

The Supreme Court is not worth it. No job is worth it. I am
not here for that. I am here for my name, my family, my life, and
my integrity. I think something is dreadfully wrong with this
country when any person, any person in this free country would
be subjected to this.

This is not a closed room. There was an FBI investigation. This is not an opportunity to talk about difficult matters privately or in a closed environment. This is a circus. It's a national disgrace.

And from my standpoint as a black American, as far as I'm concerned, it is a high-tech lynching for uppity blacks who in any way deign to think for themselves, to do for themselves, to have different ideas, and it is a message that unless you kowtow to an old order, this is what will happen to you. You will be lynched, destroyed, caricatured by a committee of the U.S.— U.S. Senate, rather than hung from a tree.

MP: Especially, perhaps the Senate?
CT: Not especially them, the media, all of them, they participated. They became a part of the mob. Thank God for people like Jack Danforth, and Senator Hatch, and Bob Dole and Bennett Johnston, and the people from the South.

MP: When you called it a "high-tech lynching," what did you mean?
CT: I meant exactly what I said. Instead of using a rope, or burning people, now you burn their reputations in the media. Now you burn it with propaganda. You become the Willi Münzenbergs,[14] the latter-day Willi Münzenberg, or the Goebbels[15] of the world, where you spread propaganda. You destroy people with calumny, with misinformation.

MP: You said in your speech that it was like the lynching of black men for sexual misconduct.
CT: I mean, you pick your reasons. Pick your reasons. We've become obsessed today with sexuality and stuff, but there are lots of other

reasons why you did it. You broke the rules. You didn't cross the street. You didn't get out of the way. You went in the wrong neighborhood. There are lots of reasons things can happen to you. When I broke a lot of rules, and they weren't the rules they were accusing me of in the end, it was all the other rules. It was not thinking the way I was supposed to, not doing what I was supposed to, not being liberal, not agreeing with the issues they agreed with. But this was the only one that they could finally gin up some momentum. You should just see it for what it is, not in isolation, but as a part of the whole. So yeah, I was the uppity Negro—that's all it was. I understood that, and that's what I said.

MP: After that, senators continued to question you.
CT: I haven't revisited all these things. I did it. I can't tell you how long it went on. I don't know how long the hearings, the questioning went on. You're numb to it by now. It just seemed like everything seemed to be part of this endless, eternal nightmare.

MP: The senators were shocked that you responded so forcefully.
CT: At this point, I had no interest in how they felt. They certainly had no interest in my reputation. I had no interest in it. What they were doing was wrong. If I were a liberal, they would literally fete me, they would be throwing rose petals at my feet. You know it and I know it. We know exactly what's going on here, and to pretend that it is for some other reason, stop. I mean, do I have "stupid" written on the back of my shirt? I mean, come on, we know what this is all about. This isn't about what they say it's about, so people should just tell the truth. This is the wrong black guy. He has to be destroyed. Just say it. Now, at least we're honest with each other.

MP: Well, it didn't work.
CT: But in a sense, it did, because they win the propaganda war.

THE PUBLIC'S REACTION
"THE DEMOCRATS HAD THE CYNICAL CONFIDENCE THAT PEOPLE WOULD BUY THIS IMPLAUSIBLE STORY"

MP: You went back to Senator Danforth's office after the hearing.
CT: We went briefly to his office, and then Ken Duberstein, who was spearheading the confirmation, came through and said that the poll numbers had changed dramatically, after I testified, and the dynamics had changed. It's like two thirds of the country is on my side.[16]

MP: Another factor I think was people were able to see the hearings on C-SPAN.
CT: I always thank God for Brian Lamb and C-SPAN, because unlike the media, which claims to be impartial, they actually just showed the hearings, gavel to gavel, and thank God for that. Because then people get to see you. At 8:00, it's drivetime on the West coast, it's primetime on the East coast, and I think more people got to see it for themselves, and said, "What the heck is going on here?"

To steal a little bit of *To Kill a Mockingbird*—the sense that the people would fall for anything, that they would believe the story. Subsequent to my confirmation, I figured it out. They had the cynical confidence that people would buy this implausible story, and they would make it plausible enough for them to buy. Their "cynical confidence," however, didn't work. That people actually were better people than they were.

In *To Kill a Mockingbird*, the argument was that the man accused had raped this white woman, and he was black, of course. But he couldn't have because one of his arms was lame. He couldn't have done what she said, it was impossible. Atticus Finch says that she tells the story with the subtle cynical confidence that members of the jury will automatically convict. And so, what I was saying, in my case, they had this story and they had the "cynical confidence" that people would automatically buy it. And the people in the country disproved that they would automatically buy, and that "cynical confidence" was misplaced.

Here's another black guy, and this is what they do, which is kind of interesting, because throughout my life, I've steadfastly tried to avoid these circumstances. I never wanted to be in that position. It touched a nerve that the very thing that you've guarded against your whole life, they gin up on you.

MP: What happened next?
CT: I came back that Saturday morning and testified again, which was exhausting. But at least I had an idea of what they were accusing me of. Not knowing is a lot worse than knowing, and knowing that it didn't happen. They say for example, you were someplace, and you did this, and you try to think of where you were, so you torment yourself trying to figure it out. But then they say, "You were in Paris"; "Oh, good, I wasn't in Paris." So at least you know. It gives you a toehold. So it was awful to come back and have to testify again. But I did it.

At the end, my wife and I went to dinner with the Danforths and the Hatches. We drove over to Tysons Corner where Morton's of Chicago was. We walked in, and we saw Ted Olson and the Borks there. We have dinner, and at the end of dinner, which Orrin Hatch paid for, the waiter said that about a half-dozen or so people had offered to pay for dinner. The people, while we were getting up to leave, applauded us. Not everybody was like the media and the interest groups. The reception was just fabulous.

MP: Then on Sunday you received a call from Mrs. Anwar Sadat.
CT: Mrs. Sadat called. I didn't know her and the White House put her through to me. She said, "They are just words, they're accusing

you of words." And then she said, "There are people doing things to women, actually doing things, all over the world." And she said something to the effect that the rest of the world is laughing at this, that they're talking about words. And I said, "But I didn't say them." And she said, "But they're still just words." Something like that, again it's been a long time. But I remember that was one of the most reassuring calls. That's what I had expected from leaders, someone who was willing to see it for what it was.

MP: Did you watch Anita Hill's witnesses testify?[17] Were you surprised by any of that?
CT: I didn't watch it. I mean there was nothing to follow. I didn't know these people, and there was no need to follow something I knew didn't happen.

MP: How about Angela Wright?[18] Did you hear about that controversy?
CT: I know I fired her, as simple as that. They [Wright and Hill] weren't together at EEOC.[19] I mean, this is laughable. These are people who said they would get even, and they did.

MP: There were a total of three other women who were not called to testify.
CT: People who don't work out, you get fired. And she said she would get even. And there was another woman, Sukari Hardnett.[20] Gil had asked me to hire her, to give her a chance, and this was on a different kind of appointment. She didn't pass the bar exam and he asked me to give her a chance, because she couldn't get a job. So I hired her. It was a term appointment, you could only have it for one year, and it couldn't be repeated. She said she would get even with me. For what? I don't know. But they did. I understand that. I don't know why people just can't see it for what it is.

MP: The other one was Rose Jourdain.[21]

CT: Rose Jourdain had been a speechwriter. She and Angela were friends. I hired them at the same time. Rose didn't do a great job. I didn't have any axe to grind with her. I helped her out. She had a daughter; it was fine. Then it didn't work out, and I dismissed both of them. Yeah, I did. And she never said anything. She never threatened, but Angela said she was going to get even, and she did.

MP: Biden didn't call them as witnesses?

CT: You need to talk to them about that. I really do not follow things that I think are disgusting and wrong. What they were doing was wrong. Here's some people that said they were going to get even when you fired them and they get even. That's pretty obvious. You don't spend a lot more time on that. And yeah, they may not have called them, I understand. Then they put our witnesses on in the middle of the night, these wonderful friends of mine, who risked their careers, and friendships and to have the courage to stand up in the storm and testify.[22] They put them on when very few people could see them. I understand what they were doing, and then they want to say later on that they're fair. This is the way it is. So yes, I have disappointments in the institutions.

MP: Did you see any of the testimony of the witnesses in your favor?

CT: I watched it years later.

CONFIRMED
"WHOOP-DEE-DAMN-DOO"

MP: Yes. Where were you during the actual Senate vote?

CT: I was at home. During the vote, I was in the tub, and finally, I was exhausted. So I got in the bath and just sort of soaked. While I was there, a young woman who worked with Virginia called to congratulate us, that the confirmation vote had been fifty-two to forty-eight.[23] And you know my reaction is still pretty much the way it is now: "Whoop-dee-damn-doo." And I wasn't really all that interested in it. I just think what they did was wrong. It wasn't about the Supreme Court. It was about right and wrong. Remember, the bottom line, it was never about the outcome. It's about the way you do it. The way they did it was wrong. What they did was wrong. If you want to say, "Look, I disagree with you on this." That's honest. "I disagree with you fundamentally, so I can't vote for you." That is honest. And if you lose on that basis, that's fair and square, but not this way. This is wrong. So you have this process and you get confirmed. The bottom line turns out ok. The bottom line doesn't change the fact that what you did was wrong.

MP: It's hard, with these attacks, to get your reputation back.
CT: My favorite prayer now is the Litany of Humility.[24] Those things don't matter. What they think of me doesn't matter, because I don't think of them. They've discredited themselves by what they did. They no longer matter.

MP: At the time of the vote, is the press still camped out on your lawn?
CT: The press is camped outside, and I go outside with my wife. It's raining. I was not going to go out and say anything to the press. I was sick of them. My wife had been trying to get me to go out. Finally, Senator Thurmond comes in, and he says, "You have to go." And then there were others there, saying, "Well, just go say a word or two. You don't have to talk to the press. You're talking to the American public. They'd like to know you're okay." So I went out. There's a picture of my wife and me with the umbrella talking outside.

MP: What happened next?

CT: Then they set up an event at the White House for the swearing in, which was great because it was more of a celebration with people who stood up. My mother was there, and my father, my son, my cousins came up, a lot of people from Pin Point, Liberty County, and Savannah were there.

We were driving to the White House, and we were in Alexandria, and we were in the turn lane on Duke Street making a left, and a big truck stopped, even though it was loaded with pipes, an eighteen-wheeler. We didn't know what was going to happen. A hand came out of the window with a big thumbs up, and then he set his brakes, rolled up his window, and took off. How he recognized me is beyond me.

During that time, the marshals required me to wear a bulletproof vest, because they thought things were getting so desperate, that it was just a matter of time before something bad happened. They were sleeping at the house.

Then I went to the White House, sat with Mark Paoletta in his little office, and had a burger and talked about the past few months. Mark had gotten to be one of the few people I talked to about the confirmation.

Then we had just a wonderful event at the White House with President Bush and Mrs. Bush. I was sworn in by Justice White.[25] It was just wonderful.

MP: You've said that it had been raining and then the sun came out that day?

CT: It had been raining for quite a bit, and suddenly there was this sunshine. It was a glorious event. It was like the quote from the Psalms, it was "joy in the morning," and it truly was. And just to be there with people who weren't trying to destroy you, as opposed to the bitter people, the people with axes to grind.

MP: You did a second official swearing in. Why was that?
CT: You need two oaths. I got the constitutional oath from Justice White. But the chief justice [William Rehnquist] had to administer the judicial oath. Chief Justice's wife, Nan Rehnquist, had just died.[26] So I spoke to his administrative assistant, who said, "If he comes in on a certain day, he says he'll swear you in." And that happened to be October 23. And so I drove over in my Chevy Celebrity with one hubcap missing, and called my wife, and Senator Danforth. They were the only ones [the chief justice] would allow to come, and he swore me in around noon on 23 October 1991.

CHAPTER NINE

ON THE COURT

"What they did was supply hope....
It was their victory"

MP: Next you had the formal investiture before the Court.
CT: November 1, 1991. That's more than a week later. We're trying
to set up shop. I've got to bring my secretaries over. I have to bring
furniture over. I have got to hire law clerks. We have a full sitting, so
I've got to get ready for the sitting, so I'm gone from one exhausting
undertaking to another exhausting undertaking, with no break.

The first thing I always take over to a new office is my St. Jude
statute. I'm sitting in there and that's basically all I have—my St. Jude
statue. Senator Danforth comes over for the swearing in, and Virginia
comes over. Senator Danforth looks at all the briefs, there's a whole
shelf of briefs, and he said, "Clarence, this looks really boring. Don't
expect me to read any of this stuff, or any of the opinions you write."
Then we walk down the hall to the chief justice's chambers, and
everything in the building is marble, and he's looking at the walls,
and he says, "Clarence, this place looks like a mausoleum." We walk
down further, and he jokes, "Clarence, where are the bodies?"

In all the bad that I saw, I got to see a really good man, and some really good people. Orrin Hatch, and Bob Dole, could not have been better. There were other senators who stood up, but Danforth was special. My wife was an absolute jewel. And Mark Paoletta, but for him, I would not have been confirmed. He was a real champion and friend. There were others. The backdrop to these great people is the unpleasantness, the mediocrity, the cowardice, and the just plain old bad people.

MP: What exactly is the formal investiture?
CT: It was by this point ceremonial because I already had both oaths. But it's important because it's your official welcome to the Court. It's literally the beginning. You can begin without it, but it's the formal beginning. It's like eloping to get married, but then having a wedding. But the wedding is a big deal. You don't tell your wife it isn't a big deal. It is a big deal. It only takes a couple of minutes. And they read your commission.[1] You have to have a commission to be appointed to these jobs where you're confirmed. You're sitting in a chair, as a new member of the Court, the John Marshall chair, off to the side, and the chief justice formally invites you to join them on the bench, where he then reads the commission, then swears you in ceremonially and invites you to take your place on the bench with your new colleagues.[2] You shake hands with your colleagues. It's your official welcome to the Court. It was absolutely wonderful. It was such a momentous event.

After that, they have a small reception in the conference room. I could only stay briefly because then I have to go and meet [with the other justices]. They've been waiting for me, the ninth justice, to decide whether to take certain cases. And so I literally had to get to work immediately after that. One of the curious things that happened, when I went briefly to this reception was that there was also another black gentleman starting that same day, who was the great-great-great grandson, at least a descendant, of the woman who brought me into the world. His name is Gary Kemp, and his fore-bear, who was the midwife who brought me into the world, was Miss Lula Kemp. He comes up to me, and he said, "I have your birth records." And by this time I'm so paranoid I'm wondering, what is this about? And it turns out, it's legitimate. He gave me a copy of her record of my birth in her books.

MP: While taking your place on the Court, did your thoughts drift back to your grandparents? Was this the end of one phase of your life?
CT: Many people take bows for other people's achievements in life—it's affirmative action, it's some welfare policy, it's some social policy, none of which had anything to do with anything. I mean, it's fine that people are thinking of these policies, but the things that matter are the people, like my grandparents and like the nuns. When we talk in law, we talk about the "but for" causation—"but for" this, this wouldn't have happened. The nuns and my grandparents are in a sense, the "but for" causation: they're the reason I'm sitting here today; "but for" them I wouldn't be here.

My grandparents, when they took us in in 1955, what they did was supply hope. You're looking at a world that looks almost hopeless. They said, "We are going to prepare you for the challenges ahead. We are going to give you a chance to do well by giving you the things you need." And people think it's just education, it's just food. It was more than that, and they understood that. They understood that you needed the things of life—work ethic, self-discipline, a set of morals, to get through life. And they supplied them. Now my grandfather had nine months total of education, my grandmother went to the sixth grade. These were poor black people in the Deep South, but they had figured out the essentials of life. It was their victory. They had won. They had been proven right.

Before my nun [Sister Mary Virgilus] who educated me died, Mark Paoletta and I would go visit the nuns in Tenafly, New Jersey. Sister Mary Virgilius had gone in the convent at the age of sixteen and died at the age of one hundred. When we visited, I was an exhibit of why their sacrifice mattered—of their faith and their hope for us. Just imagine us in this little segregated Catholic school in Savannah, Georgia. And in 1955, when I went there, Sister Mary Dolorosa was there. We were doing the Baltimore Catechism, and I came from the tenements, and I wasn't Catholic. And she said, "Why did God create you?" "God created us to know, love, and serve Him in this life and to be happy with Him in the next." So this was the completion of something they started. It wasn't the end of a phase so much as the proof positive that they had been right, and it was their victory.

THE ROLE OF A JUDGE
"YOU HAVE TO REALLY BE CAREFUL NOT TO SUPPLANT WHAT IS THERE, WHAT WAS RIGHTFULLY DONE, WITH YOUR OWN VIEWS, SIMPLY BECAUSE YOU DON'T THINK IT'S A GREAT RULE"

MP: How do you approach judging a case?
CT: I was talking recently with Justice Scalia's son Father Paul Scalia in Virginia. Justice Scalia always wondered why we were so much alike when we come from such different backgrounds and very, very different lives. I think it perplexed him and interested him. Paul Scalia said it was our Catholic formation, that we were taught that

Clarence Thomas's
mother, Leola Williams.
Courtesy of Leola Williams

Myers Anderson,
Clarence Thomas's
grandfather. "Boys,
the damn vacation
is over." *Courtesy of
Clarence Thomas*

Clarence Thomas's grandmother Christine Anderson. "My grandmother was as sweet as she could be." *Courtesy of Clarence Thomas*

Clarence Thomas and his brother, Myers Thomas, circa 1956, wearing blazers from St. Benedict's, the all-black Catholic school they attended in Savannah during segregation. *Courtesy of Clarence Thomas*

The home of Clarence Thomas's grandparents in Savannah, where Clarence and his brother Myers went to live in 1955. "For us, it could have been a palace."
Courtesy of Clarence Thomas

A St. Benedict's school class trip. Sister Mary Virgilius Reidy, the school's principal and Clarence Thomas's eighth-grade teacher, is standing between the other two nuns.
Courtesy of the Catholic Diocese of Savannah

Eighth-grade graduation from St. Benedict's, May 1962. Clarence Thomas is the second student from the left in the second row.
Courtesy of the Diocese of Savannah

Clarence Thomas (left) and Richard Chisholm, the only other black student at St. John Vianney Minor Seminary (high school) in 1964.
Courtesy of the Catholic Diocese of Savannah

Working on the St. John Vianney yearbook in 1967.
Courtesy of the Catholic Diocese of Savannah

CLARENCE THOMAS
"T.C."

Savannah, Ga.
St. Benedicts Parish

Business man for *The Grail* and Seyf's partner on *The Pioneer* ... Bob Hayes' idol ... "Tops" ... Mmwuaa-haahaa ... blew that test, only a 98 ... Hey boey! ... base fiddler in the "schola" ... likes to argue

Clarence Thomas's senior photo in the St. John Vianney yearbook: "Blew that test, only a 98."
Courtesy of the Catholic Diocese of Savannah

St. John Vianney Minor Seminary graduation, 1967. "We've grown up and gone through trials and tribulations together." *Courtesy of the Catholic Diocese of Savannah*

Class photo from Immaculate Conception Seminary in Conception, Missouri, 1968. Thomas is in the third row, sixth from the left. *Courtesy of Immaculate Conception Seminary*

Clarence Thomas's ID card from Holy Cross College.
Courtesy of Clarence Thomas

Myers Thomas, Clarence Thomas's brother, in his Air Force uniform. "He was a beacon of stability." *Courtesy of Clarence Thomas*

Wedding photo of Clarence Thomas and his first wife, Kathy Ambush, in Worcester, Massachusetts, on June 5, 1971, the day after Thomas graduated from Holy Cross. Also pictured are his mother, Leola Williams (right), and his grandmother Christine Anderson (left). *Courtesy of Clarence Thomas*

Yale Law School graduation, May 1974. *Courtesy of Clarence Thomas*

Clarence Thomas holding two-year-old Jamal in the spring of 1975. "I knew one thing, nobody was going to have some social experiment and throw my son in there." *Courtesy of Clarence Thomas*

Thomas with Senator Jack Danforth, when he was working as a legislative assistant in Danforth's office. *Courtesy of John Danforth*

Clarence Thomas with Jamal. After his divorce, Thomas raised Jamal as a single parent. "Being with him was my happy place." *Courtesy of Clarence Thomas*

Clarence Thomas in front of a "Don't Tread on Me" flag. "The only thing I have to do is stay black and die." *Equal Employment Opportunity Commission*

Clarence Thomas with Jay Parker, who, when Thomas was reluctant to take the civil rights job at the Department of Education in 1981, told him, "Put up or shut up." *Department of Education*

Clarence Thomas, EEOC chairman, with his staff in 1984. *Courtesy of the National Law Journal*

Thomas with President Ronald Reagan in the Oval Office in 1986, when Thomas was EEOC chairman. *Courtesy of the Reagan Presidential Library and Museum*

Clarence Thomas and Ginni Lamp in 1987, a week before their wedding. "She was a gift from God that I prayed for." *Courtesy of Clarence Thomas*

Ginni and Clarence Thomas on their wedding day at St. Paul United Methodist Church in Omaha, Nebraska, May 30, 1987. *Courtesy of Clarence Thomas*

Thomas at his son Jamal's high school graduation in June 1990. "My grandfather raised me in a way that I could raise Jamal the right way." *Courtesy of Clarence Thomas*

Clarence Thomas on July 31, 1991, in Washington, D.C., with his ninety-one-year-old cousin Jack Fuller, one of a number of relatives and friends who travelled from Pin Point and Savannah to show their support on the same day that the NAACP voted to oppose Thomas's nomination. *AP Photo/John Duricka*

Senate Judiciary Committee Chairman Joe Biden asks questions during the hearings into Anita Hill's allegations. *AP Photo/Greg Gibson*

Clarence Thomas testifying before the Senate Judiciary Committee on October 11, 1991. *Consolidated News Photo/Newscom*

Anita Hill being sworn in to testify before the Senate Judiciary Committee. *AP Photo/Greg Gibson*

Clarence Thomas testifying in response to Anita Hill's allegations. "A high-tech lynching." *AP Photo/Greg Gibson*

Justice Byron White administers the constitutional oath to Clarence Thomas on the South Lawn of the White House on October 18, 1991. *Courtesy of the George H. W. Bush Presidential Library and Museum*

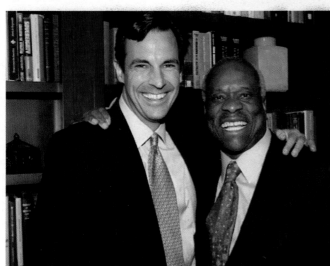

Clarence Thomas and co-author Mark Paoletta, who worked on the Thomas confirmation as a lawyer in the White House Counsel's office. *Courtesy of the Heritage Foundation*

Justices Clarence Thomas and Antonin Scalia at the 2014 Federalist Society Annual Dinner. "We had a trust from the very beginning." *Avonlee Photography*

Justice Thomas with his clerks in his chambers. *Courtesy of Manifold Productions*

Clarence Thomas and Thomas Sowell. *Courtesy of Clarence Thomas*

Clarence Thomas and co-author Michael Pack speaking during a break on the set of *Created Equal: Clarence Thomas in His Own Words*, produced and directed by Pack. *Courtesy of Manifold Productions*

Justice Thomas in his chambers at the Supreme Court. The portrait is of Frederick Douglass and the bust is of Thomas's grandfather. *Courtesy of Manifold Productions*

Statue of Sister Virgilius and two students at Maryrest Cemetery in Mahwah, New Jersey, where more than two hundred Missionary Franciscan Sisters of the Immaculate Conception are buried. *Courtesy of Mark Paoletta*

The bust of Myers Anderson, Clarence Thomas's grandfather, commissioned by Ginni Thomas. "Old man can't is dead, I helped bury him." *Courtesy of Manifold Productions*

you did things a certain way. My grandfather was like that. You did things a certain way. You planted corn a certain way, you fed the hogs a certain way, you pull the fence line a certain way, you plow the field a certain way, and it always had to be the right way. Similarly, when you did math problems, and you did it a certain way and there was a right and a wrong way. There was a moral way. There was an ethical way, and you didn't skip steps, you didn't cheat.

The way I approach judging is you look at: What are the rules that you apply? What are the facts? What is the right way to apply those rules to those facts? And then you accept the results of that. In other words, there is a way of judging that you look for the conclusion based upon the application of law to fact. And you have to be honest. My grandfather said something in 1955 that I use. When my brother and I went to live with him, he said, "I'm not going to tell you boys to do as I say. I'm going to tell you to do as I do." So one of the things I say to my four law clerks is, "Just watch me." And I promise them when they're done with the job, they will have clean hands, clean hearts, and clear consciences. Watch me so that we always do things in an honest way, so if I have a strong feeling, for example, about a case, I will say, "Here's my reaction to this: I don't like this or something," and then that's pretty rare, but I say, "Whatever you do, don't let me decide on that basis, watch me and make sure that has no role in the way we decide things."

MP: Do you think about what the law meant at the time?
CT: If you're looking at a written law, not common law, which is unwritten, but at a written law, you look at the text. The legislature said at this corner, there shall be a stop sign. It says stop. Well, you might think that's really a stupid stop sign. But does it say stop? So you don't rewrite the sign because you think it ought to be something

else. You thought it ought to be go, or no sign at all. It said stop. And it may be ridiculous, but that's what it says.

I think you have to really be careful not to supplant what is there, what was rightfully done, with your own views, simply because you don't think it's a great rule. So that's why we start with the text, and when the text is unclear, you look at the tradition, the history. If you do that in the areas of written law, of contracts, of regulations, then you do it in the broader sense when you have formative documents like the Constitution. You don't want to displace that because it's a written constitution, unlike England's.

COLLEAGUES
"HE NEVER ASSUMED HE KNEW WHAT I SHOULD THINK"

MP: What is your relationship like with the other justices, especially Justice Scalia?
CT: They're all wonderful people. I like them. I have warm relationships with everybody on the Court and especially with my colleagues, but Justice Scalia was special in that he had been at the Court about five years when I got there, when I was forty-three years old and had only been a judge about a year and a half, so this was all new to me. That Court was together for eleven years. It's pretty special to me, and Justice Scalia is the special of the specials. I came of age on that Court. It's very different when you've been here a long time. You have warm relationships, but I'm not the new guy. So I have been very close to Justice Alito. Justice Kagan and Justice Ginsburg, I'm close to as a colleague. Justice Breyer is wonderful man, I am very close to him as a friend. Justice Kennedy is such a good man. He is the only member of the Court who was there when I got there, so we've spent most of

our career together. He is an elegant, bright, decent man. The chief justice I've known for quite a while. I knew him before as an advocate, and actually, I knew him when he was at the Justice Department and I was a nominated to the D.C. Circuit. Justice Gorsuch, I knew as a law clerk; he clerked for Justice White. Justice Sotomayor, I met her early on when she was a new judge on the Second Circuit.

But on Justice Scalia, we had a trust from the very beginning. They've painted this image of him as kind of this intellectual bully. Unlike so many of the people that you have talked to me about that had a notion of what I should be, what I should think, he was never that way. He was always fascinated by me.

The one criticism he had was that I would not go hunting with him. If he would try to get me to go hunting, I would ridicule him for killing unarmed animals. I said, "How could a guy from New York and New Jersey go out in the woods?" And he was, oh my goodness, he was into it. He did not understand how I was from rural Georgia and didn't hunt. And I explained to him that I had used up all my good fortune, and I had never gotten hurt in the woods, and never got bitten by a snake, or anything like that, and I wasn't planning on going into the woods. I did all my hunting at the supermarket, and he just thought that was just ridiculous, but we would have this running joke about that.

He never assumed he knew what I should think. He never had a conclusion for me. Think about the people who know what I should think. How is that different from any gross stereotype? That you're black, therefore—. That you're black, you should—. That you're black, your opinion should be—. On, and on, and on. He never did that. To him, I was entirely free to reach my own conclusions. I loved it. He was a very, very dear friend.[3]

MP: On natural law, Justice Scalia and Harry Jaffa from Claremont would not agree because Justice Scalia is closer to being a positivist.

He's closer to wanting to stick to acknowledge the letter of the Constitution and not refer back to the Declaration. Did you argue with Justice Scalia about the place of natural law as a factor in analyzing a constitutional right?

CT: Justice Scalia was someone who liked being challenged, and who was willing to be shown, to be persuaded. In this town, people who claim that, "Oh, I'm against bullying." They are the bullies. They love to bully people who don't agree. What do you think they do to me? What do you think this is all about? It is just bullying. It's about beating you, whipping you into shape. You couldn't bully him into shape. Now you could persuade him. I never had a problem with him, ever, because I respected his right to disagree, and he knew I respected it. He asked me one day, and it was really kind of funny, he said "Clarence, you really don't care for other people's opinions, do you?" I said "No, Nino, I do care for them, but I prefer my own." He thought that makes all the sense in the world. And he preferred his opinion. Now is he willing to listen to mine? Am I willing to listen? Yes. That's the respect that we learned in liberal arts education, in a civil society. This is what you do. You debate things.

MP: Were there often times when he convinced you, or you convinced him, about an issue?

CT: Oh, I think it went both ways. But I was pretty relentless. He was my friend, and he listened to me, unlike much of what goes on in this city, and the so-called tolerant crowd who never listen because they're convinced theirs is a religion. His was more an intellectual exercise. How we got to the answer was really important. To them, the answer was more important. It didn't matter how you got there. If you have a group of people in this city, where the bottom line, whether they're for this particular issue, affirmative action, abortion, whatever, the outcome is the most important thing. How you get there is irrelevant.

You can tear down all the trees you want, as long as you give them the answer they want. That wasn't him. And I agree with it. It's how we get there. And when you meet a person like that, we're on common ground. We can debate things. But if you tell him, you must arrive at that answer, then that's where the fight begins.

MP: So, I know you don't like labels, but would your jurisprudence be textualism or originalism?
CT: Well, I think in a sense we're all textualists and originalists. When we ride down the street and we stop at a stop sign, we're textualists. It said stop. Josef Pieper did that piece on the use and abuse of language.[4] He makes a point that the purpose of language is to communicate fact or truth. If you don't use it to communicate those things, then for what purpose do you use it? He suggested it's to gain power over people, marketing a manipulative propaganda. And I think we have to be really careful that language doesn't lose its meaning or that we pervert it in a way in order to gain advantages over people. Stop means stop. We know what it means, and that makes us all textualists, or there's no way for us to communicate.

MP: What are examples of a law that you disagreed with on a policy level but was nevertheless legal or constitutional?
CT: When we had the Haitian refugee cases back in the early nineties, at the end of President Bush's administration and beginning of the Clinton administration, the Haitians were leaving Haiti and were out on the high seas. They would divert them to the base at Guantanamo Bay. There was some question as to the president's authority to do that. And my own personal view was more along the lines that they should let them in the country, these poor people.[5]

We had a case involving whether or not medical marijuana in California could be regulated by the national government, even though it was totally in-state in California, whether the national government had the authority under the Commerce Clause to regulate this medical marijuana.[6] I wrote a dissent pointing out that it could not be regulated. There was no authority under the Commerce Clause. Now, do I think people should be walking around smoking marijuana? Not particularly, but that's not the point. The point is who gets to regulate it? And the national government has no police powers.

Now people are interested in letting people in Denver and California smoke their marijuana, but at the same time they're interested in a very expansive Commerce Clause that says the national government can regulate the very conduct that they say now that California should be able to do. It's fascinating to me. To me, the policy isn't the point, it's the authority to make the decision. You might agree or disagree with the decision. It isn't about that. It's about who gets to decide.

THOUGHTS ON THE DECLARATION
"I THINK THAT THE DECLARATION INFORMS THE CONSTITUTION"

MP: You frequently quote Lincoln saying, "The Declaration of Independence is the apple of gold, and the Constitution, the frame of silver around it." Do you see it that way too?
CT: I'm a big fan of Lincoln, as he freed the slaves, I've got a vested interest in that. I hate to be parochial, but that's another "but for" causation.

I think that the Declaration informs the Constitution. It makes sense when you understand the Declaration. I just finished reading a book on the Tudors, and earlier a book on the Plantagenets. What I'm interested in is the development of English common law because

England becomes the backdrop that informs the Founding of this country. There are many things in England that the Framers adopted. They were Englishmen. There were also things they rejected, there were things they were concerned about. You will understand the Cruel and Unusual Punishment Clause if you understand some of the punishments that were used in England at the time.

Similarly, you would understand what they were upset with the king about, and what they were guarding against. This king has already told them, "I'm going to hang all of you," and they really did bad things. The king is really ticked at them, and he wants them to pay for the cost of their own policing, their own defense, with these taxes. They don't want to do it. They don't want him overruling them. They want to be self-governing. So they take precautions so that whoever becomes a leader in this country does not become another King George III.

I went back and took a look at Henry VIII. Henry VIII was a really rough guy, and Elizabeth was tough, too. This is sixteenth century but the Framers know this. They're in the eighteenth century. This is a part of their history, and I think they're guarding against that. So they break up the government. They break it into three parts so you don't wind up with the Star Chamber, or a centralization of judicial authority, legislative authority, and executive authority in one place.

MP: In the Declaration of Independence, Jefferson was also trying to derive natural rights from a source other than the king, from the laws of nature and nature's God. How do you see that?
CT: What were they trying to do? To get a framework, a structure and they were trying to protect your rights. Let's say we agree that we have these rights that are transcendent, and the source of those rights [is] transcendent, and the king can't take those away, but we're

trying to keep whoever's governing from interfering with those. That's what I think they were trying to do. And then when you structure the Constitution, what is it trying to protect? It is trying to protect our liberty, and then we can debate about what the liberty is, but we have a framework within which to do that.

If you go back and look at a lot of Justice Scalia's separation of powers cases, it is fascinating. We were totally different in approaches, but the touchstone is the same thing—individual liberty. And then what's the source of that. And that's why, if you notice from time to time, I would cite the Declaration, not so much as positive law, but rather as informative of what the law was intended to do.

AFFIRMATIVE ACTION—*GRUTTER V. BOLLINGER*
"SHOW ME IN THE CONSTITUTION WHERE YOU GET A RIGHT TO SEPARATE CITIZENS BASED ON RACE"

MP: I'd like to focus in on the affirmative action case from 2003: *Grutter*, where the University of Michigan had an admissions policy that gave preferential treatment to minority applicants.[7]

CT: The whole point that I have made in these race cases is the same point that [Justice John] Harlan was making in *Plessy* [*v. Ferguson*].[8] Had I sat on *Brown* [*v. Board of Education*], I would have said, "Show me in the Constitution where you get a right to separate citizens based on race."[9] The Constitution guarantees equal treatment to all citizens. You have to show me where you get the authority to do this, and why this doesn't violate the Fourteenth Amendment.[10]

I think what we've become comfortable with is thinking that there is some good discrimination and some bad discrimination. Who gets to determine that?

If you look in the briefs in the race cases, the segregationists, the people who thought you should have a separate system, they said that they thought it was good for both races.[11] They thought it was good discrimination. People think there's some benefit to doing what they want done. Just because they want it done, doesn't mean it's a benefit. Doesn't mean it's constitutional, just because you like it.

I am a huge Nebraska football fan. Actually, my favorite teams now are volleyball and women's basketball. I think those coaches have it right. But at any rate, I'm a huge Nebraska fan. So, let's just say, in sports, judging is refereeing: the judge on the field is the referee. If there is a call against Nebraska, do you think I'm analyzing, "Well, this referee really had the right angle and he looked at it. This is analytically right when he called a charging call or something?" No, he made a call against Nebraska. It is wrong, and that's what people do. They look at the outcome, they look at what they want, and then that tells them whether or not the ruling was done properly.

And I think that's what we are doing in our society. We're saying, "Is this a policy I like? If I liked that policy, then it's got to be constitutional." That's not the case. A bad policy can be constitutional. A good policy can be unconstitutional. I think we have to be really careful because what we do, the next generation will do it. If we do it for what we think is good, you're now authorizing or empowering somebody to do it for something that's bad.

MP: In your *Grutter* dissent, you made the point that racial discrimination to create a positive result that everyone thinks is a positive result is still racial discrimination, and contrary to the Declaration and the Fourteenth Amendment.[12]
CT: It distorts the Constitution. Just because you do what you think you want doesn't make it constitutional. And that is willfulness because you're using authority that you don't have. You're using a

document that doesn't authorize it to do something that you want. And those policies, like fads, change. What is popular today will be unpopular tomorrow.

It's fascinating to have lived at a time when segregation was popular and then live long enough to see another policy, diversity, is now popular. I remember when it was popular to build huge high-rise public housing complexes, then it was not popular to build those. So fads, policies, change. The whole point of what the Framers were doing is saying, you can change your policies, but there's going to be stability and a rock of things that you can't alter, or it's going to be difficult to alter, in order to preserve liberty.

MP: Would you say affirmative action is one of these instances where people are using racial discrimination to achieve a specific objective they think is best?

CT: To be honest with you, I don't even know what affirmative action is. People come up with euphemisms, everybody is for something that affirmatively acts—to do what, I don't know. Most people don't know. Whatever it is, it's often redefined as equal opportunity, then it's redefined as, "Let's help the poor." We could have done this easily by helping poor people. Let's say we're going to have classes on Saturday morning. I remember suggesting that back in the sixties and seventies. Okay, we're going to have study halls on Saturday mornings that are monitored and with tutors. That's affirmative action. That'll catch you up in chemistry and math, et cetera. How many people would actually say, "Let's go?" "Oh, no, no, no, I can't do that." But that's affirmative action, that's taking extra steps. So I think that we could have done it in ways as a policy matter that would not have run into the Constitution.

MP: In *Grutter*, in particular, you called the University of Michigan's law school's efforts for diversity an "aesthetic concern."[13] And you

pointed out that they could have achieved it by lowering their LSATs, lowering their standards.

CT: Well, the University said they were a state school, and they wanted diversity. Well, the community colleges are diverse, but they are not elite. But they wanted to have a school that was elite and diverse. You've got two things at war. I was pointing out that if diversity was your goal, there were other ways to do it that didn't discriminate.

MP: You pointed out that other public law schools, like Berkeley, had that rule, "You can't discriminate in admissions," and they didn't lose their elite status.

CT: Well, Berkeley is really interesting, but there are lots of schools. This is a big country. I don't like the idea that we ennoble ourselves with this pretense that we're doing good; that's why I called it "aesthetics." I've lived through segregation. Now, it's diversity. I think people should be asked to show what it has produced. We have done some damage in our society, particularly to the people who could least afford the damage. You go back to communities. You go back to the schools. They shut down schools in the name of integration, like my high school in Savannah, St. Pius X High School. They irreparably changed the black teaching profession, and these policies irreparably changed our communities, like my old neighborhood in Savannah, which was a stable, hardworking, but poor neighborhood.

The women in the movie *Hidden Figures* were more like the people around me.[14] You always had those people, exceptional people, around, people who were just brilliant, and they were black. Suddenly they turned us all into helpless victims. I don't think creating that attitude is good, that sense of a permanent victim status, like we're serfs or something. I don't think it's good now, and I think it's counterfactual and ahistorical.

MP: In the conclusion of your *Grutter* dissent, you wrote, "For the immediate future, however, the majority has placed its imprimatur on a practice that can only weaken the principle of equality embodied in the Declaration of Independence and the Equal Protection Clause. 'Our Constitution is colorblind and neither knows nor tolerates classes among citizens.' *Plessy v. Ferguson*, (Harlan dissenting). It has been nearly a hundred and forty years since Frederick Douglass asked the intellectual ancestors of the law school to 'Do nothing with us,' and the Nation adopted the Fourteenth Amendment. Now we must wait another twenty-five years to see this principle of equality vindicated. I, therefore, respectfully dissent from the remainder of the court's opinion and judgment."[15]

That is a great paragraph. It was a long time ago, but I'm assuming you still subscribe to it?

CT: Principles don't vacillate. People who are congratulating themselves, they're going to pay a price when they wake up one day and they have no Constitution.

MP: You allude in that conclusion to Justice John Harlan's "colorblind Constitution" statement in *Plessy*.

CT: If the Constitution isn't colorblind, which color? Which one does it mention? There's that great scene in the movie *Gettysburg*, where [Confederate General George] Pickett, who's finished with his charge and straggles back across the field, whipped, and he sees [General Robert E.] Lee.[16] Lee tells him to pull together his division. He looks at General Lee, and says, "General Lee, I have no division." If we keep it up, we're going to look around and someone will say, "I want my constitutional rights," and they'll be told, "We have no Constitution." I think we have to be really, really careful.

We talk about formation, the things we believe in. Until the mid-1980s, I was not someone who focused that much on the Constitution itself. Having been in government for a while, I saw what government could do and what people would do with governmental power. I began to wonder what was the Constitution meant for? How was it formed? And that's when I had Ken Masugi and John Marini come in to work at EEOC. It wasn't to become a judge; it was merely to understand it as an informed official, an informed citizen. We're running the risk of one day not having a Constitution, and hence not having a country. We're going to pay a price. People forget what happened to the great empires of the world: the Ottoman Empire, gone, fragmented; the Habsburg Empire; the Roman Empire. And the one thing that we have is this long-lasting written constitution, that should be, for us, like the Holy Grail: to be protected. Our desires don't amend the Constitution, that's the touchstone for everything. It allows us to live in a free society, but it doesn't guarantee us the best position in that free society.

MISMATCH
"WHY WOULD YOU DO IT TO THESE LITTLE BLACK KIDS, LITTLE MINORITY KIDS WHO CAN LEAST AFFORD IT, WHO REALLY DO NEED TO BE ABLE TO KEEP HOPE?"

MP: In *Grutter*, you discussed the problem of "mismatch" in an effort to get this aesthetic goal of diversity. Are these policies benefiting the people that they're admitting?
CT: Think about it, people have multiple kids and they have different abilities. You try to match their abilities with the challenges that they have. One is particularly athletic, you want them to do athletics, but

if you have one who's gangly and uncoordinated, you don't put that kid in a situation where that kid is always failing. It might be fun at a certain level, but you wouldn't have them doing AAU basketball, and for obvious reasons. Why would you do that to kids who can perform very, very well at one level? And then what we have done in these programs is put them at levels where they're guaranteed to fail, or close to being guaranteed-fail.

Let's say, for example, a kid had a 1000 on the SATs and the median score at school is 1400. We know we wouldn't do that to our own kid. You put them in a situation where they're certain to be at the bottom of the pool from the very beginning, or, at best, fighting an uphill battle every day, as opposed to putting them in a situation where they are competitive with the kids around them. Why would you do it to someone else's kids? And why would you do it to these little black kids, little minority kids that can least afford it, who really do need to be able to keep hope? And it's very hard in these schools, particularly when you don't fit in, to keep your hope and to keep going. And why would you overburden them with all these extra things, things that are totally unnecessary? I'd prefer a kid to excel at a community college than to fail at Harvard.

MP: You have a feeling for these struggling kids that other people don't have. Does that come from your own life experience?
CT: I think it comes from a sense of do unto others as you would have them do unto you. I wouldn't want anybody to do that to me, to be less than honest with me, to put me in a situation where I'm almost certain to fail.

The nuns knew what we were capable of. I was thinking of Sister Mary Virgilius, my eighth grade teacher, and when she saw my entrance scores to high school and she saw my performance in the eighth grade, she looks me in the eye in 1962, and says, "You lazy thing, you." In other words, I was underachieving, and years later, she would try to apologize. I said, "Oh, no. You were absolutely right." But then I think we should apologize to these kids that we don't prepare for these challenges.

They may have the ability, so the solution may have been to prepare them for that opportunity, not to throw them into a fight they couldn't win, that they were not prepared for. And when the preparation just took extra effort, the nuns prepared us for it. My grandfather and my grandmother prepared us for the challenges. They knew it was going to be difficult. They knew that we were going to need an education, so they sent us to parochial schools. They knew we were going to need self-discipline. My grandfather would always say when we were on the farm or doing anything, "I'm gonna teach you boys how to work." In other words, build in you a way to make the effort because he knew it was going to be an uphill battle, and it was going to take an almost Herculean effort to do it.

So why don't we, instead of being self-congratulatory because we put these kids in this school or that school, why don't we do the preparation part? The hard part. Instead of going, "Oh, I am for this." That's easy. It's harder to actually do the work. The nuns did it. They devoted their lives to doing what other people congratulate themselves for, and not doing.

WHAT THE GOVERNMENT CAN'T DO
"YOU KNEW WE LOVED YOU"

MP: The nuns and your grandparents could do one set of things. But what should be the role of the government?

CT: Does the government know you? Who is the government? I asked Sister Mary Virgilius, "What was the key to their success?" And she said, "We lived with you." They lived in the neighborhood. They were right there. And the other thing she said was, "You knew we loved you." And someone who loves you, they can get you to do hard things. When was the last time you said to yourself or anyone: "Oh, the government loves me. The government knows me. The government sat with me when my mother died. The government was there when I was on my last leg." No one. We don't even know who we're talking about. The nuns—I have faces. Sister Mary Virgilius was my eighth-grade teacher, Sister Mary Dolorosa, my second-grade teacher, and I can go on, Sister Mary Jean, Geraldine, Sister Mary Francis. They are real people; they are actual people.

MP: Does this relate to that great quote from Frederick Douglass, which we discussed earlier: "Leave us alone. Do nothing with us. Your doing has already played the mischief with us"?[17]
CT: What Frederick Douglass was saying was: Leave people alone. People are grown, they can figure things out. My grandfather may not have been educated, but he didn't need somebody in Washington to tell him how to raise his boys. When people would come to him, and they would be upset with what he was doing with us because he had very strict rules and was very firm about the way he did things, he would say, "They got a lifetime to get pleased." And that's where my attitude, "Go away" comes from. We have now replaced the old physical form of slavery with a new kind of slavery to these policies. Give in, let somebody lead us, leading us into this new form of bondage.
The Constitution guarantees liberty. Now liberty gives you the liberty to succeed, liberty to fail, liberty to be mediocre, liberty to be outstanding. It doesn't guarantee either, but it does guarantee your

right that the government isn't going to tell you what to do every day. But we have given up. We are supposedly governed by consent, and when somebody else is telling you what you can do and what you can't do, is that your consent or are you being ruled? And there is a very fine line. It's a line that is monitored by the Constitution of the United States, not by my preferences. All I'm saying is that you are overriding a constitutional provision to do something that you have no authority to do, that is, in addition, harmful.

MP: It's ironic that people who are jealous of protecting their own liberty are concerned that others will use their liberty in ways they don't like.
CT: Well, that's the idea of liberty. I was talking to someone the other day about when you raise kids, when they're small, you get to dominate. As they get older, they go their own way and parents have to live with their decisions. That's the truth when it comes to liberty. You may not like the way this person is using his or her liberty, but they are free, and they get to use it. And the nuns, that's the way they used to talk. We don't talk about it anymore. We talk about all this determinism and how we're controlled by this or that. I mean, determinism was a big deal when I was in school taking these courses back in the sixties. It's become a part of our fabric of our society as we become less religious. But when I was in school, when I was a kid, it was free will—that you made a choice—you could go left, you could go right, you choose.

But at some point you've got to make a choice to do things. And I think we've pushed free will aside, and we've pushed aside people's right to fail. The nuns never did that and neither did my grandfather. You had a right to try, even if you failed. You can't assure people that they're going to be successful. You can give people security, but it comes at the expense of liberty.

ACCUSATIONS THAT THOMAS BENEFITTED FROM RACIAL PREFERENCES
"IT'S DEFAMATION. YOU LOSE THE ARGUMENTS, SO YOU ATTACK THE PERSON"

MP: Your critics, especially African-American critics, say about cases like *Grutter* and *Fisher*, that you benefited from a kind of preferential policy that you now attack.[18] What do you say to those critics?

CT: They have run out of arguments. They don't know me, they don't know anything about me. I really don't spend a lot of time on them. We have reached a point where people want to pull you into the swamp. Particularly with many of the elites, they want to maintain a sense of superiority: there's no way I could be their equal. I think time will properly identify them for exactly what they are. I had a young man come up to me, a young white kid, at the University of Georgia. He started out his question by apologizing for my poor education in the South. That was the premise. He wasn't being mean or anything. He wasn't being a jerk or anything. That's what he had been taught. And I said to him, "I don't know what education you're talking about. When I finished high school, for example," I didn't go through the whole curriculum, but I said, "I had three years of Latin, and two years of German, and two years of French, mathematics, physics, chemistry, all these things." And he stops. And he says, "You know, I took AP courses, I had none of that." And I said, "You don't have to denigrate the education," which is basically what many of these theorists have to do. They have to denigrate it in order to say they're doing something beneficial. My point to him was I could've had a vastly superior education, and segregation would've still been unconstitutional and still morally wrong.

It's like saying those women in *Hidden Figures* needed affirmative action to perform at NASA. They did not. They needed to be treated fairly. They needed to be treated in a way consistent with the Constitution and humanity. And that's what I think is required. But I just think it's really interesting to me, that people you don't know will displace all the effort of the nuns, of my grandparents, of myself, and yet they wouldn't be humble enough to take credit for the damage they did with other ideas of theirs, like public housing, like the fact that LSD is good for you. Oh yeah! You remember all those Timothy Leary arguments? If this is working so well, then why are minorities, particularly blacks, so bad off?

MP: In *Grutter,* you reference how these liberals deny there is a stigma with affirmative action, but then they apply it to stigmatize you.
CT: Come on, we're not stupid. I mean, come on. We know what's going on. This is the old defamation. This is the whole thing when you were asking about my confirmation, and they were smearing me. One of the reasons I kind of resist that is we know what it is. We should know what it is. It is a tactic. It's defamation. You lose the arguments, so you attack the person. I understand that.

They are what they say they are not. They are precisely what they say they're not. They are the stereotypers. They are the ones who have taken the superior position, "Oh, let's just help these little people, these minority kids, to give you the pat on the head and we'll give you your affirmative action." Yeah, well, give me an old coat, too, while you're at it. It's nonsense. We know what's going on.

THE ATTACKS CONTINUE
"THE IDEA WAS TO GET RID OF ME, AND THEN IT WAS—AFTER I WAS THERE—IT WAS TO UNDERMINE ME, MY CREDIBILITY, MY EFFECTIVENESS"

MP: After you were on the Court, those same groups that opposed you during confirmation continued their attack. Did that surprise you?

CT: Nothing they do surprises me anymore. It's just unpleasant, but that's life. It was unprecedented. But everything about what had happened with my confirmation—everything was unprecedented.

In my first term on the Court, the suggestion was quickly made that Justice Scalia was leading me around. It's the same thing. I understand that. He was very upset about it. I remember going over and sitting with him, and he said, "Clarence, they're saying I'm leading you." I didn't know him. I just met him that year when I got to the Court. And he's a funny guy, and he enjoys the laughter, and I said, "Nino, look, you're white and I'm black. And that basically means you're the boss and I'm the hos [horse]. You tell me what to do. That's the white man's burden." And that was it. That's the last discussion we had on it.

I think it started with the New York Times. I don't read the New York Times. I think that's what my clerks said. They started this narrative that I was being led around by him. I couldn't possibly think of these things by myself, but that's precisely what they accused people in the South of doing. And yet it never happened to me in the South. It's absolutely fascinating, and I'm sure there are people who were around me who had stereotypes, but it really never happened. It didn't happen from my teachers. It didn't happen from my fellow classmates. It didn't happen from the white ladies at the libraries, or the black ladies at the Carnegie Library. So it's fascinating that the very people who put themselves up as superior are doing precisely what they're saying they're not doing. They're the absolute worst. In my lifetime, they've been the worst.

MP: You mean in using racial stereotypes?
CT: Well, it's stereotypes draped in sanctimony and self-congratulation.

MP: In some ways, it's more remarkable to keep attacking a Supreme Court justice than a president.

CT: I don't know if it is more remarkable. We used to say that when President Obama was elected, we all were supposed to be in line and it's our president. It's a different set of rules for different people. If you criticize certain people, you're a racist, you're sexist, you're a homophobe. If you criticize a black person who's more liberal, you are racist. Whereas you can do whatever to me, or to now Ben Carson, and that's fine because you're not really black, because you're not doing what we expect black people to do.[19] That's just the way it is. But that's been true since I was at EEOC. None of this is new.

You see things for what they are, that's what I do; I see it for what it is. The idea wasn't the merits of anything. It's a tactic. It is a way to get rid of me. I understand it. It is what it is. The idea was to get rid of me, and then it was—after I was there—it was to undermine me, my credibility, my effectiveness, and certainly to somehow affect the next person.

ON *STARE DECISIS*
"THAT'S BEEN DECIDED, EVERYBODY FALL IN LINE. WELL, THEN WHY ARE WE HERE?"

MP: **Many people point to the independence of your opinions, and you are less bound by *stare decisis*.**
CT: With these notions like *stare decisis*, we say, that's been decided, everybody fall in line. Well, then why are we here? Are we supposed to stop thinking? I fought this back when I was in school: blacks were supposed to all have Afros, so I refused to have an Afro. Who came up with that? We're all supposed to listen to Hugh Masekela. I don't want to listen to Hugh Masekela. Maybe I want to listen to country and Western, or I want to listen to the Brandenburg Concertos. Why

do I want to do what everybody says I ought to do? So I didn't do it, and it's the same thing now. We do it with notions like *stare decisis*. Oh, it has been decided, or you know, conventional wisdom is this. Well, goodbye. I'll think on my own. That was the beauty of why many of us found libertarianism appealing when I was in school because at least it freed me up from all these people telling me what to do. And it said: you think for yourself. If you read *Invisible Man*, you see all these stereotypes that we're supposed to be. You have to go underground sometimes just to be yourself.

THE ADMINISTRATIVE STATE
"IT COMES AT THE EXPENSE OF THE VERY STRUCTURE OF THE CONSTITUTION"

MP: Let me ask you about another set of issues that have come up. You've been a leader in the administrative state cases.[20] What is at stake there? It seems to be a question of liberty again.

CT: The very people who say they don't want the government in their lives want this sort of expansive administrative state, which is in their lives, and then every aspect of their lives. And a lot of it comes at the expense of the very structure of the Constitution that is intended to prevent the government from coming in. The separation of powers, the enumerated powers, federalism. The whole point was to keep the government in this box. Justice Scalia and I often talked about that, that the structure was the main way to protect your liberty. The danger in the administrative state is seeing those powers all coalesce again in various agencies. If you think about your life today, there's very little major legislation that comes from the legislature. The legislation comes in the form of regulations from agencies. They tend to have all three powers. They have the executive power, the enforcement power, they have administrative judges to adjudicate, so they have all three. And the question for us is, where do they fit in the constitutional structure?

When a private right is somehow intruded upon by one of these agencies, what is the role of the federal courts? If we simply defer to the agencies, which is what we do now, in many cases, aren't we doing precisely what happened when it came to the royal courts of the pre-Revolutionary era? How does that make us any different? You've got this creation that sits over here outside the Constitution, or beyond the Constitution. How does it fit within our constitutional structure? How's it limited and what is the risk that it will actually vitiate the constitutional protections that we have?

We have a form of government where we've limited the national government in what it can do. We've separated the powers. You've got enumerated powers. One of the ways that we've limited the national government is to divide the power. You said, "Here's the legislative power, here's the judicial power, here's the executive power. That structure was very important to keeping the national government at bay. You also had federalism, in other words, that the states had most of the authority, and certainly the local authority, beyond what was in the Constitution and the rest remained with the individuals.

MP: I think it was James Madison who said that if you combine the executive, legislative, and judicial in one person, or branch, it's the very definition of tyranny.
CT: That's wonderful rhetoric, and it plays out that way when people look at agencies, and they think, "Of course I have no way to defend myself against an agency." And what we have simply been trying to

do is to raise the question of what are the limits of that. There are different views about it. But at least when you look back at guys like [Frank] Goodnow[21] or Woodrow Wilson[22] or the Progressives at the close of the nineteenth century and in the early twentieth century, at least you have the advantage of them being candid. To some extent, they meant "progress"—to progress beyond the Constitution. And how that is consistent with the Constitution is something I think is worth discussing.

MP: They were clear, too, that they believed in experts and agencies rather than in traditional legislating by elected members of Congress.
CT: I think to some extent they thought that the quaint ideas that the Framers had were anachronistic, at best, and that you could have someone who understood how a government should operate or how a policy should operate.

Once you lose the notion of self-governing, that of self-governance, then where are we? And I think the stark choices are between government by consent and being ruled. And perhaps some people think that we can have a little of both. But good luck! I think the tendency throughout history is that once people get authority to rule, they tend to rule more, not less.

MP: When people use the expression, "the administrative state," what does that mean?
CT: I think that's their way of saying we're being governed by administrative agencies. And it's like affirmative action, who knows? You get a sense of what they're talking about, but I think we have to be more precise in defining the relationship between, say, a specific agency and the constitutional protections.

I think most people don't follow administrative cases and they don't think about the role of these financial boards or the environmental boards. People like a particular policy. Then they'll argue about the policy and not think about how you got to that policy. And I think how you got there, and by what authority, is the more important question for us, not the policy itself.

MP: The phrase "the administrative state," itself, implies that each of these little agencies has some particular role, but when you accumulate all of them together, it looks like almost a fourth branch of government.

CT: I don't know which agencies are little anymore. I ran EEOC and it was small. But look at the reach and the effect that you could have. I ran that little Office of Civil Rights at the Department of Education, look at the reach and the things that it could affect. So the reach is nationwide.

THE SUPREME COURT AT WORK
"WHEN THAT OPINION IS IN DRAFT FORM,
IT CIRCULATES. THAT'S WHEN THE REAL WORK
IS DONE"

MP: People are interested in what a Supreme Court Justice does with his day. What's a daily or weekly routine for you on the Court?

CT: Most of your time is spent just reading, writing, and reviewing drafts. Because it's appellate work, it's in writing. It is mostly seat time.

On a day that we have arguments, I usually start around 4:45 a.m., and then I leave home around 6:00 and I usually work downtown until we're done. Get home, and then I usually work until close to midnight.

MP: When a particular case comes in, you do the readings first? When do you talk to your clerks about it? What is the process?
CT: Most of these cases are repeats of cases that you've had before. It's just another iteration. We have decided to take the case because someone is asking a question that we think we should answer. Having been on the Court so long, it is rare that you get one that's completely new. I've written opinions in a lot of these areas and certainly joined or dissented from opinions in a lot of these areas.

You have to petition us to come to the Court.[23] The law clerks write summaries called "pool memos," and I usually review those on the weekend. There might be 200 or 300 of those on the weekends. And then I have a process within my chambers with my four law clerks to take various looks at those.

We usually have our conferences on Fridays, and we vote. Four votes, we take the case. Now, that's your first look at that case. When you grant a cert. petition, the case is now coming to the Court.

The appellant files a brief (which isn't so brief, they're usually in the fifty-page range). Then there will be a response from the opposing party and then the appellant gets to reply, he or she gets two shots. Then you have people who can participate, they're called "friends of the court," *amicus curiae*, so they file amicus briefs and you read those.

Then we have a process in chambers with my law clerks doing summaries. Then we have a packet that we call bench memos, and then we have disposition memoranda, et cetera. Now I start by reading the cert. petition, then the briefs, and then some of the relevant amicus briefs. Then I look at what my law clerks have written. Then we have a clerk conference about it. Then I go to oral argument, then we come back and we'll talk about it again.

Then, we'll finalize a disposition memorandum. The cases that we hear on Mondays, we decide on Wednesday afternoon. The cases that we hear on Tuesday and Wednesday, we decide on Friday mornings. You go to conference and you vote.

MP: Please describe the long discussions with your clerks, all together, about each case.
CT: One of the joys is I hire four new clerks every year. They go back into the files, and they see the continuum. This is my twenty-seventh year, so they see the consistency.[24] They see that when we have seen something that we may not have gotten right, we say it's not right. And then we try to get it right.

I've always, since the beginning, believed that all four clerks should always be engaged on every case. Before I decide a case, I meet with my law clerks for maybe an hour or so. Now our docket is so slim, only a couple of cases a day. In the old days there were four cases a day. Then, we will have lunch for two or three hours and chat about different things, but you always chat about work. It always leads right back to work and what's going on in these cases, but it's informal because it's a way of life. It's a part of what I do. It's who I am. So you can drift from substantive due process, the dormant commerce clause, from the Eighth Amendment to the Fourth Amendment, and it's seamless. You're not compartmentalizing. It's just a way of life.

So it doesn't just have to be in the context of the case. You chit chat with your law clerks about it because they're self-described law nerds. It requires you to be willing to do the intellectual part of it beyond just the cases in order to understand where we're going, and that includes reading books, reading articles, et cetera.

MP: After oral arguments, there's a conference where all nine of the justices discuss the case together. What is that like?

CT: The way it works at the Court is, intramurally we are called the conference. When we go on the bench, we are the Court. We meet in the conference room, and we vote in descending order of seniority, starting with the chief justice, so he sits at the head of the table. Then the senior associate justice is Justice Kennedy; he sits at the foot of the table directly in front of the chief justice. Then it starts on the more senior side of the table. I'm next to Justice Kennedy. Then Justice Ginsburg next to me, then Justice Breyer. So the three of us on that side, there are four on the junior side of the table. So that would be Justice Alito, Justice Sotomayor, Justice Kagan, and Justice Gorsuch, and then we vote in descending order of seniority.

MP: Even before you vote, do you talk about the case?
CT: The chief justice announces the case, gives his reasoning and votes. Then Justice Kennedy gives his reasoning, votes, and same with me, and then you go around the table. There might be some discussions, but it normally doesn't change anything at conference. The way things are changed is when the senior member in the majority assigns who writes the opinion, when that opinion is in draft form, it circulates. That's when the real work is done because now you see, it's in writing.

Early on in my tenure, when we had so many more cases, someone would vote a certain way. They would try to write a draft, and I remember coming back once, and it could have been Justice White, and he would say, or one of them would say, "That dog won't hunt," or "That opinion won't write, that I thought that made sense, but when I sat down to draft it, it does not write. It doesn't work." It's like in the business of documentaries, you might have an idea and then you try to make it work and it doesn't work. So usually the work is in the draft, and that's where the negotiations and the real work takes place.

On Asking Questions during Oral Argument
"The referee in the game should not be a participant in the game"

MP: Some people say you don't ask enough questions during oral argument. What's your response to all that?
CT: That stuff is ridiculous. If you look at the history of the Court, the Court was a very quiet Court. Justice Brennan rarely asked questions. Justice Powell rarely asked questions. This is all new. When I got to the Court, people actually listened: Justice White, Chief Justice Rehnquist, Justice Blackmun. Justice Marshall wasn't on the Court with me. But I heard by and large they were pretty quiet. We've gotten very hyperactive now. I think it's unnecessary, and I don't think it befits the Court, and it doesn't advance the process.

I think that an advocate should be allowed to advocate. We are judges, not advocates. We should act accordingly. Yeah, we might have opinions, but it's not my job to argue with lawyers; it's their job to make their cases and there's an advocate on each side. The referee in the game should not be a participant in the game. There might be things you want to flesh out, but we cannot cross the line between advocacy and judging.

Imagine a Thanksgiving dinner. Imagine nine people at the table. Imagine everybody talking simultaneously. What do you learn? Nothing. It's a Tower of Babel. The beauty of having order, and having people listen, is that everybody gets to say something coherent. When I first went on the Court, you had many conversations between the members of the Court and the lawyers. Many conversations—not rapid-fire questions, not questions headed in two different directions. And I liked that. It advanced the ball, it made you think about things.

We've gotten very comfortable with this "gotcha" mentality. I don't find that helpful.[25]

The lawyer should be able to say at the end of that case, go out on the front steps of the Court, and say, "You know, I may not win. I know I have an uphill battle, but isn't this a great country where I get to be heard and to say my piece?" The salve on any wound is, "I got to say my piece." Now imagine that very same lawyer, same case. He got to the Court, and we never let him get his points out. What do you think he says on the front steps? He said, "They never let me make my argument." I don't think that's good for the country. I don't think it's good for our process.

MP: There have been, of course, many famous and well-known cases during your time on the court: *Citizens United*,[26] the Obamacare case,[27] *Obergefell*,[28] *Kelo*,[29] *Clinton v. Jones*,[30] and *Bush v. Gore*,[31] to name a few. Do any of them stand out in your mind as significant that you want to comment on?

CT: As you probably gathered, I really don't think about it a lot when I'm done. I think about it in the context of understanding the Constitution and its limitations. I don't see it as a sporting event, or a news event. You see it as a continuum. This is our Constitution. I don't go back, and I don't see these cases as trophies. I don't grade them, like this is more important to me than the other. We don't even count the number of opinions I write. What's really important to me is when we are deciding those cases is to do them the right way. I've been there a long time. There are lots of cases that generate a little bit more interest than others. But I contrast that, though, with this: *Plessy* was not considered a big case when it was decided. There were very few, if any, law review articles on it, and there weren't big spectacular news articles about it. And yet, in our history, it's considered a big deal. That's because of the effect of this case on our Constitution and our fellow citizens and structure of our country. I think any case, even the smallest, could turn out to be an important case. Every one of them is important because any of them could seriously change the way that we live our lives, the way that we protect our liberties.

LEGACY

CHAPTER TEN

LEGACY

"What makes us one anymore?"

MP: Do you think the overall direction of the courts is positive? Are we now doing a better job of protecting our liberties or is it more of a problematic moment?

CT: I think we as citizens have lost interest and that's been my disappointment. That certainly was something that bothered Justice Scalia, that people tend to be more interested in their iPhones than their Constitution. They're interested in what they want rather than what is right as a country.

MP: Do you think that a loss of interest in their Constitution and their liberty on the part of citizens is a burden for the Supreme Court?

CT: No, it's a burden on them, the citizens. They're going to lose their liberties.

MP: But you guys are there protecting them, aren't you?

CT: No, we're not. You protect your liberty. It's your country. We are one part of the effort, and it is the obligation of the citizens to at least know what their liberties are and to be informed. I think we are allowing ourselves to be ruled when we turn all that over to someone else and we're saying, "Rule me." Does it mean we get to make all the decisions? No. We have a system for doing that, but a part of that is our role in it, and our informed role in it, not what is said on TV, not what is said by some half-informed person. You mentioned earlier, Madison—think about these guys. There's a book called *Ratification* and it's about the ratification process that we don't talk about much anymore.[1] We think of the drafting of the Constitution, we think of Philadelphia. There was no Constitution yet; it had to be ratified. You go back and look at the debates among the citizens about that Constitution and ask yourself whether we could have similar debates today.

MP: The Supreme Court is the least democratic branch—
CT: It was supposed to be the least dangerous. When you delegate your responsibilities to someone else, you're asking to be ruled. When you say, "I don't have time. I'm too busy playing fantasy football to understand my constitutional rights. I'm too busy listening to snippets on TV, or with little tweets, two-sentence analysis, because I have to get over and have me a cup of chai with a bunch of buddies or go to the football game." So you made your choice: "I want to be ruled. I don't want the responsibility of understanding it myself." But the Supreme Court has a role in it. I agree with you—but it is not the ruler, and I think that people shouldn't see the Court as a ruler. But a part of that is being self-governed and ruling yourselves.

MP: We talked about your relationship with Justice Scalia, a little bit. I like the anecdote that you have told about his phrase of this "freedom-destroying cocktail."
CT: Well, I forget the opinion I had written, it was one of the Fourth Amendment ones—either swabbing, or an anonymous tip case where

he didn't agree with me. He and I often disagreed on the Fourth Amendment, and he wrote in his dissent this wonderful line. He said that my approach and my decision was a "freedom-destroying cocktail." And at the end of the term, this was the end of his last full term because he would die the next term, we went to a restaurant in D.C. with his law clerks and my law clerks. We had done that a lot in the past when this restaurant A.V.'s was around, but it's long gone. And so we're at this restaurant and we're upstairs, having pizza, and he loved the anchovy pizza. And he's going over the menu and he can't make up his mind, unlike him. He can't figure out a cocktail, and I said, "Why don't you get you a freedom-destroying cocktail to start?" And he thought that was the funniest. And he blamed his law clerks for that line and they're all, "Oh no, you came up with that on your own." But I loved that. He was just a good guy and he would come up with these quips like that.

THE ALLEGATION IS EVERYTHING
"FACTS DON'T MATTER, IT'S THE SERIOUSNESS OF THE CHARGE"

MP: In discussing your confirmation, you have mentioned the phrase, "Facts don't matter." How did that come up?
CT: Whenever we would rebut something during my confirmation, some charge against me, they would say, "The facts don't matter. It's the seriousness of the charge." That's the point where we're at. People don't ask for facts anymore. They just simply say, "Give me a story, give me a narrative that fits what I like." It's fascinating to me.

MP: We have gotten used to cases where the charge is everything.
CT: Well, that's it. That's what I was saying then: *J'accuse.* You don't have to have it proven. That was what really was worrisome. You

know what is coming down the pike if this gains legitimacy. Are we against the fact that in our society that if "A" says something about "B," then "A" has the burden of demonstrating that in the court of law? Again, people sit passively by and let it happen.

MP: In many cases, especially in yours, the left doesn't give up. At the end of the confirmation hearings, a poll showed that the American people believed you by a margin of two to one. Over the next twenty-five years, with an endless amount of attacks, and movies like *Confirmation*, and they've changed the narrative. They've changed the public's perception.[2]

CT: They create a myth. They create an image. It's a tactic and when people see it being successful, they don't realize they're going to be the next ones in the Tower of London. It is just a matter of time. You allow this to be a precedent in your society, and people might say, "Oh, it's wonderful. This particular guy is getting tarred and feathered." Well, there's a lot of tar and there's a lot of feathers, and eventually you will be there.

UNINTENDED CONSEQUENCES
"THE POLICIES DESTROY PEOPLE"

MP: You have talked a little today about how life in the black community has not been improved by many well-intentioned social programs. Do you think, in some sense, it is worse than when you grew up?

CT: It's a disaster. When I grew up, you had family, you didn't have drugs, you didn't have gang-banging. You could walk down the street.

There was a change in our society. I think that these programs certainly had an impact. Just go back to Savannah and take a look around you. Our worst fears were realized. We didn't want to be right; we wanted to be wrong. It wasn't about winning an argument. No, we wanted to lose the argument. We did not want the damage to occur; that's why we were involved. I don't particularly like public life; I never wanted to be in public life. I'd like to go to football games. I'd like not to make decisions about other people's lives, but what drags you into it is when you see these principles being undermined, which leads to such destruction. The policies destroy people, and, ultimately, I think, we're going to destroy the very thing that allows us to have liberty and to have a free society.

MP: So the heirs to those movements, like Black Lives Matter, focus on other things: mass incarceration, police brutality. What do you think of the current movements for racial justice?
CT: I don't really follow the movements *du jour*. I don't quite understand them. It's fascinating to me that the radical groups in the sixties, that we all were aware of and fond of back then, like the Black Panthers—that's kind of mainstream now. But we knew they were more marginal back then. I don't know what to say about this. But if you look at some of the things that still are problematic, like bad education, unsafe neighborhoods, drugs, alcohol, breakdown in families, it seems like these are things that we warned about back then. We were told, basically, take a long walk on the short pier. And I understand that. I understand people not wanting to hear an opposing view. But at the same time, we're not taking ownership of these policies' having a significant role in the damage that's been done.

MP: You've made many trips back to both Pin Point and Savannah. When you return, do you reflect on your life? Do you reflect on how it is now?

CT: I don't reflect a lot about these sorts of things. A lot of this is depressing, and it didn't have to happen. The Savannah that I return to is not the Savannah I grew up in. There are good parts, you're free to move about. You don't have the segregation, but you've got pathologies that we didn't have before. You've got the crime we didn't have before. You've got the disintegration of families that you didn't have before, disorder you didn't have before. And they were things that were avoidable. You didn't have to do that to poor people, and it's just heartbreaking. Something has changed, so it's kind of hard to go back.

My grandfather would always talk about how do you help people without turning them into wards of the state, turning them into people who don't help themselves? He would have this line, "You help people help themselves." And there was a difference between helping, or helping to help themselves. Now we could do it individually because we did it all the time. It was not only our Christian obligation; it was the way we lived. That's the way our community lived. You have fish and somebody else has beans, they bring you beans, you give them fish, or vice versa.

But what happens with people who can't help themselves? And my grandfather's line was, "There are people who won't help themselves, and the people who can't help themselves." And he wanted to help people who couldn't help themselves versus those who wouldn't. And how do you make that distinction? Well, you live there. It's a part of your community; it's family, it's your neighbor. You know that this person refuses to work, versus that person who's disabled, or that person had just had another kid and can't go to work right now. But you don't know that from a distance.

When people have these sort of macro policies and they have unintended consequences, they don't fess up to it. When you tear down a neighborhood in order to replace the housing, you have changed the neighborhood. That little church that used to be there that people went to on Sundays, that little community house, or whatever, is suddenly gone.

MP: Why do you think these activists promote these policies? Don't they have good intentions?

CT: We were talking before about people will push a policy that makes them feel good. "Oh, I feel good about myself because I put you all in public housing." When my grandfather saw all these high-rises for public housing, he thought it was awful. I remember when we visited a relative in New York who lived in one and he said, "Boy, this don't make no damn sense: pilin' po' people on top of po' people." And it turned out he was right. They tore down Cabrini Green [a housing project in Chicago] and many of these notorious high-rise public housing projects. They made a prophet out of him because he thought it would just create more problems. And yet the people who pushed it never say, "Oh, we made a mistake." And they never take account of the fact the damage they did to the people with their grand experiment, the gangs they created, the drug dealing they accommodated, the destruction of the family that was exacerbated. All this was not necessarily caused, but at least influenced in the wrong direction by the artificiality of the neighborhoods they created.

The experts don't live in the neighborhood. They don't know what effect it had when you tore down that little shoe store because you say it was in a sub-standard building. It's the same thing. When we had school integration, the unintended consequences is the effect it had on the black teachers and also the neighborhood schools. You walked to school, your parents went to that school, and what happens when you break those bonds?

MP: Good point. The unintended consequences are significant.
CT: My grandfather said something one day when we're riding around on the oil truck, and they're beginning to tear down the old substandard housing, and supposedly putting up new things. Well, they never got around to putting up that part. So when they started tearing down some of the dilapidated houses in our neighborhood, he said "Boy, they're tearing down neighborhoods and building buildings." That phrase has just stuck in my mind. There's a difference between a neighborhood and a building. And it may be a subtle difference, particularly when you're young, that you miss. But as life goes on, you see that a building and a neighborhood are two entirely different things. You can have really nice buildings and a horrible neighborhood, and you can have awful buildings and a wonderful neighborhood. And that was his point about our neighborhood. Our neighborhood was fine. But geniuses came in—the experts—and started tearing down buildings and tearing up the neighborhood.

MP: It's amazing that he saw that.
CT: My grandfather had to see life on his own terms. He had to deal with what was, not what he wanted life to be.

MP: Government policies, particularly at the national level, can have devasting impacts on communities.
CT: I'm not saying you don't pursue the policy, but you consider the unintended consequences when you're the working poor. It is really hard to keep going. We were trying to say this when they started sending minorities to these schools in New England. It is hard to be the only black kid, it is hard to show up in a classroom and not look like anyone else. It is hard to not have the income, or to not understand what they're saying when you go to school in Massachusetts.

That doesn't mean you don't do it but recognize that it puts a lot more pressure on the kid, and that not everybody can do it.

And then when it happens, don't blame it on something else. So those of us who went through it warned them that this is really, really hard. I was the only black kid, and I'm not saying it can't work, but it is really hard, and most people can't do it. But, of course, there was the deaf ear to that. Now you've got a problem, you see kids who feel isolated on these campuses or you see kids who can't really handle it.

Similarly on these social programs, they may have meant well, but they had unintended consequences. And then when I go home, when you go back to your family, to your neighbors, you see it. I grew up there with the substandard housing. And you saw it, and you saw some of the effect. You saw the effect on families. You sit there and run studies on it? No, you live it, and it becomes a part of the fabric of your life and you didn't have to do it. So that's what I'm talking about. It's fundamentally changed Savannah. Again, it goes back to the question that Juan Williams asked me in December of 1980, "Why are you so concerned about it?" Because I'm watching the effects of it, and it is not good. I'm not saying you do away with it but come up with another way of doing it.

ROAD TRIPS IN THE RV
"ONE DAY I'M GOING TO SEE GEORGIA, AT LEAST"

MP: Let me ask a little bit about your life outside the Court and in the summer. You're well known to take RV trips with Ginni. How did you get into that, and why do you do it?
CT: Well, let's just start with this baseline. When I grew up, because of the way the world was, we did not venture beyond beaten paths.

My grandfather wasn't adventurous. The race problems in south Georgia were such that you didn't want to get caught up someplace where you didn't know what the informal rules were. We went from Chatham to Bryant to Liberty County and back. So that's a distance of about thirty miles or so. We didn't do much traveling beyond that. We went up to the Bronx, New York, twice during my childhood, that was it. In your mind, you say, "One day I'm going to see Georgia, at least."

About twenty-plus years ago, an older gentleman, who was a photographer and who had been a successful businessman, had bought a motor home to travel and take photography. He said to me at a reception one time, "The best people in the country are in the RV park." My initial reaction was, "Yeah, well good luck with that. I'm not doing that." And he sent me some magazines, saying, "You should just take a look at it." And I said, "This man's got a point." And I began to look at it and decided that I was interested in a bus. And eventually we got it, and we've had it for now eighteen and a half years.

What it does is it gets me beyond the confinement of my youth, it opens up not only Georgia, but the entire nation. I think we've done close to forty states in this bus and we've seen the rural areas. We've been to east Tennessee and Sevierville, and Gatlinburg and we've been to Nashville; we've been to Utah; we've been to Wyoming, Nebraska, upstate New York, New England. So you get to see the entire country in a different way and I enjoy that. And you get to be around regular people. You get to go to Walmart parking lots, and truck stops. Most people pass a Flying J truck stop, a Pilot, a TA, Love's, never think twice of it. But for us, we've been there. And you go into rest stops, you go in the RV parks, you see nice people from all different walks of life. It's truly a democratic place when you go into RV parks.

MP: Do any of your trips stand out in your memory?

CT: I remember early on when we weren't that familiar with it, and we were having trouble letting out our awnings or putting them back in. Everybody around, like good neighbors, came over, like we had a barn raising or something, to help me with the awnings. Now today, that's almost embarrassing because it takes, like, five minutes to put all the awnings out. I remember we were at a camp ground about ten, fifteen years ago, sitting at the campfire with a gentleman and he said, "What do you do?" And you know, I told him, "I'm a lawyer" and he says, "Where?" I said, "In D.C." And we talked and he just went on about something. It was fun because you get to talk to people and they don't know who you are. You're just a guy who pulled up next to them on the coach.

We were at a truck stop, and I mean this is a diesel bus; this is actually a bus. People think it's just a regular motor home that I'm talking about. No, it's a bus that's been converted to a motor home and has always been a motor home, but it's an actual bus. It's a Prevost Chassis. So I'm in there with big truckers, the eighteen wheelers. I think it was a Pilot truck stop in Pennsylvania. And you have to go through a process—you put on your fueling gloves and you have to kick the tires. I never figured that out, but you do it because you're a professional. I was walking to pay, and this black trucker comes over. He looks at me, and says, "You that judge?" And I said, "Yeah." I said, "Shhhh! Don't tell anyone." And he said, "Wow. You know, I heard you a big rig man like us, but I didn't think I'd ever meet you." And he said, "Can I get a picture?"

I was headed down to Florida the week after *Bush v. Gore*, and things were a little dicey then. And I was at a truck stop north of Jacksonville, just outside of Brunswick, Georgia, at a Flying J. This trucker comes over, after I'm fueled up, and he looks at me—squints, they always, they love to squint for some reason—and he says to me, "Anybody ever tell you you look like Clarence Thomas?" And I said, "Yeah." And he said, "I bet that happens all the time, doesn't it?" And then he goes on about his business.

Then I was at another Flying J, my wife and I. A black gentleman, he was driving an eighteen wheeler, walks by a couple of times. And then he looks at me and he says, "Anybody important on that bus?" And I said, "No, it's just my wife and me." And he says, "You sure?" "No, I'll go check." [laughs] No, I didn't say that. I said, "No, just my wife and me." He goes off, and he comes back again. "You sure there is nobody important on that bus?" I said, "No, just my wife and me." He comes back with his card and he said, "Look, I'm sure there's somebody important on there. If you need help driving that person, here's my card, I'm available." So you get that sort of thing, and it's really entertaining. For the most part people are delightful. You have occasional problems with your coach or something like that. But other than that, it's been a wonderful experience.

MP: Many of your colleagues go to Europe and resorts in the summer. Why don't you?
CT: I don't have any problem with going to Europe, but I prefer the United States, and I prefer seeing the regular parts of the United States. I prefer going across the rural areas. I prefer the RV parks, and I prefer the Walmart parking lots to the beaches and things like that. There's something normal to me about it. I come from regular stock, and I prefer being around that.

GETTYSBURG
"WE CANNOT ALLOW THESE PEOPLE TO HAVE DIED IN VAIN"

MP: I am told that you take your clerks to Gettysburg every year. Why do you do that?

CT: That started some years ago and then I started doing it with my bus. What if Gettysburg had turned out the other way? What is it that we will make a Pickett's Charge for? The Civil War is a central part of our history because you got a divide, you've got two constitutions. You've got the pre–Civil War Constitution, and then you have the Civil War Amendments—you have the Thirteenth, Fourteenth, and Fifteenth Amendments. You've got a series of laws after that. So you have a different country after the Civil War than you had before the Civil War. It is a pivotal point in our history, and Gettysburg is a crucial battle.

MP: And, of course, there's Lincoln's Gettysburg Address. Do you and your clerks reflect on that?
CT: Well, we do. It's as though we cannot allow these people to have died in vain, and it is up to us to keep it going, to keep the country going, to keep the grand experiment going. "For us the living," as he said.[3] The Gettysburg Address, the Civil War, Reconstruction. You cannot understand the Fourteenth Amendment, in particular, which is crucial, without understanding the Civil War and Reconstruction.

MP: Lincoln in that address is very concerned with fulfilling the Founder's vision and a Nation dedicated to a proposition...
CT: "All men are created equal." After *Dred Scott*,[4] and the Kansas–Nebraska Act,[5] Lincoln gets back into politics. People forget that the Republican party was the anti-slavery party. Lincoln makes a point about the Republican Party being anti-slavery and pro-Union. It was really fascinating against what Chief Justice Taney had written in *Dred Scott*, which most people do not read or think about, but it is crucial. In *Dred Scott*, Chief Justice Taney says that blacks could never

be citizens for the purpose of diversity or any other reasons. Well, the Fourteenth Amendment answers that, and this isn't something that is really written about: It defines citizenship. It makes you a citizen of the state you are born in and the United States. Okay? If you are born here, or if you become a citizen, it says that no state can deprive you of the privileges or immunities of citizenship. And it is that Privileges and Immunity Clause that is so important. The Fourteenth Amendment provides what Taney said was not in the Constitution.

There are certain rights that you are born with that are inherent, and the government can't take them away. The nuns believed in that. And, certainly, the Framers believed in that: that you had these God-given natural rights, and then you gave up some of those rights in order to be governed.

GRANDFATHER'S LEGACY
"TO BE ABLE TO SAY TO HIM THAT I LIVED UP TO MY OATH AND DID MY BEST"

MP: At the end here, I want to come back to your grandfather and his legacy. You've mentioned earlier that when you were confirmed and sworn in as a justice that that was a victory for your grandfather. But now twenty-six years have gone by. Do you still think that, overall, what you've done, from the confirmation to now, is a victory for him and his values?

CT: Oh, yes. You know, I keep a bust of my grandfather that my wife had made, over me and I've done since I've been at the court. One of my objectives is always to be able to say to him, "I lived up to my oath and did my best." And just the idea that he would say, "It's a job well done. You do things the right way."

I remember when we had this old Ford tractor. He would give me some water and some gasoline and send me back off in the distance to plow. One of my great reactions and feelings was when he would look over what I had done later on in the day and said, "Boy, that's really nicely done." That's about all you could get out of him.

My grandfather would never have anticipated that I would have been on the Supreme Court. My grandparents, I think, would've been satisfied that I was here and would've been confident that I was raised the right way. And I remember what he said when I was at EEOC, and I was complaining to him about getting beat up, about getting criticized and all sorts of things were happening to me, and people were saying things, and the media was after me, and he was very clear. He just simply said, "Boy, you have to stand up for what you believe in." He was uncorrupted by modern thinking. When you can't read and write, you take life as it is. And that's it. There was no more, no less. And I think that that's what I've tried to do.

MP: **It's clear that you have done that. But do you also think that your values are his values, and that the things in particular, that you stood up for were the things that he would have wanted you to stand up for?**

CT: Let's just take race, for example. He was a lifelong member of the NAACP—went to all the meetings, he contributed to get the protestors during the sit-ins out of jail. He was the one who put his property up for bail, that sort of thing. He wasn't one of these people who sat around and did nothing. When you asked him about people and race, he said, "Son, in God's eyes, we're all the same," or, "It takes all kinds to make a world." That would be it.

So yes, I would be able to look him in the eye and say that the law applies equally to everybody, and it may work in your favor sometimes, and it may work against you sometimes, but it is the law and it is applied equally. We grew up in a world in which it did not apply equally. Was it supposed to solve all your problems? I think that's overpromising, just like these social policies won't solve all your problems. But to apply it equally, he would absolutely be for that.

MP: "In God's eyes we're all the same" is something like the Declaration's notion of equality, or Lincoln's notion of equality, as opposed to egalitarianism.

CT: It's also consistent with the nuns. "In God's eyes." I've heard that a zillion times when we were living under segregation. When I was discriminated against getting a driver's license, or my grandfather got a ticket for having too many clothes on, or when he couldn't get a license for a cinder block–making plant, we knew what was going on, and we knew why, but the fallback was, at least in God's eyes, we were equal. And that was consistent with the Declaration.

MP: What do you want your legacy to be?

CT: I never think of it. I think that the most that you hope for in life is that they will say you did your job, and you did the best you could, and you did it honestly.

MP: It seems to me you enjoy your job at the Court, Justice Thomas.

CT: I do. My grandfather used to say, "If it's honest work, it's good work." And to be a part of this country and this Constitution, there is a sense of fulfillment that you get to write, and to think about, and to defend the very thing that protects our liberties. I have been so blessed to have an opportunity to participate in this government, at this level, and in this way.

EXCERPTS FROM INTERVIEW WITH GINNI THOMAS

MP (Michael Pack): Where were you born and raised?
GT (Ginni Thomas): I was born in Omaha, Nebraska, in the middle of the country. I was the fourth child of a couple who were very civic-minded. My mother was very political. She ran for the state legislature and was a Reagan delegate in '68. My father was a civil engineer who owned his own small business. I'm clearly my mother's daughter. I caught the bug in terms of political activism from my mother.

MP: I know you have visited Pin Point. What was it like?
GT: My husband's childhood was so unlike mine in the sense that he was truly disadvantaged and being of a generation where he was coming out of segregation in the South. His experiences were unlike anything in my childhood. So the things I've learned about his childhood have stretched my understanding of our country and of the social environment that he was in and how somebody like that gets through a societal change.

245

My husband, the wingspan of Clarence, I think of it this way: From the people in Pin Point that I've met, and that he knows, and that are a foundational part of his life to the people that have been successful in their life that we interact with now, he has this great wingspan that he can interact with and talk with. He changes dialect down there sometimes. I'm just thrilled that he still keeps focused on the people who were close to him at one point, and he can communicate complex things in simple ways, and yet interact with people that are very wealthy, or very successful, right now.

MP: Have you heard him speaking Gullah to these people?
GT: There have been times where I honestly cannot understand what's happening, as they talk in different dialects. I know when I first went down to Pin Point and Savannah with Clarence, there were times we would go into very small, very warm, heated homes out in the country, and they were talking to me, and I came out and I said, "Clarence, I can't understand a word that they just said," because they talk in a dialect. So I just try to listen and smile.

MEETING CLARENCE THOMAS
"THAT'S WHEN I HEARD HIS LAUGH FOR THE FIRST TIME"

MP: How did you meet him?
GT: We met in 1986, up in New York at a conference that was sponsored by the B'nai B'rith on how long does America need race preference policies to get over slavery. And I was going as someone who worked as a lobbyist for the U.S. Chamber of Commerce on civil rights and some labor issues. And he was going as head of the EEOC, and when I heard him, it was a small group of probably twelve of us

that day talking. I was in my twenties from white Nebraska, and his experiences were so resonant and so powerful and so genuine. I was struck by him. I was taken by his understanding of what we were talking about that day. And we became friends that day, and we rode to the airport together in a taxi, and then became professional friends. And by the time we then went to lunch, and then went to an early movie, it was just starting for me to be something bigger than a professional friendship.

MP: What was the next step?
GT: The next step was that he called me, and we went to lunch, and we ended up going at some point to an early movie, *Short Circuit.*[1] And that's when I heard his laugh for the first time, and it was pretty powerful, pretty resonant, pretty infectious. And I was taken by his laugh. We went to dinner afterwards, and the more I got to know him, the more I realized I was talking to someone who was maybe the best man I'd ever talked to in my life given his qualities, his values, how he treated people in his life, what he thought about people, how he ingested the lessons of his life. I knew from that dinner that I was very attracted.

MP: His laugh is amazing. It seems to express a genuine joy in existence.
GT: A lot of people take a lot of joy from Clarence's laugh, and I do too, because it fills the room, and it makes you feel better. And I don't know where it comes from, but it's a blessing.

MP: When we first met Justice Thomas, my wife, Gina, observed that he is particularly skilled at finding the commonality with people.
GT: He learned as a child when he was the first black in an environment, whether it's school, or whatever, that you look for what you have in common, not your differences. And when you can find that, it makes

everything smooth and comfortable. I have learned so much from him in that regard because I've watched him do it on many occasions.

THE EEOC YEARS
"HE JUST SPEAKS HIS MIND"

MP: He was at EEOC when you started dating him. What do you recall about his time there?
GT: As we were starting to date, Clarence was testifying a lot on Capitol Hill. I would go and watch him sometimes, and I was astounded because he would be very confrontational with some of the chairmen that he would testify in front of. He did that once before the Senate Aging Committee, and I had never seen anything like it from an administration official. And I said to him after, "There's going to be repercussions for this." And sure enough, there was two years of a General Accounting Office investigation, and lots of investigations and trouble for him.[2] But he handled it all well. He just speaks his mind when he goes to the Hill.

MP: Not a common practice. After you were married, in Washington, he still had lots of controversies, people attacking him in the press.
GT: Ever since I met him, left-wing leaders, or black leaders, have attacked him. That's just part of our life together. I love how he handles it. He lets it drip off of him like a duck. Clarence just puts things in perspective. It's painful, and it hurts, and stings, but you have to learn to accept it, and decide are you going to bend to please them or are you going to be your own person?

MP: When he was at EEOC, he hired two Claremont professors, Ken Masugi and John Marini, as speechwriters.

GT: When Clarence was at EEOC, one of the best things, looking back, that he did was to hire two speechwriters who worked with him on reading Founding documents and understanding American exceptionalism. So John Marini and Ken Masugi were anchors for what came out to be his jurisprudence, now that he's on the Court. It was the beginning of an educational process where he thought with them, and talked with them, and argued with them, and went back and forth in a way that probably had a lot to do with forming his thoughts.

MP: The other thing about hiring them, that always struck me, is that many people who run agencies think they're too smart to ever want to learn anything anymore.
GT: When Clarence was head of EEOC, he was in the midst of a lot of controversial things. He was dealing with hearings and press issues and a lot of management issues in the agency. To take time to work with, and learn from, these two scholars, who were hired as speechwriters, but were really his retreat into thinking deeply, getting out of the morass of current events, and thinking about things that were important, ended up being a huge asset to him later in life.

MP: Do you think that the attacks of the liberal groups on him were worse than the attacks on any other Reaganite appointee in those days?
GT: The liberal groups have a particular focus on ensuring that any black conservative doesn't advance because they would become more resonant with the population. So it was important for them to destroy Clarence Thomas and any other black conservative.

MP: And Justice Thomas has mentioned that he didn't like being told by other people in the Reagan administration what to do. He bristled at that.
GT: I can tell you as his wife that Clarence doesn't like to be told what to do, from the moment I met him in '86. Whether you're his wife, or

whether you're the Justice Department in the Reagan team, he will say in a minute, "All I have to do is stay black and die." He's going to go his own way.

MP: I think that's a defining characteristic. It's enabled him to get through these things and find his way.
GT: There's been people who have said to me, "There should be more Clarence Thomases on the Supreme Court," and when I tell him that he goes, "If there was, I would disagree with him." Because he's a contrarian.

MP: During this time period, he seemed to be moving back towards his Catholic faith.
GT: When he would have hard days, he would find time to go to Mass, or to go into a church and just be quiet. He's always been very personal, very devout, and focused on his faith. So he would quietly find his way to church and to daily Mass. He would find peace in a chaotic time from going to church.

When we got married in 1987, in the Methodist Church in Nebraska, we carried on our faith life in Protestant churches or in nondenominational churches in the Washington area. As I look back, I realize that was because of me. He was going to Protestant churches because of my faith. He was pulled to the Catholic faith again. It was a big decision, and it was a big comfort to him.

MP: What was your daily life like during this EEOC period? You were in the Department of Labor during that period.[3]
GT: Clarence and I would ride to work together every morning and come home together, and he would inevitably call me once or twice during the day too.

MP: When Justice Thomas was nominated to the D.C. Circuit, how did the confirmation process go?

GT: When Clarence was first nominated to be on the court of appeals, the liberal groups made it very clear that they were going to make it as hard as possible. The message was, "Don't you even think of going further than the Court of Appeals, even if you can get through this barrage."

The left always had their machinery aimed at taking him out, one way or another, because he had diverged from what he was supposed to be as a black man rising in America. They did not want him to succeed or to be elevated because he hadn't kissed the rings of the black liberal icons that you're supposed to. He was his own person and he was not going to be controlled. So that was highly offensive, apparently, to the left. And so they would do anything they could to bring him down.

NOMINATION TO THE SUPREME COURT
"WE NEED DIRT ON CLARENCE THOMAS"

MP: What did it feel like when he was nominated to the Supreme Court?

GT: It was tremendous. When Clarence was in Kennebunkport being nominated for the Supreme Court, it was a high point, and he made it a high point. And knowing his life, I knew the whole trajectory.

MP: During his preparation that summer, what was your day-to-day like?

GT: When he was prepping at home, I would go to work. But honestly when I came home, I could feel a big cloud over the whole area because he was trying to study and focus, but phone calls would come with press inquiries that had to continually be batted down, something that was being alleged by a friend, or by a journalist. And so for him it was the conflict between the urgent versus the important, studying and focusing, and reading, and absorbing, and thinking, versus battling the current event.

MP: Didn't he have some White House people helping with this, dealing with all these rumors and allegations?
GT: There was a team at the Justice Department that helped him focus and study. There was a team at the White House who was helping bat down the allegations that were cropping up every day. Every day there was something new, from a divorce record that they wanted to open or a charge of some employee, or some position that he had that was mischaracterized. It was a constant fire that was happening that summer.

MP: Were interest groups fanning out looking for stuff?
GT: We knew that journalists had said, "We need dirt on Clarence Thomas."[4] And so that's just their modus operandi for those that they want to destroy and discredit. It's not like a celebratory time where people wanted to tell the good side of Clarence Thomas—they'd have none of it. There was no acclamation, no "this was a national hero." None of that.

You can hear when you're the subject of their scrutiny. You get calls from people who are getting calls, telling you what they're asking about. We could tell they were after him and would look for anything.

Every day there were people with lines of attack that were trying to find people in Clarence's life that would validate whatever their story was. So we were constantly, every day, trying to bat back things that were popping up, almost all of them were just totally false, but they'd have to be handled and responded to. And it was very time-consuming, and very tiresome.

MP: The press were also heading down to Pin Point and talking to his mother.
GT: Leola had a number of reporters who were trying to get into her home with various stories. And I remember she was distraught several times and brought to tears by the things they were trying to make her say that just weren't true. She was feeling sorry for us, and she was feeling sorry for her son at a time that she was also supposed to be so proud.

MP: The women's groups were worried that he was going to reverse the *Roe v. Wade* decision. Why did they think that?
GT: All I can say is that after the hearing, there was a young woman who came to my door at the Heritage Foundation and asked if she could talk to me. She had worked for Patricia Ireland of NOW [National Organization of Women], and she had a religious experience in her life and became a Christian. She wanted to come and apologize to me on behalf of what happened to my husband. She said, "We all believed that he was going to take our life away from us—our ability to have abortion. We thought that that justified anything we could do to your husband." And she said this with tears streaming down her face in front of me as if I was someone that could relieve her guilt. So I was honored to have that window into what motivated our adversaries during the confirmation.

MP: The left was not buying the biography either. They claimed he exaggerated it, he's exploiting it, and he's leaving things out.
GT: The left even wanted his mother to believe that she only had two children, not three. So the left's attack on the biography and the story of his life was laughable. And yet he did rise from really desperate circumstances.

Part of the strategy of the White House and the people who were supporting Clarence's confirmation was to help always remember the background from which he came.

There were people who came up to celebrate Clarence's confirmation process, who made all the difference in the world. So the bad people may have been coming together, but thankfully there were people from Clarence's past who came to us from Savannah.

There were conservative groups who were marshalling activists from around the country to come in and line the hallways in the Senate. And when we came out of Senator Danforth's office, and we were going down the hallway, and all these people were clapping, and very excited. And he said to me, "Who are those people?" And I said, "I think they're angels," and they were.

They ended up being Eagle Forum women from around the country. My mother was an Eagle Forum woman with Phyllis Schlafly early on. You get encouraged by the people who show up, and a lot of good people showed up in the midst of a lot of the bad.

MP: During the summer, how was he doing with all the attacks?
GT: I could tell that the press inquiries and the liberal groups on the outside, the activists, and the things that were being said in the batting down of stories, this was taking a toll on him personally leading up to the hearings.

BEFORE THE SENATE
"AND SO THIS WAS THEIR CHANCE, AND WE KNEW IT WAS IN THE LIONS' DEN"

MP: The first day of hearings was September 10, 1991. What did it feel like walking into the Committee hearing room?
GT: After a summer full of preparation and pushing back on various stories, coming to the hearings felt like you were getting to the end. When you walk into that room, it's a circus feeling. The klieg lights

are up. The media starts popping with the cameras. The senators are up there being nice and wanting to shake hands. And so I walked in with him and was happy to find my seat. And we had family there from Savannah, and Jamal was there.

MP: What was Senator Danforth's role?
GT: Senator Danforth was amazing throughout the whole process. He was working senators independently. He was the full-time angel next to Clarence Thomas going through the Senate ordeal. It was a Democrat Senate, and Jack Danforth was the perfect partner for this because he's not as ideological and he is liked by both sides. And he knew Clarence from Yale onward.

MP: The senators were focused on trying to get him to say something about *Roe*.
GT: It felt like the senators were asking any number of things that were designed to trip him up or make an issue out of his answers. On *Roe v. Wade*, he honestly hadn't focused much on it. I know it was a big cultural, social issue, and people thought it was the dividing line. But honestly from his life in rural poverty in Georgia, to being at the edge of economic sustainability, abortion was not something that he had thought much about.

MP: They also pursued questions about natural law, especially Senator Biden. Because Justice Thomas believed in natural law, they implied that he would use it as a justification to institute a conservative agenda.
GT: It's perplexing. There was so much focus on natural law because in the Declaration of Independence, the country assumes that man has inalienable rights, and that those rights come from God, not from government. So that wasn't any extreme view, that was simply what our Founding Fathers put in the Declaration of Independence.

MP: For example, the phrase "all men are created equal" is very important to Justice Thomas.

GT: You know it's natural for Clarence to have come out of segregation and cling to the notion of "all men are created equal," to hold on to what's now cast as natural rights, and carry that into the confirmation process, and everything he does as a black man in America. So it wasn't controversial. It was what his nuns told him, it was what his grandfather told him, and it was bizarre to see Democrats find something wrong with that.

I wish the whole hearing was about how a man that grew up as Clarence grew up and got to this point in his life. I certainly wish that more people could have come to absorb his story as something that helps all of us in America rise up against whatever adversity, or poverty, or circumstances that start our life off but then ultimately come to a different place. It felt like the confirmation process wasn't respectful of that story—it was trying to trip him up.

MP: How was Justice Thomas holding up during the hearings? I mean it was a very grueling eight days.

GT: We had power bars for him, and we just tried to support him around the edges. But he knew he was going into the trial of his life with the Senate run by the Democrats, and they were after him. They've been after him since I met him. And so this was their chance, and we knew it was in the lions' den.

ANITA HILL
"I COULD SEE THAT A STORY WAS BEING TOLD THAT COULD RESONATE WITH MANY, MANY WOMEN IN THE WORKPLACE"

MP: The first time Justice Thomas heard that Anita Hill was alleging sexual harassment, is when these FBI agents came to your home.

GT: Clarence was shocked that Anita Hill was the person that was making allegations because he had helped her. He had done everything he could to help her professionally, and he thought of her as an ally and friend. So it was stunning to him, devastating, that she would be the one coming out from the shadows to launch an attack against him in any way.

MP: Was the name Anita Hill new to you?
GT: Anita Hill was just one of many names that I would hear at home, and I knew that Clarence had worked with Dean [Charles] Kothe in Oklahoma to help Anita get a job at a law school in Oklahoma.[5] So it was totally shocking, such a surprise that this was a person that had anything negative to say about my husband.

Anita Hill worked with Clarence at the request of his friend Gil Hardy at the Education Department, and then she wanted to follow him to EEOC where he was going to be the chairman. She wanted to continue her career working with him. And Clarence allowed that to happen and honestly never assumed that there was any problem with Anita Hill and all the other people he was employing and helping. He was an advocate against sexual harassment at EEOC. He was working on policies and disciplining employees that were crossing the line. So sexual harassment and Anita Hill was never something that he would have put together until the FBI was at our door saying that she was making accusations.

MP: What was your reaction to these allegations?
GT: I know the man. I know the people in his life. I know his character. I know his nature. I know what he's like with everyone in our world, and everyone in the workplace. He has thousands of people that he interacts with. So to hear someone, one person, come from the dark recesses of her imagination and tell a tale about him that contradicts every other person's experience of my husband was highly offensive.

MP: One of the striking things in contrast with other sexual harassment charges is that there wasn't a pattern of harassment.
GT: There was no pattern of sexual misconduct in the workplace.

MP: The only one they ever found was Angela Wright, who didn't alleged sexual harassment, but she did allege inappropriate comments.[6]
GT: There were a few people that Clarence had fired or let go that started joining in with Anita Hill to say that there was some pattern. But honest to God, if you know what I know, the breadth of his life, the breadth of the people who worked with him, there was no pattern in his life of any sexual misconduct, and in fact he was an adamant proponent of fixing anything that was nefarious in the workplace.

MP: Then Anita Hill's statement was leaked to the press. How did you find out about that?
GT: When Nina Totenberg [of NPR] and probably Senator Howard Metzenbaum's staff were conspiring to get Anita Hill's story out into the public, it just took it to a whole other level of seriousness in the public's mind.

MP: The press were planted outside your home.
GT: The press outside were getting increasingly numerous. There were just a lot of them out there, and we lived in a very small lot in Alexandria, with a very short driveway, so you really couldn't come and go. I would be the pigeon and I'd make strategic ventures out for food. Neighbors were bringing food products by, really amazing things were coming. The mail was filled with people sending Bible verses, and positive things. People don't know how sustaining it can be to people in the midst of this to get words of encouragement, and Bible verses, from other people.

MP: Before Anita Hill's allegations were leaked to the press, Joe Biden said that he would be Justice Thomas's biggest defender.

GT: Joe Biden made it clear to both of us. I was on the phone listening to him talking to Clarence, that if the allegations came up, he would be Clarence's biggest defender. And having gone through the first round of hearings, having seen that he wasn't a man of his word, I took a spoon out of the cabinet, and kind of gagged myself in front of Clarence, because I just didn't believe that man anymore.

MP: Do you remember watching Anita Hill's press conference on October 7?
GT: When I saw the press conference, I was more worried because it looked like a story that could be sold and packaged and believed by more people than I expected, based on what he had told me their relationship was, so I could see there was a problem.

    Emotionally, he was at the end when he went for the first time to the Senate Judiciary Committee and got done with the hearings, and we were so glad that he was done. We couldn't ever imagine going back for any reason, much less this reason. So emotionally, I was now on full alert about whether my husband could do this physically.

MP: You've also mentioned in articles that you too were sexually harassed at work.
GT: I had been sexually harassed when I was at one of my early workplaces, and it was awful. I never named the person, and I never went to the H.R. department. But I could see that a story was being told that could resonate with many, many women in the workplace.

MP: In your case was it a physical assault?
GT: When I say I know what sexual harassment is, mine was physical, and was personal. Mine was someone above me in the line of command, taking advantage of a young girl in a very vulnerable place. It wasn't like saying that there is pubic hair on a Coke can. That's not

sexual harassment, and anyone who says that it is degrades the notion of sexual harassment for others in the workplace.

MP: You mentioned to me that Washington is a tough town for young women.

GT: For single women in Washington, in a professional setting at that point, I really thought that it was a sea of sharks. So I was glad to find the best man walking the face of the earth and to cling tightly to Clarence Thomas.

THE SECOND ROUND
"I DIDN'T KNOW HE HAD IT WITHIN HIM TO KEEP GOING"

MP: As you both are getting ready for the committee to convene again on Friday, October 11th, you arranged for Justice Thomas to have a haircut.

GT: Yes, I did. So . . . [voice breaks], he clearly needed a haircut. And our neighbor was a hairdresser. She came over, and at our kitchen table cut his hair to get him ready. But honestly, he was not in a good place. He was just really beaten up by the false charges. So it was just challenging.

MP: Justice Thomas has described the experiences as Kafka-esque, where suddenly you're charged with something that you don't even know exactly the charges, and you can't defend yourself and you can't prove a negative. How did it feel for you?

GT: For me it just felt like a nightmare... [voice breaks] because people were believing something so wrong, and so false about my husband. But somehow because of the prayers, and what we were doing from a spiritual point of view, it felt like a nightmare we were riding on a magic carpet through. It just felt like we were a little bit above the nightmare that was unfolding.

MP: When the Senate Judiciary Committee did decide to reconvene, Justice Thomas wanted the chance to clear his name. He believed it was necessary.
GT: He may have thought it was necessary to go back in front of the Senate, but honestly from his wife's point of view watching the man who is my loved, beloved husband, I didn't know he had it within him to keep going.

MP: Was it around this point that you form this prayer group too?
GT: It was during the Anita Hill time of the confirmation process. We brought in two families who were particularly devout Christians, and they helped us in our home, read through the Bible, find verses of relevance, and learn about spiritual warfare, and put on the armor of God, and bring the Holy Spirit into a very secular and political space because it felt like the demons were loose.

MP: Talk about the process of him preparing his opening statement.
GT: The clock was ticking when it was time for him to have a statement. And I honestly didn't know from watching him where that statement was going to come from inside of him. He always wrote his own stuff and did his own speeches. This was such a difficult experience, but the clock was ticking so he was trying to get his thoughts together. He was so tired.

He needed a nap, and he went up to take a nap. And when he came back down, we cleared the table. It was filled with paper on the kitchen table, and I told him, "You do one page, and I'll go type it." And so that's how we worked for as long as it took. He wrote in longhand on a yellow pad, and I would type it at the computer upstairs and bring it down until it was all done.

MP: This takes you into the wee hours of the morning.
GT: We were not conscious of whatever time of the day it was; we just were trying to get through hour by hour, to the point where we could be done with the Senate.

MP: And then you return to the hearing room. What's that like?
GT: When we came into the hearing room, honestly those senators looked very small to me, because I was very much in Clarence's space, in his corner. It was now the two of us against the world. I have to tell you from my perch behind him, I was just watching the senators and feeling rage towards them. And I especially focused on Senator Kennedy, and the things that I knew he had done in his life, and the nerve of any of this to come out against a man like I know and I love. And I probably had the wrath of anger coming out of my eyes, because that's what I felt protecting my husband, and seeing how they were mistreating him, and how Anita Hill was telling lies about him.

MP: And then, after his opening statement and some arguing between the Senators on how to proceed, Justice Thomas was dismissed by the committee and Anita Hill was brought forward to testify.
GT: When Clarence was done, we went home. He had to rest, he had to sleep if he could. I was the one that tried to watch what was going on for as long as I could, and it looked bad. It looked like it could be credible. She was painting a compelling picture and yet coming up with different iterations from what we had been told her allegations were, so it was growing. Someone had worked with her, or she had found new aspects of her story that she was putting out there.

MP: Did Justice Thomas watch any of her testimony?
GT: Clarence couldn't watch any of it.

MP: And what did he say when you told him about her testimony?
GT: Well, as she got more specific, it gave him comfort that it couldn't be true. He had been racking his brain—was there something he inadvertently said that was misunderstood? But as soon as the details started coming out, then it oddly gave him more comfort, since he knew it wasn't true. This was a set of lies.

MP: Were you shocked in any way by Long Dong Silver and talking about the size of his penis and all these things she said he said?
GT: Honestly, it was a nightmare to hear about any of her charges, whether it was the pubic hair on the Coke can or Long Dong Silver. It was all jarring. It was all so wrong. It was so shocking. And I'm sure America was tuning in to C-SPAN, and it was horrendous because it was so untrue.

There was a group of people who sidled up to Anita Hill and took her off and prepared her for testimony. I don't know where she got the new facts she alleged, contrary or beyond what she told the FBI.[7] So it didn't surprise me later on to find that there were various law cases that talked about some of the things that she talked about, whether it's Long Dong Silver or whatever.

MP: What was the effect on people watching the hearings on C-SPAN rather than watching snippets on the nightly news?
GT: C-SPAN was the best ally for all of us on this side of the world because people were able to absorb the whole hearing and hear it unfiltered from the media propagandists that are so everywhere now.

MP: The Republican senators questioned many inconsistencies in Anita Hill's story. What was your response?

GT: Honestly, I didn't listen. We were, again, just trying to survive and we assumed, that there were others that were part of the battle, so to speak.

I appreciated anyone who was able to bat down this, as well as the other things that were coming out of the darkness at Clarence. There was an army of people trying to help him. And all I was trying to do was keep him upright.

MP: The media and left had attacked him for many years on affirmative action and other issues. But these Anita Hill charges were of a different kind.

GT: This was a kill shot. We could feel it. So, they were coming to destroy my husband, not just discredit him or differ with his point of view. This was the kill shot.

MP: What was his state of mind?

GT: Once it got so bad, he knew he couldn't pull away. He was going to go through with it to make sure that they didn't take his reputation away. He was in it for the long term, but it's not like he coveted the job.

MP: Did he think about his grandfather's saying: "Stand up for what you believe in"?

GT: Whenever anything got hard in his life, he would go back to his grandfather's sayings [voice breaks], and his grandfather's foundational tips for life that were commonsensical and steadying, and important to him as a man. That's where he really gets his strength.

A HIGH-TECH LYNCHING
"CLARENCE, IF THAT'S WHAT YOU THINK, SAY IT"

MP: Anita Hill's testimony ends late in the day. Then Justice Thomas goes to Senator Danforth's office, sleeps there for a bit, and then he tries to pull his thoughts together. What's that moment like?
GT: After Clarence has given as much as I thought he was humanly able to do, he was in Senator Danforth's office taking a nap on the couch, and the lights were low, and Senator Danforth came over and sat next to him. I was across from the two of them. Clarence got up and said, "Jack, this feels like a high-tech lynching." And Jack said, "Clarence, if that's what you think, say it. That's exactly what you should say." So Clarence was encouraged by Jack to be as authentic and genuine as he could be in this final chapter of this ordeal. And that's what happened. Senator Danforth was a friend, a priest, a mentor, and a colleague. And he knew what was going on. So as somebody that knew Clarence's best interest, and Clarence as a human being, that was his advice.

MP: Was Justice Thomas working with the White House handlers at this point?
GT: Most of their handlers were discordant voices during the end of this confirmation process to Clarence. They were a disappointment in some ways. It just wasn't working with us, with Clarence. He was in a different place. He was trying to survive. And it was very personal, and it was also very religious, and so Jack Danforth was the perfect man in all of his life to help him, being a senator and a priest. It was just what my husband needed at that time.

We saw it as a spiritual battle from a certain point onward. And that's the only way we could get through. We didn't want to talk politics or hear any political advice from friends or people who were trying to help.

MP: So then Justice Thomas goes back again into the hearing room at night to respond to Hill's allegations.
GT: You know, Clarence and I, [voice breaks] even at that early point in our marriage, we were, "Two became one." And so as I sat there, I had all sorts of emotions and rage really about what these people were doing to my husband. As I watched him, I was watching for their reaction to his words because I was so with him in everything he was doing.

When your loved one goes through a battle, and it's unfair and it's so personal, and they're touching on things that only you know about your husband, you're hurting me too. You're in my world, you're in my bedroom, and I hated what they were doing.

When Clarence gave the high-tech lynching speech, I knew how little of my husband was sitting in front of me. [voice breaks] And I knew that God was with him because I knew he wasn't doing that on his own, because I knew how weak he was at that point.

MP: What was your reaction to his saying this was a "high-tech lynching"?
GT: When Clarence called it a "high-tech lynching," he said that because they were doing anything they could to kill this man. He had no wealth, he had nothing else but his reputation. This was a murder. This was a defamation and a murder attempt. And so he called it a "high tech lynching," and that harkened back to what happened to blacks in the South when you got out of line as a black man. And he was right.

Black conservatives have a whole different level of vitriol put on them. They become social outcasts to people who are expected to be your friends, your allies, your kind. It's ostracizing. It hurts. But Clarence's grandfather told him that whatever he believes, he's got to be his own man against whatever odds come up in his life. So that's what he was, but that doesn't mean it didn't hurt.

MP: He did say in that very statement that they're taking away his reputation. There's no way to get it back.
GT: Clarence Thomas has been hounded by his adversaries all his life. I love what Shelby Steele calls him, "The freest black man in America,"[8] because he has kept to his ideals despite pressure. He is a man true to his own convictions, and his grandfather would be proud of him.

MP: He has said he felt let down by the institutions that were supposed to protect him.
GT: So much time has passed now. You end up realizing that a lot of people go through injustices, and things that shouldn't happen. You learn how to deal with that in different ways, but you just have to not dwell on it. I have to say years later it's hard to go back to that place because I wasn't as wise and capable. I was just angry and afraid that my husband was at the end of his life.

MP: Did you watch the rest of the hearings?
GT: I was not watching the rest of the hearings, Clarence wasn't watching. Honestly, we were done at that point. So whatever was going to happen was going to happen.

I didn't see the group of women testify in the middle of the night on Clarence's behalf.[9] That was my favorite panel, though, because it depicted the truth about his life and what he was like in the workplace and in his life. People who could have been taken advantage of, and women who worked with him closely, they saw the real Clarence Thomas, and they saw that he was offended by sexual harassment and inappropriate behavior in the workplace—he's just a good man.

They made these women testify in the middle of the night. I'm sure most Americans didn't see this clarifying, fortifying, edifying, panel that was filled with people from the left and the right who had worked with him, and there could have been hundreds more.

MP: Many of those women were not conservative, and more than one had experienced sexual harassment herself—Janet Brown, I think.
GT: The panel of women from the left and right, people who knew him a long time and a short time. Janet Brown, who worked for Senator Danforth and was a colleague of Clarence's, experienced sexual harassment, and went to Clarence as a big brother to support her and buck her up, and to sustain her at the worst point of her life.

MP: The White House staff or Ken Duberstein must have told you that in fact public opinion was turning. Did you hear that?
GT: You know, we were not inclined to care about public opinion one way or another, whether they believed him, or whether they didn't. We were in a place just trying to get through hour by hour, and day by day.

MP: He has described it as hell, those days.
GT: It was hell. It was a hellish time. We didn't care about anything but surviving.

MP: And where were you when you found out he had been confirmed?
GT: We were emotionally drained and just hanging out at the house. So, when the vote happened, someone who worked with me called and told me that he won. And I went and told Clarence, and he was in a bathtub. I gave him the count and he said, "Whoop-dee-damn-doo." Because that's where we were. It was just getting through ritual defamation, the lies, the process, some institutions that had let

us down, and allegations that came from the depths of hell. He had gone through a war and he was still in pretty bad shape. But at least he got in, which is more than Bob Bork experienced when he went through his battle.

MP: Must have taken many years to recover from that intense and horrific experience.
GT: False allegations can cast a pall over anyone's life, and especially someone who has nothing but his reputation. But we've both processed it as well as possible, so that you can function. You watch false allegations all around you, and you have a certain sympathy for the victims, and perhaps a refinement that makes you stronger for the bad things that happen in your life.

MP: What do you think motivated Anita Hill?
GT: I don't really know why Anita Hill did what she did. We may never know what Anita Hill's motivation was. Maybe she's just a liberal activist who wanted to bring him down and wanted to help her allies, ideologically. I don't know her motivation, but she's living a lie. And at some point, lies catch up with liars.

A lot of people don't know the specifics of the allegations Anita Hill leveled against my husband. They were words that offended her, she said, and she built it into more. But it was never where Harvey Weinstein or Bill Clinton or Matt Lauer took sexual harassment or the things that happened in my life.

But I do live in hopes that one day she will explain why because Clarence did everything he could to help her professionally and personally. I'm hoping one day it becomes obvious why she did, or that she asks for forgiveness. That's why I did call her one time to leave a message. I do hope that one day this personal cloud over Clarence's life could be lifted by her.

MP: We were talking about Anita Hill's motivations. At the time you thought maybe she was in love with Justice Thomas. Do you no longer think that?
GT: There's a very good shot that she was interested in my husband romantically at some point, and that now it's just evolved into her liberal cause.

I know as somebody who experienced sexual harassment myself that the last thing you do is follow the perpetrator job to job. The last thing you do is to call them to congratulate them on their wedding or seek professional help from them. And Anita Hill's story kept changing. I can tell you as his wife, and the women in his life professionally and personally know, that she was telling a lie. He is a man who treats women with the utmost respect and dignity. The lies were told about something that was allegedly said in the workplace, and it continues to cast a pall over a good man. And it really hurts, I have to say.

MP: It hurts now, but it must have been even more painful twenty-six years ago.
GT: As the lies were being told about my husband, it was very hard to go live your life and realize that a lot of people were going to believe a lie about my husband. So learning to live with a lie being cast about my husband about a very private aspect of our life, it took me years to really overcome what that felt like. It certainly puts me in touch with others who have felt injustice and false accusations in their life.

MP: Does it bother you now that Anita Hill is back? In some ways these charges are out there again uncontested.
GT: Institutions let us down, whether it was journalism, or whether it was the Senate. There was truth to be found and the truth is that she was telling a lie and now she's back again. What she even alleges was mere dirty talking in a workplace, that was not what Harvey

Weinstein did. It was not what Bill Clinton did, or Matt Lauer did. So I'm appalled that she has the capacity to rise up again in any social movement in our country and be a credible force.

THE SUPREME COURT
"CLARENCE'S JURISPRUDENCE IS COURAGEOUS"

MP: What was the White House swearing-in ceremony like?
GT: When Clarence got sworn in, it was a beautiful day on the South Lawn at the White House that was a gift from God. President Bush and Mrs. Bush were delightful and welcoming and gracious to all family members, many more family members than we ever knew existed until that day at the White House. And it was great. It was just a wonderful capstone of a very difficult time for both of us, but especially Clarence.

MP: I've seen footage of Justice Thomas's formal first walk down the steps of the Supreme Court.
GT: Every justice gets that opportunity to walk down the front steps of the Supreme Court. It's a beautiful moment. It's a ceremonial moment and it's a tradition that is very special. The justices all were so kind and so welcoming and so comforting as Clarence began his time inside that building.

MP: Justice Thomas is one of the few justices to have worked in all three branches of government.
GT: Clarence's wingspan from where he grew up, to all of his life experiences, to working in the executive branch, to working in the legislative branch for Jack Danforth, to working for a state attorney general. He just has a breadth of experience that's pretty unique, and wonderful for what he's doing.

MP: How would you describe his jurisprudence?

GT: Clarence's jurisprudence is courageous. It's independent. It's carefully crafted from his life experiences as a black man growing up in the South. But beyond that, he talks about his Catholic formation as putting him in concert a lot with Justice Scalia's Catholic formation and view of the world. Whether it's affirmative action, or the administrative state, or abortion, or guns, or just the way the separation of powers in our country works, or the way that the Court interprets the Constitution, either in line with the Founding or an expansive version, all of that comes from his life experience and what he knows hurts from an expanded, aggressive government.

MP: How does his personal experience affect his views on the race cases?

GT: Clarence's view of race is that somewhere things started going wrong in our country where we took race into too great of an account. We started only looking at the superficial, immutable characteristics of people, not treating them as individuals and it's easy to do for policy makers. But there are long-term devastating consequences for individuals, and somebody has to start saying, "Wait, stop. There is something going wrong with our policy." And I love that my husband has had that courage.

MP: What was his response to affirmative action at Yale Law School during his time there?

GT: Clarence put a fifteen-cents sticker on his Yale law degree certificate because he found when he started looking for a job after he went through the work of Yale Law School, that people were thinking he was only brought into Yale because of his skin color. And they didn't credit his achievements, his accomplishments, his work. And so when he saw that, he understood more dramatically the dangers of affirmative action. It wasn't just a theoretical issue, and it didn't even help people that it's supposed to help. It was harming him in a very tangible way. And that's why that certificate stays in our basement with a fifteen-cents sticker on it in the bathroom.

MP: Justice Thomas refers in his *Grutter* dissent to the desire of the University of Michigan law school to have diversity as an "aesthetic consideration." They wanted to look a certain way, rather than really help anybody.
GT: Clarence sees that universities and others are sprinkling people around into classrooms by skin color as a social experiment, not really caring about the individual and what they might be feeling or experiencing or needing in their personal life to succeed.

His Law Clerks
"Clarence Picks Clerks in a Very Different Way"

MP: Justice Thomas is well known to have a special relationship with his law clerks.
GT: His clerks are his joy in life. He loves the four clerks that he gets every year. It's beyond a year's experience. It becomes a lifetime relationship, as they ask him for guidance in their career, and look up to him for advice on decisions in their life. And it's a joy for us to have hundreds of young people and now middle-aged people, all former clerks, sprinkled around the country who are doing amazing things, both personally and professionally—judges, and teachers, and lawyers, and even housewives who are spending their time with their children. It's really exciting to watch what they're doing.

MP: How does Justice Thomas pick his clerks from outside Harvard, Yale, and the other top ten schools?

GT: Clarence picks clerks in a very different way. He has people that are watching for the best people, whether they're in schools, or other clerkships at the Court of Appeals level, certainly. And then there's former clerks who become vetters, so to speak. And then they get in to talk to him eventually and he's watching the chemistry, whether he likes them, whether they're a jerk or not, whether they're comfortable with other people who he's picking. And he always has such good taste because they're such good, nice people that you want to spend time with.

When Clarence started picking non–Ivy League clerks, some people would call them "third tier trash" and those clerks who were clerking for Clarence took it as a badge of honor, that they had to prove something if they were from Rutgers, Creighton, the University of Georgia, or B.Y.U. And they performed well. So he continued the practice of looking for people who are smart all over the country, not just the Ivy Leagues.

Clarence also likes finding clerks that come from disadvantaged backgrounds. So if they've had middle class, working class families, where this is something amazing that one of the children has been succeeding in college and law school, and getting to be a clerk, that's an affirmative action hire for Clarence, because there are people who appreciate how you can rise in America.

MP: What is it like being a Thomas clerk?
GT: Justice Byron White told Clarence early on to get a system, and the system that Clarence ended up getting is seemingly different from a lot of other justices. All four clerks are engaged with all cases. Instead of giving one clerk one case, and being siloed in that way, they have to edit each other, they have to discuss and debate each other, and it becomes the five of them working through every single case that he has on his plate. So it is a different clerkship, and they all come away appreciating the humbling ability to be edited by other people who are also smart.

MP: **Many have recently gone into the Trump administration. That must be satisfying at some level, too.**

GT: Since President Trump has become president, there's been a number of Thomas clerks that have been elevated to the bench. Thank God. Also, there are many throughout the Justice Department and in the White House Counsel's Office, the Treasury Department, the Transportation Department. It's really exciting to watch. He used to tell them, you're going to be future leaders, it's coming your way, you're going to be next. And now they are.

MP: **How does he stay in touch with former clerks?**

GT: He has lunch with his former clerks monthly, if they're in the D.C. area. We're going to a retreat this summer out in Utah with their families and with all of them. There's a lot of connective tissue between and across the years of the clerkships. So people that clerked in '91 may call on people who clerked in 2017 for advice on moving to a state, or getting a new job, or going to teach in a law school. It's very exciting what the Thomas clerk network has become.

I have put a directory together so they can find each other. I send emails that show who's having a baby, who's getting married, their jobs that have changed, so I get to watch some of the social interactions and help build that connective tissue across the years.

THE COURT FAMILY
"THE TIMES THAT YOU SHARE WITH THESE PEOPLE THAT SOME ONLY KNOW THROUGH HISTORY BOOKS"

MP: **You told me once that Justice Scalia said that Justice Thomas was more an originalist than he was.**

GT: Justice Scalia called Clarence a "bloodthirsty originalist." He took that as a compliment.

MP: What do you think Justice Scalia meant?
GT: There were times when Justice Scalia and Clarence would have disagreements over different things, maybe *stare decisis*, things that Clarence was more willing to go back and revisit than Nino was.

MP: He also had a great friendship with Justice Scalia.
GT: Justice Scalia and Clarence were like brothers. They had a very warm and wonderful relationship, as can happen up there when you're working with people that you tend to agree with so much. A very close relationship. We really miss Nino.

MP: What are his relationships with the other justices like?
GT: He has a great relationship with all the others, whether it's Steve Breyer or Ruth Ginsburg. I mean it crosses ideology because they're working on so many things that are not ideological all the time. They're just people working together in the same place.

MP: It seems like he has a good relationship with Justice Gorsuch, the newest justice.
GT: Yes, Neil Gorsuch has become a real friend. Sam Alito has been a wonderful friend, even probably closer since Nino has passed away.

MP: Do you get together with them in groups? Do you see their wives and families?
GT: The Supreme Court family is a special one. Everybody's different, and living in their own world, but we have spouse lunches quarterly, or as many as you can gather on the day and we help host, some of us. There are parties when people join the Court, when they're retiring. I still remember there was one time that we did a conga line when Justice Blackmun was retiring. We were all in one of the rooms, and after dinner there was entertainment. It is amazing thinking back

on the times that you share with these people that some only know through history books.

MP: I heard Justice Thomas was particularly close to Justice White in the beginning. Is that right?
GT: Justice White was particularly warm and said to Clarence, "Everything that happened on the outside is over; now you're here. This is where you'll determine the next part of your life." That was characteristic of Byron and Marion White, who were completely wonderful, welcoming, gracious, and made us feel at home with them.

TRAVELS IN THE RV
"WE JUST PREFER, BOTH OF US, BEING IN AMERICA"

MP: You and Justice Thomas travel in the summer in an RV. How did that come to be?
GT: One of Clarence's biggest loves is when he can get away from Washington, D.C., and be on the road in his motor home, our bus. We found motor homing years ago, probably twenty years ago, through a friend who said, "You're flying over the best parts of the country, Clarence. Here's how you could do it differently." And he showed him motor homing and gave him some catalogs that are readily available. And eventually Clarence found the one he wanted in Phoenix, Arizona. And we got it. And we've done probably thirty-eight states now, over nineteen years. And he loves being out on the road. He knows how to tinker with the machine if something's wrong. You meet different people who don't know who he is and what he does for work. I've heard him describe himself as a government lawyer to people who are neighbors in the campground.

MP: That runs so counter to what most of us think Supreme Court justices are doing in the summer, like jetting to the south of France or something.

GT: Some justices like to go the south of France, or other places in Europe, for the summer, or to go away and teach in a beautiful place. And we've done some of that too. We just prefer, both of us, being in America, in campsites, seeing friends across the country, seeing new places—beautiful parts of the country.

MP: Do you have any stories about RV living?

GT: When we first got the motor home in Phoenix, Sandra Day O'Connor had us stay overnight at her house. She gave us as a gift the Lucy and Desi Arnaz movie *The Long, Long Trailer* [a 1954 comedy about a newly married couple on a road trip with a car and a trailer].[10] She thought it would be highly appropriate as we launched from Phoenix, near her house. It was our first day really driving, and we hit snow in the mountains in New Mexico, and cars were on the side of the road and Clarence was just going carefully up, with forty feet of all of this bus behind him, up this road and this really bad weather where it was treacherous. We put on the CB radio and we heard truckers behind saying, "Who is that stage coach up front of us?" And we were just doing everything we could to stay on the road. Fortunately, we made it through our first day of driving, but we had every piece of weather that God could throw at us.

There was one time when we were driving in New York, to upstate New York, along [Interstate] 87 by Lake George and suddenly on a busy highway, the red light came on and the engine went down and it stopped. And Clarence pulled over to the side and I was like, "Uh-oh," and was getting ready for a long time sitting on the side of the road. And he got out of the driver's seat, and he went to the back of the bus on the outside. He came back inside. I was thinking of, "Who do I call for help?" He turned on the key, and it went. He said,

"It was just a fan belt. I had an extra one." I said, "No justice could do what you just did." He is a tinkerer. He knows how to mechanically fix things that go wrong, often with motor homes or big equipment like that. It's a rolling condominium, it's got a TV for him watching sports, and a TV for me watching public affairs. We've got enough room to cater to all tastes and it's a great life.

MP: Are there any encounters you had with people at RV campsites that come to mind?
GT: Last summer, we were in a campground in Michigan. There was a man who kept coming by with his pet and noticed that Clarence was a Nebraska fan. One day when we were sitting near a campfire at our bus, he came up and started ribbing Clarence about Nebraska football, and Clarence would rib him back about his team. And this continued and it was a really fun, interesting exchange. And I've never seen Clarence do this, but at the end when we were leaving, he took one of his pieces of Court stationery and wrote a note to the guy and put it in his mailbox on the way out so that he knew later what Clarence's job was, and who he was fiddling around with. It was kind of fun.

MP: Justice Thomas seems to relate to the ordinary men and women of America.
GT: Clarence can find what piques someone's interest, what they're good at. He listens for what's their passion and he listens well, and that's a gift to him and to anyone who comes in contact with him because he'll give you the time, he'll find what's fascinating, and he'll be fascinated by what you're fascinated by.

MP: It seems to me he still thinks of himself as one of them, one of the regular people of America, not so much an elite, even though clearly he is very distinguished.

GT: When you're Clarence Thomas, when you refer to the Litany of Humility after every Mass, you're constantly trying to not put on a cloak of elite righteous arrogance that can often come in Washington D.C., in the halls of the Supreme Court, or any powerful place where decisions are made. When we go out into the country, it fills his sails and reminds him of what's really going on beyond what he reads every day for casework.

MP: He often says that his grandfather was the greatest man he knew. His grandfather clearly was poor and had a third grade education, so maybe that leads Justice Thomas to feel wisdom can come from that kind of person.
GT: That's very intuitive. I never thought about it like that. But if you really believe that every human being has value, and is worth listening to, you listen to them. Clarence's grandfather is the perfect example of an anchor in his life that was not seen by the elites as having value because he had such poor education. He was illiterate. But for Clarence, the wisdom from that man and the experience, and the way he lived his life, did make him the greatest man in his life. So he has a natural capacity to hear more than most of us do from regular people.

MP: What's a typical day for you and Justice Thomas?
GT: Clarence is a wonderful best friend to be married to. I think he should give brown bag lunches for other spouses, actually. When it's birthday time, or anniversary time, or Valentine's Day, he will spend hours at the Hallmark store going through every card to see what he can pick and bring home. And he hides—we probably hide twenty cards around the house for each other on such days where it's just a joyous place. It's a loving, happy, laughing kind of place where he comes up with names for me and makes fun of me in a loving way. We have lots of friends in our life. Our faith is important to us. He reads a lot. My world is very political and activist. His world is very

legal and, to me, kind of boring. So it's just different lives coming together, but all under a roof of such warmth and love.

MP: It is wonderful to hear him speak of you. He always says you're the center of his life.
GT: I think he's the best man walking the face of the earth, okay, let's just be clear. But what happened when we came together? I feel like he stretches me. He makes me wiser. He makes me a better Christian. For him, I guess I fill gaps that he has. I don't know what I do for him, but I'm really happy that it's worked this way because it's been thirty-one years almost, and it just gets better with time as we get to know each other and have memories together.

MP: You mentioned his reading. I've been struck in talking to him that he takes on a subject and then reads everything about it.
GT: He goes on journeys of reading that are beyond the wife. You'll have to ask him more about his reading. He likes any Nebraska sports especially. He used to be Oklahoma affiliated, but then at the wedding altar in Nebraska, he shifted allegiances and ever since we were married, he's been a very good Nebraska advocate. It's RVs, sports, reading, a lot of friends, a lot of laughter. That's what makes our life sing.

MP: You mentioned earlier the prayer for humility. What is it and how does he use it?
GT: The Litany of Humility is a Catholic prayer. I don't know when he started using it, but I've certainly noticed every time he takes Communion, he'll pull it out and reflect on it. It just helps him not focus on what praise might come his way, what criticism might come his way, to cast off what other people think, and instead focus on what God wants him to do in his job on that day, in that week in his life.

MP: There surely is a shortness of humility in this city.
GT: Yeah, he should send it around to others, I think.

A CONTINUED, RELENTLESS ASSAULT
"THEY REALLY DON'T LIKE CLARENCE THOMAS"

MP: Over the last twenty-six years of his time on the court, there's been a continued, relentless assault on Justice Thomas.
GT: Yes. Certainly, the left is relentless at driving a narrative. During all the time that my husband has been trying to be just a justice, there are people working feverishly at building the narrative and telling a story the way they want it to be told. It happened to Ronald Reagan, it happened to many conservatives. They really don't like black conservatives. They really don't like Clarence Thomas. They really don't like his jurisprudence and his ideology. So they do anything through movies, through arguments, through articles, through attacks to drive their narrative. America has to just see it for what it is. It's an ideological battle going on through journalists and through the culture.

MP: You, too, also get attacked.
GT: There have been efforts to take me down based on the things that I have been doing ever since I was in my twenties, before I met Clarence. I've been a pretty political person, and it is what I've been doing, as my mother's daughter. They've tried to stop me from being an advocate for issues that I care about in the public square. But it works out. There've been other judges who have had spouses in the political sphere and who have run for office—Ed Rendell was head of the Democrat National Committee and his wife was on the Third Circuit.[11] So it happens, it's just not supposed to happen for conservatives.

OUTREACH AND LEGACY
"CLARENCE WANTS TO DO HONOR TO HIS GRANDFATHER"

MP: It's about ten years ago that he chose to write his memoir, *My Grandfather's Son*. Why did he do that and what was that process like?

GT: Writing Clarence's memoirs was really challenging, very hard for him. It took so much time and so much thought, and he put everything into it. He was doing research into newspapers of different times, and in many places that could remind him and refresh his memory as he thought through different phases of his life. It was new, it was challenging, it was all-consuming, and he vowed he would never write another book after he got done because it was so hard. But I'm glad he did it. He was probably under pressure from me and other people who love him to get the story down so that others could see that only in America could you rise from where he began to where he is now.

MP: People have no idea that he speaks to a lot of outside groups and especially ones that focus on young people, like the Horatio Alger Association.[12] Why does he do it?

GT: My husband really comes alive when he talks to disadvantaged kids, and that happens every year for the Horatio Alger Association, which he was fortunately inducted into in '92. And it's become a place that honors and respects the paths that disadvantaged people can take in America to success later in life, and so we love that organization. He spends so much of his time with those kids. I'm sure he busts up the schedule that they have for these kids who come to Washington because he'll take every question. He thinks that the longer he can stay with them, some of them will find more courage to approach him with whatever is really inside of their heart. He says the thing that he's asked most frequently is, "How did you do this without a father?" Because fatherless children really still need something that substitutes for that anchor in their life and they're asking him, begging him for answers to that and many other things that only he can impart to people also struggling.

The interactions Clarence has with kids are numerous now, it started right after he got on the Court—they come to the Court or when he goes to campuses. He'll spend time with the black students at a college, and they never protest. The protests seemed to come from a couple of faculty who are working with outside people, but maybe that'll change. But honestly, the black students and Clarence, they have very special conversations, and it's magical.

MP: That would be black students of any political persuasion, I'm assuming.
GT: He's had great success talking with black students and any students across the ideological divides because he listens well and once he really hears them, he responds to whatever they're asking. He helps them grow from wherever they are, when they first meet him into something beyond.

People are surprised by that when they come to visit him. They are used to members of Congress who may have ten or fifteen minutes, and often times Clarence will end up spending two or three hours with a person or their family. It's a constant refrain I hear.

MP: Do you think that he has lived up to his grandfather's values and realized them in his life?
GT: I so wish his grandfather was still alive to be proud of who he raised, and who he created, and who is serving our country, and who is blessing my life. He would love our home. Clarence often talks

about his appreciation for modern appliances, like dishwashers, and it comes from what he didn't have early on. And so it's this wingspan that he has that has taken him from so much he didn't have to everything that he has today.

MP: What do you think that his legacy will be?
GT: His legacy will be multi-pronged. His clerks that are out there moving around knowing how to have courage in the public square, how to be independent, principled in whatever they're doing. Some will view his jurisprudence as beacons in a dark world. But everyone who knows him will take various lessons of how to be a good friend, how to be a good person, how to be a good Christian. And I certainly know I have the best husband.

MP: How do you think he wants to be remembered?
GT: Clarence wants to do honor to his grandfather, and he hopes that when he gets to heaven that his grandfather and others would say, "Well done."

THE LITANY OF HUMILITY

Lord Jesus, Meek and humble of heart, *Hear me.*

From the desire of being esteemed, *Deliver me, Jesus.*

From the desire of being loved, *Deliver me, Jesus.*

From the desire of being extolled, *Deliver me, Jesus.*

From the desire of being honored, *Deliver me, Jesus.*

From the desire of being praised, *Deliver me, Jesus.*

From the desire of being preferred to others, *Deliver me, Jesus.*

From the desire of being consulted, *Deliver me, Jesus.*

From the desire of being approved, *Deliver me, Jesus.*

From the fear of being humiliated, *Deliver me, Jesus.*

From the fear of being despised, *Deliver me, Jesus.*

From the fear of suffering rebukes, *Deliver me, Jesus.*

From the fear of being calumniated, *Deliver me, Jesus.*

From the fear of being forgotten, *Deliver me, Jesus.*

From the fear of being ridiculed, *Deliver me, Jesus.*

From the fear of being wronged, *Deliver me, Jesus.*

From the fear of being suspected, *Deliver me, Jesus.*

That others may be loved more than I, *Jesus, grant me the grace to desire it.*

That others may be esteemed more than I, *Jesus, grant me the grace to desire it.*

That, in the opinion of the world, others may increase and I may decrease, *Jesus, grant me the grace to desire it.*

That others may be chosen and I set aside, *Jesus, grant me the grace to desire it.*

That others may be praised and I unnoticed, *Jesus, grant me the grace to desire it.*

That others may be preferred to me in everything, *Jesus, grant me the grace to desire it.*

That others may become holier than I, provided that I may become as holy as I should, *Jesus, grant me the grace to desire it.*

—Rafael Cardinal Merry del Val[1]

ACKNOWLEDGEMENTS

The authors, together, want to thank, first and foremost, Clarence and Ginni Thomas, without whom, quite obviously, this book would not exist. We appreciate their trust and cooperation throughout what they both hoped would be a much shorter and easier process. Leonard Leo has been essential to the both the film and the book, lending his support from behind the scenes, consistently and patiently. James Rosen, Greg Mueller, Erik Jaffe, and Brandon Stras reviewed the manuscript at various stages; we are grateful for their sensitive suggestions, careful edits, and overall advice. Brandon also was very helpful on running down facts and citation checking, and he was always ready to work at a moment's notice. Elizabeth Kantor and Laura Spence Swain, our editors at Regnery Publishing, were everything editors should be but seldom are these days. Needless to say, all the final decisions on what to include and how to organize the books are ours alone.

Michael Pack would like to thank his wife, not only for her enthusiasm for the book, but also for her dedicated work on the film. He also wants to thank all those who helped craft the film, which included the interviews that form the basis of this book, and also the donors to this project, without whose generous support neither the film nor the book would have been possible. Readers who want to watch, or re-watch, *Created Equal: Clarence Thomas in His Own Words*, should visit ManifoldProductions.com, which includes links to the platforms currently streaming the film.

Mark Paoletta would like to thank his wife, Tricia, and their children, who were steadfast in their support and encouragement of this book.

NOTES

Chapter One: Childhood Years

1. The Baltimore Catechism was the national Catholic school text of Catholic doctrinal teaching in use from the 1880s to the 1960s. "Baltimore Catechism," Wikipedia, https://en.wikipedia.org/wiki/Baltimore_Catechism.

2. St. Benedict the Moor Catholic School in Savannah, Georgia, served the black community during segregation. The school opened in 1907 and closed in 1969 at the time of integration. "St. Benedict the Moor Catholic Church: Mother Church of Black Catholics in Georgia," Georgia Historical Society, June 16, 2014, https://georgiahistory.com/ghmi_marker_updated/st-benedict-the-moor-catholic-church/.

3. Pin Point, eleven miles southeast of Savannah, Georgia, was settled in 1896 by former slaves from Ossabaw, Green, and Skidaway Islands. "Pin Point Community," Georgia Historical Society, June 16, 2014, https://georgiahistory.com/ghmi_marker_updated/pin-point-community/.

4. Ossabaw Island lies approximately twenty miles south of Savannah, Georgia. "Island Overview," Ossabaw Island Foundation, https://ossabawisland.org/island_overview/.

5. Henry Mercer (music) and Johnny Mercer (lyrics), "Moon River" (RCA Victor, 1962), sung by Audrey Hepburn.

6. "The Gullah Geechee people are descendants of Africans who were enslaved on the rice, indigo and Sea Island cotton plantations of the lower Atlantic coast.... Gullah Geechee is a unique creole language spoken in the coastal areas of North Carolina, South Carolina, Georgia and Florida." "The Gullah Geechee People," The Gullah Geechee Cultural Heritage Corridor Commission, https://gullahgeecheecorridor.org/thegullahgeechee/.

7. Harper Lee and Horton Foote, *To Kill a Mockingbird*, directed by Robert Mulligan (Universal Pictures, 1962). The film starred Gregory Peck as Atticus Finch and is based on the 1960 Pulitzer Prize–winning novel of the same name by Harper Lee.

8. Myers Anderson's grandmother was Annie Allen, who was born in 1850 or 1851 into slavery in Liberty County, Georgia, and died in 1924 at the age of seventy-four. Ken Foskett, *Judging Thomas: The Life and Times of Clarence Thomas* (New York: William Morrow, 2004), 34.

9. The nuns are the Missionary Franciscan Sisters of the Immaculate Conception, who ran St. Benedict's school. The order was founded in 1873 by Elizabeth Hayes. Among other missions, the Franciscan Sisters help the country's needy and poor. Marie Puleo, "Missionary Franciscan Sisters of the Immaculate Conception: How Did I Get Here?," *The Boston Pilot*, November 13, 2015, http://www.thebostonpilot.com/article.php?Source=Archives&ID=175210.

10. "It originally opened in 1914 as the Colored Carnegie Library, one of twelve segregated public libraries in the south funded by philanthropist Andrew Carnegie and one of the earliest African American public libraries in Georgia. It was added to the National Register of Historic Places in 1974. Though temporarily closed in the late 1990s, it reopened in 2006 after a major restoration and expansion project." Matthew Griffis, "East Henry Street Carnegie Library, Savannah, Georgia (1914–)," Black Past, February 12, 2018, https://www.blackpast.org/african-american-history/east-henry-street-carnegie-library-savannah-georgia-1914/.

11. Joe Archibald, *Crazy Legs McBain* (Philadelphia: Macrae Smith, 1961).

12. J. Edgar Hoover was director of the Federal Bureau of Investigation from 1935 to 1972.

13. The National Association for the Advancement of Colored People was formed in 1909 to advance civil rights in the United States. "NAACP," Wikipedia, https://en.wikipedia.org/wiki/NAACP.

14. *The Crisis* is the official magazine of the NAACP.

15. Harper Lee, *To Kill a Mockingbird* (Philadelphia: J. B. Lippincott & Co., 1960).

16. Harper Lee wrote *To Kill a Mockingbird*. She died in 2016.

17. Allison Schroeder and Theodore Melfi, *Hidden Figures*, directed by Theodore Melfi (20th Century Fox, 2016).

18. Peter Silverman and Robert Caswell, *Something the Lord Made*, directed by Joseph Sargent (Home Box Office, 2004).

19. Mark Brown, *Barbershop*, directed by Tim Story (MGM Distribution Co., 2002.)

20. "The war on poverty is the unofficial name for legislation first introduced by United States President Lyndon B. Johnson during his State of the Union address on January 8, 1964." "War on Poverty," Wikipedia, https://en.wikipedia.org/wiki/War_on_poverty.

Chapter Two: In the Seminary

1. A minor seminary is a high school seminary established and run by a Catholic diocese as a preparatory school for young men who have an interest in entering the seminary and becoming priests.

2. St. John Vianney Minor Seminary.

3. St. Pius X High School was the segregated school that Thomas attended his freshman year.

4. Robert Frost, "The Road Not Taken," *Mountain Interval* (New York: Henry Holt, 1916).

5. Otis Redding died on December 10, 1967, in a plane crash in Madison, Wisconsin, at the age of twenty-seven.

6. Otis Redding, "(Sittin' On) The Dock of the Bay" (Stax Records 1968).

Chapter Three: Radical Years

1. Simon & Garfunkel, "Homeward Bound" (Columbia Records, 1966).

2. President John F. Kennedy was assassinated on November 22, 1963, in Dallas, Texas.

3. Civil rights leader Martin Luther King Jr. was assassinated on April 4, 1968, in Memphis, Tennessee.

4. Robert F. Kennedy, a U.S. senator from New York who had been the sixty-fourth attorney general of the United States, was assassinated on June 6, 1968, at a presidential campaign appearance in California.

5. Michael Harrington, *The Other America* (New York: Macmillan Publishers, 1962).

6. Father John E. Brooks was a Jesuit priest who served as the twenty-eighth president of Holy Cross College, from 1970 until 1994. He died in 2012 at the age of eighty-eight.

7. Ralph Ellison, *Invisible Man* (New York: Random House, 1962).

8. Richard Wright, *Native Son* (New York: Harper & Brothers, 1940); Ayn Rand, *The Fountainhead* (Indianapolis, Indiana: Bobbs Merrill, 1943); Ayn Rand, *Atlas Shrugged* (New York: Random House, 1957).

9. Ayn Rand, *The Fountainhead*, directed by King Vidor (Warner Bros., 1949).

10. In the movie *The Fountainhead*, the character Howard Roark, who is an architect, states, after rejecting demands to change the design of his building, "I'd rather be a day laborer, if necessary" to support himself.

11. "What the Black Man Wants: An Address Delivered in Boston, Massachusetts, on 26 January 1865," reprinted in J. Blassingame and

J. McKivigan, eds., *The Frederick Douglass Papers: Volume 4, Series One: Speeches, Debates, and Interviews, 1864–80*, The Frederick Douglass Papers Series (New Haven, Connecticut: Yale University Press, 1991), 68.

12. Richard Wright, *Outsider* (New York: Harper & Brothers, 1953); Richard Wright, *Black Boy* (New York: Harper & Brothers, 1945).

13. Richard Sander and Stuart Taylor, *Mismatch: How Affirmative Action Hurts Students It's Intended to Help, and Why Universities Won't Admit It* (New York: Basic Books, 2012).

Chapter Four: Lessons from Yale Law School
1. George McGovern was the Democratic Party presidential nominee for president in 1972. He lost to President Nixon.

2. Thomas Sowell, *Black Education: Myths and Tragedies* (Philadelphia: David McKay Company, 1974).

3. Thomas Sowell, *Race and Economics* (Philadelphia: David McKay Company, 1975).

4. Thomas Sowell, *A Conflict of Visions: Ideological Origins of Political Struggles* (New York: William Morrow & Co., 1987).

5. Thomas Sowell, *Knowledge and Decisions* (New York: Basic Books, 1996).

6. Ernest Tidyman and John D. F. Black, *Shaft*, directed by Gordon Parks (Metro-Goldwyn-Mayer, 1971); Phillip Fenty, *Super Fly*, directed by Gordon Parks (Warner Bros. Pictures, 1972).

7. Doug Atchison, *Akeelah and the Bee*, directed by Doug Atchison (Lionsgate, 2006); Peter Silverman and Robert Caswell, *Something the Lord Made*, directed by Joseph Sargent (Home Box Office, 2004).

Chapter Five: Entering the Arena

1. Sidney Buchman, Lewis R. Foster, and Myles Connolly, *Mr. Smith Goes to Washington*, directed by Frank Capra (Columbia Pictures, 1939).

2. *The Fairmont Papers: Black Alternatives Conference, December 1980* (Institute for Contemporary Studies, 1981).

3. Juan Williams, "Black Conservatives, Center Stage," *Washington Post*, December 16, 1980, A21.

4. Thomas Sowell, "Blacker Than Thou," *Washington Post*, February 13, 1981, A19.

5. Thomas Sowell, "Blacker Than Thou (II)," *Washington Post*, February 14, 1981, A23.

6. Ernest Holsendolph, "Skills, Not Bias, Seen as Key for Jobs," *New York Times*, July 3, 1982, 5.

7. Juan Williams, "EEOC Chairman Blasts Black Leaders," *Washington Post*, October 25, 1984, A7.

Chapter Six: Birth of an Originalist

1. Pamela Talkin served as marshal for the U.S. Supreme Court from 2001 to 2020.

2. "Abraham Lincoln, Cong. Candidate, Ill., A Fragment on Slavery (1854)" in Joe Rubinfine & Ryan Lord, *Exceptional Manuscripts in the Harlan Crow Library*, 56 (2010).

3. Paul Johnson, *Modern Times: A History of the World from the 1920s to the 1980s* (London: Weidenfeld & Nicolson, 1983).

4. Allan Bloom, *The Closing of the American Mind: How Higher Education Has Failed Democracy and Impoverished the Souls of Today's Students* (New York: Simon & Schuster, 1987).

5. Ayn Rand, *Atlas Shrugged* (New York: Random House, 1957).

6. Ayn Rand, *The Fountainhead*, directed by King Vidor (Warner Bros., 1949).

7. William Roberts, *The Magnificent Seven*, directed by John Sturges (United Artists, 1960).

Chapter Seven: Supreme Court Nomination

1. Justice Thurgood Marshall, the first black Supreme Court justice, who was appointed by President Lyndon Johnson to the Court in 1967, announced his retirement from the Supreme Court on June 27, 1991.

2. In *Morrison v. Olson*, the Court concluded that it was constitutional for a three-judge panel to appoint an independent counsel. Justice Scalia dissented, arguing that this panel violated the Appointments Clause and the separation of powers. In his dissent, Justice Scalia wrote: "That is what this suit is about. Power. The allocation of power among Congress, the President, and the courts in such fashion as to preserve the equilibrium the Constitution sought to establish— so that 'a gradual concentration of the several powers in the same department,' *Federalist* No. 51, p. 321 (J. Madison), can effectively be resisted. Frequently an issue of this sort will come before the Court clad, so to speak, in sheep's clothing: the potential of the asserted principle to effect important change in the equilibrium of power is not immediately evident and must be discerned by a careful and perceptive analysis. But this wolf comes as a wolf." *Morrison v. Olson*, 487 U.S. 654, 699 (1988) (Scalia, J., dissenting).

3. Robert Bork, a distinguished professor of law at Yale Law School, former solicitor general of the United States, and a judge on the D.C. Circuit, was nominated by President Reagan to the Supreme Court in 1987, but the Senate rejected his nomination by a vote of 58–42.

4. Robert Bork, *The Tempting of America: The Political Seduction of Law*, 2nd ed. (New York: Free Press, 1990).

5. Michael Pertschuk and Wendy Schaetzel, *The People Rising: The Campaign against the Bork Nomination* (New York: Thunder's Mouth Press, 1989).

6. Franz Kafka, *The Trial* (Berlin: Verlag Die Schmiede, 1925).

7. The ABA Standing Committee on Federal Judiciary gave Thomas a mixed rating, with twelve voting to give him a "qualified" rating, two members giving him a "not qualified" rating and one member recusing. Saundra Torry, "ABA Panel Judges Thomas 'Qualified' for High Court," *Washington Post*, August 28, 1991.

8. The ABA's Standing Committee on Federal Judiciary gave Bork a mixed rating, with ten members giving Bork its highest rating, "well-qualified," four giving him a "not qualified" rating, and one voting "not opposed." Stuart Taylor, "A.B.A. Panel Gives Bork a Top Rating But Vote Is Split," *New York Times*, September 10, 1987, 1.

9. Ernest Holsendolph, "Skills, Not Bias, Seen as Key for Jobs," *New York Times*, July 3, 1982, 5.

10. At the time of Thomas's nomination, Democrats held a 57–43 majority in the Senate.

11. The Office of Legal Counsel (OLC) in the Department of Justice provides legal advice to the president and executive branch agencies. It is regarded as having some of the most accomplished attorneys in the area of constitutional law.

12. In *Roe v. Wade*, 410 U.S. 113 (1973), the Supreme Court held that the right to privacy includes a woman's right to an abortion.

13. In *Griswold v. Connecticut*, 381 U.S. 479 (1965), the Court held that prohibiting contraceptives violates the right to marital privacy.

14. "Nomination of Judge Clarence Thomas to Be Associate Justice of the Supreme Court of the United States: Senate Hearing 102-1084" (Washington, D.C.: Government Printing Office, 1991), part 1, 107–10, https://www.govinfo.gov/content/pkg/GPO-CHRG-THOMAS/pdf/GPO-CHRG-THOMAS-1.pdf.

15. Norman Whitfield and Barrett Strong, "Smiling Faces Sometimes," recorded by The Undisputed Truth (Motown Record Corporation, 1971).

16. Clarence Thomas, Speech before the Pacific Research Institute, August 10, 1987, reprinted in *Nomination of Judge Clarence Thomas to Be Associate Justice of the Supreme Court of the United States: Senate Hearing 102-1084* (Washington, D.C.: Government Printing Office, 1991), part 1, 150–67, https://www.govinfo.gov/content/pkg /GPO-CHRG-THOMAS/pdf/GPO-CHRG-THOMAS-1.pdf.

17. Senator Biden's question: "In the speech you gave in 1987 to the Pacific Research Institute you said, and I quote: 'I find attractive the arguments of scholars such as Stephen Macedo, who defend an activist Supreme Court that would'—not could, would—'strike down laws restricting property rights.' My question is a very simple one, Judge. What exactly do you find attractive about the arguments of Professor Macedo and other scholars like him." Id., 111. Later in the hearing, Senator Hatch read the entire Thomas quotation, which clearly showed Biden was taking it out of context to make it appear that Thomas was endorsing Macedo's position: "I find attractive the arguments of scholars such as Stephen Macedo, who defend an activist Supreme Court which would strike down laws restricting property rights. But the libertarian argument overlooks the place of the Supreme Court in the scheme of separation of powers. One does not strengthen self-government and the rule of law by having the nondemocratic branch of the government make policy." Id., 148.

Chapter Eight: Anita Hill

1. Lee Liberman Otis served as an associate counsel to the president in the Office of the White House Counsel from 1989 to 1993.

2. Anita Hill submitted a statement to the Senate Judiciary Committee on September 23. In her statement, Hill claimed that Thomas pressured her for dates, commented on her appearance in a sexual

way, and spoke with her in detail about pornographic films. Arlen Specter, *Passion For Truth: From Finding JFK's Single Bullet to Questioning Anita Hill to Impeaching Clinton* (New York: Perennial, 2001), 362–63.

3. Tim Phelps's *Newsday* story on Hill's allegations was published on the evening of October 5, and Nina Totenberg's interview with Anita Hill was broadcast on the morning of October 6.

4. After receiving Anita Hill's statement on September 23, the Senate Judiciary Committee made a request to the White House and DOJ that the FBI investigate Hill's allegations. The FBI interviewed Anita Hill on September 23, two former EEOC colleagues, Allyson Duncan and Nancy Fitch, on September 24, and Clarence Thomas on September 25. Neither Duncan nor Fitch corroborated Hill's allegations. Peter Fleming, "Report of Senate Special Counsel Peter Fleming on Leak of Anita Hill's Charges against Judge Clarence Thomas," http://anitahillcase.com/wp-content/themes/anita/pdf/Fl eming-Report.pdf. After receiving the FBI's summary of the interviews, Senator Biden decided to proceed with the committee's vote on Thomas's nomination. On September 27, 1991, the Senate Judiciary Committee, composed of eight Democrats and six Republicans, voted seven to seven on the nomination of Clarence Thomas. Senator Denis DeConcini of Arizona broke ranks with his fellow Democrats to join the six Republicans on the committee and vote for Thomas. The committee then voted to advance the nomination to the full Senate for consideration.

5. The full Senate was scheduled to vote on Thomas's nomination on October 8.

6. The Senate appointed Peter Fleming as special counsel to investigate the leak of Anita Hill's allegations. He did not determine who leaked the statement. *Report of the Temporary Special Independent Counsel* (Washington, D.C.: Government Printing Office, 1992), Document 102–20, May 13, parts 1 and 2. The report can be found at the website anitahillcase.com, a site created and maintained by

Mark Paoletta, http://anitahillcase.com/wp-content/themes/anita
/pdf/Fleming-Report.pdf.

7. Harper Lee and Horton Foote, *To Kill a Mockingbird*, directed by
    Robert Mulligan (Universal Pictures, 1962).

8. Juan Williams, "Open Season on Clarence Thomas," *Washington
    Post*, October 10, 1991, A23, https://www.washingtonpost.com/arch
    ive/opinions/1991/10/10/open-season-on-clarence-thomas/1126ce5b
    -c63c-447b-b496-545b198d4dcd/. Here is an excerpt from Williams's
    op-ed. "The phone calls came throughout September. Did Clarence
    Thomas ever take money from the South African government? ... Did
    he beat his first wife? Did I know anything about expense account
    charges he filed for out-of-town speeches? And finally, one exasperated
    voice said: 'Have you got anything on your tapes we can use to stop
    Thomas.' The calls came from staff members working for Democrats
    on the Senate Judiciary Committee.... The desperate search for
    ammunition to shoot down Thomas has turned the 102 days since
    President Bush nominated him for a seat on the Supreme Court into a
    liberal's nightmare. Here is indiscriminate, mean-spirited mudslinging
    supported by the so-called champions of fairness: liberal politicians,
    unions, civil rights groups and women's organizations. They have been
    mindlessly led into mob action against one man by the Leadership
    Conference on Civil Rights. Moderate and liberal senators, operating
    in the proud tradition of men such as Hubert Humphrey and Robert
    Kennedy, have allowed themselves to become sponsors of smear tactics
    that have historically been associated with the gutter politics of a Lee
    Atwater or crazed right-wing self-promoters like Sen. Joseph
    McCarthy."

9. Anita Hill held a press conference on October 7, 1991, at the
    University of Oklahoma Law School.

10. The Senate leadership agreed to postpone the full Senate vote on
    Thomas's nomination for one week, from October 8 to October 15.

11. The Senate Judiciary Committee reconvened hearings to consider Anita Hill's allegations beginning on October 11, 1991. The hearings ended on October 14 at 2:03 a.m.

12. Clarence Thomas appeared before the Committee and gave his opening statement. Before questioning by senators commenced, Chairman Biden announced that he would not allow senators to use the statement previously submitted by Anita Hill on September 23 to question Clarence Thomas. Senator Biden said Hill had requested confidentiality about her statement and "did not release the statement, she says, and she wants her story told by her." Senator Hatch objected to this restriction and said he intended to use Hill's statement in his questioning of Thomas, since it had been submitted to the Committee. If he could not use it, Hatch threatened to resign from the Committee. After some very tense exchanges, Senator Biden recessed the hearing to discuss this matter with Committee members outside the hearing format. Senator Biden reconvened the hearing, and despite his promise to allow Thomas to go first, he announced that Thomas would be excused and Anita Hill would testify first. Thomas would be called back to testify after Hill's testimony. *Nomination of Judge Clarence Thomas to Be Associate Justice of the Supreme Court of the United States: Senate Hearing 102-00* (Washington, D.C.: Government Printing Office, 1991), part 4, 27–29, https://www.gov info.gov/content/pkg/GPO-CHRG-THOMAS/pdf/GPO-CHRG -THOMAS-4.pdf.

13. Anita Hill's opening statement to the Senate Judiciary Committee on October 11 was significantly different from her original September 23 statement that she had submitted to the Senate Judiciary Committee and also from what she had told the FBI in her September 23 interview. In his memoirs, Senator Arlen Specter, the lead Republican Senator to question Anita Hill at the hearings, wrote that Hill's testimony at the hearing "was explosive—substantially expanded and different from her earlier statement to the Judiciary Committee and the FBI" and asked, "Why did Hill give one set of facts on September 23 and then a

different set on October [11]?"; Arlen Specter, *Passion For Truth: From Finding JFK's Single Bullet to Questioning Anita Hill to Impeaching Clinton* (New York: Perennial, 2001), 356–66.

14. Willi Münzenberg was a propagandist for the Communist Party of Germany in the 1920s who set up several front groups in the West. "Willi Münzenberg," Wikipedia, https://en.wikipedia.org/wiki/Wi lli_M%C3%BCnzenberg.

15. Joseph Goebbels was the chief propagandist for the Nazi Party. "Joseph Goebbels," Wikipedia, https://en.wikipedia.org/wiki/Jose ph_Goebbels.

16. A *New York Times*/CBS poll taken on October 13, after Thomas and Hill had testified, found that respondents believed Clarence Thomas by a margin of 58 percent–24 percent. There was no significant gender gap in the polling: Only 26 percent of women believed Hill more than Thomas, compared to 22 percent of men. Elizabeth Kolbert, "The Thomas Nomination: Most in National Survey Say Judge Is the More Believable," *New York Times*, October 15, 1991, 1.

17. Four witnesses testified on Anita Hill's behalf: Susan Hoerchner, Joel Paul, John Carr, and Ellen Wells. For more information on their testimony, see the website AnitaHillCase.com, created and maintained by Mark Paoletta.

18. Angela Wright was a political appointee at the EEOC during Thomas's tenure. According to Thomas, he fired her when she called a male colleague a "faggot." *Nomination of Judge Clarence Thomas to Be Associate Justice*, part 4, 254. See also Mark Paoletta, "Anita Hill and the Smokeless Gun," *Washington Examiner*, March 21, 2016, https:// www.washingtonexaminer.com/anita-hill-and-the-smokeless-gun. Wright claimed Thomas made comments about her body and asked her out on a date. Wright was interviewed by the Senate Judiciary Committee staff and was then subpoenaed to testify at the hearing. At the last moment, Wright decided not to testify, and Biden released her

from the subpoena. Instead, Biden placed Wright's interview with committee staff into the hearing record. *Nomination of Judge Clarence Thomas to Be Associate Justice*, part 4, 254. Wright agreed to this arrangement, memorialized in a letter from Senator Biden to her, which both Biden and Wright signed. Ibid., 440. For more information on Angela Wright, visit "Anita Hill: Why Her Case Never Added Up," www.AnitaHillCase.com.

19. Anita Hill worked at the EEOC from September 1982 to July 1983. Angela Wright worked there from March 1984 to April 1985.

20. Sukari Hardnett worked at the EEOC from 1985 to 86. She filed an affidavit with the Senate Judiciary Committee that did not allege Thomas engaged in any sexual harassment. Rather, Hardnett wrote that in her opinion women who worked at EEOC "were being inspected and auditioned as a female." *Nomination of Judge Clarence Thomas to Be Associate Justice*, part 4, 1023–24, https://www.govin fo.gov/content/pkg/GPO-CHRG-THOMAS/pdf/GPO-CHRG-TH OMAS-4.pdf.

21. Rose Jourdain was a speechwriter at EEOC from November 1983 to March 1985 who, like Angela Wright, was fired by Thomas. Jourdain was a friend of Wright's and was interviewed by committee staff. Jourdain said she spoke with Wright at the time about Wright's interactions with Thomas, but her characterization of events did not match Wright's. Her interview with committee staff was also entered into the hearing record. She was not called to testify. "Nomination of Judge Clarence Thomas to Be Associate Justice," part 4, 512–51, https://www.gov.info.gov/content/pkg/GPO-CHRG-THOMAS/pdf /GPO-CHRG-THOMAS-4.pdf.

22. Twelve women, most of whom had been Thomas's colleagues at the Department of Education or the EEOC testified in support of him. One panel consisted of Diane Holt, former secretary to Thomas at the Department of Education and the EEOC; J. C. Alvarez, special assistant to Thomas at the EEOC; Phyllis Berry Meyers, special assistant to Thomas at the EEOC; and Nancy Fitch, Special Assistant

to Thomas at the EEOC. A second panel began their testimony well after midnight and finished testifying just after 2:00 a.m: Patricia Johnson, Director of Labor Relations at the EEOC; Pamela Talkin, former chief of staff for Clarence Thomas at the EEOC; Janet Brown, former press secretary for Senator John Danforth; Linda Jackson, research associate at the Department of Education; Nancy Altman, formerly of the Department of Education; Anna Jenkins, a former secretary at the EEOC; Lori Saxon, former assistant for congressional relations of the Department of Education; and Connie Newman, Director of the Office of Personnel Management. Not a single colleague of Anita Hill's at either the Department of Education or the EEOC supported her allegations. For more information on these witnesses, visit "Anita Hill: Why Her Story Never Added Up," www.AnitaHill Case.com.

23. Eleven (of fifty-seven) Democratic senators voted to confirm Thomas, and two Republicans voted against him.

24. The Litany of Humility is a Catholic prayer asking for the virtue of humility. Cardinal Rafael Merry del Val, the author of the prayer, was the Vatican Secretary of State from 1903 to 1930. Justice Thomas has this prayer framed on a wall in his chambers at the Supreme Court. See Appendix B for the full text of the prayer.

25. Justice Byron White was appointed to the Supreme Court by President Kennedy in 1962.

26. Natalie "Nan" Rehnquist passed away on October 17, 1991.

Chapter Nine: On the Court

1. A commission is signed by the president appointing the justice to the Court.

2. Chief Justice John Marshall was the fourth chief justice and served from 1801 until his death in 1835.

3. Justice Antonin Scalia passed away on February 13, 2016.

4. Josef Pieper, *Abuse of Language, Abuse of Power* (San Francisco: Ignatius Press, 1992).

5. In *Sale v. Haitian Centers Council, Inc.*, 509 U.S. 155 (1993), the Court held that the president could send asylum-seeking Haitians back to Haiti, as neither the Immigration and Nationality Act nor the United Nations Protocol Relating to the Status of Refugees restricted the President's power to do so. While the treatment of the asylum-seeking Haitians concerned the Court, it found that "there is no solution to be found in a judicial remedy." Justice Thomas joined the majority opinion.

6. In *Gonzales v. Raich*, 545 U.S. 1, 58 (2005), the Court held that Congress could prohibit the local cultivation of medical marijuana under the Commerce Clause. Justice Thomas dissented, finding that this allowed Congress to regulate "virtually anything—and the Federal Government is no longer one of limited and enumerated powers."

7. In *Grutter v. Bollinger*, 539 U.S. 306, 350 (2003), the Court held that the University of Michigan Law School's affirmative action policies did not violate the Equal Protection Clause. Justice Thomas dissented, arguing that the "Constitution does not, however, tolerate institutional devotion to the status quo in admissions policies when such devotion ripens into racial discrimination."

8. *Plessy v. Ferguson*, 163 U.S. 537, 563 (1896) held that it was constitutional for a law to provide "separate but equal" accommodations for people of different races. Justice Harlan famously dissented, finding Louisiana's law "hostile to both the spirit and letter of the constitution of the United States.... Our Constitution is color-blind and neither knows nor tolerates classes among citizens. In respect of civil rights, all citizens are equal before the law."

9. In *Brown v. Board of Ed. of Topeka, Shawnee City, Kan.*, 347 U.S. 483, 495. (1954), the Court unanimously decided that "separate but

equal" laws are "inherently unequal." The decision declared public segregation unconstitutional.

10. The United States ratified the Fourteenth Amendment to the Constitution on July 28, 1868. Section One provides: "All persons born or naturalized in the United States, and subject to the jurisdiction thereof, are citizens of the United States and of the State wherein they reside. No State shall make or enforce any law which shall abridge the privileges or immunities of citizens of the United States; nor shall any State deprive any person of life, liberty, or property, without due process of law; nor deny to any person within its jurisdiction the equal protection of the laws."

11. Justice Thomas is referencing the group of lawsuits in the 1950s challenging the separate but equal laws in public schools, including *Brown v. Board of Education*. Brief for Respondents at 22-27, *Bolling v. Sharpe*, 344 U.S. 873 (1952) (No. 413) 1952 WL 47258. You can find a copy at: http://blackfreedom.proquest.com/wp-cont ent/uploads/2020/09/bolling5.pdf.

12. The Declaration of Indepedence provides: "We hold these truths to be self-evident, that all men are created equal...." The Fourteenth Amendment provides that no state shall "deny to any person...the equal protection of the laws."

13. From Justice Thomas's *Grutter* dissent: "'[D]iversity,' for all of its devotees, is more a fashionable catchphrase than it is a useful term, especially when something as serious as racial discrimination is at issue. Because the Equal Protection Clause renders the color of one's skin constitutionally irrelevant to the Law School's mission, I refer to the Law School's interest as an 'aesthetic.' That is, the Law School wants to have a certain appearance, from the shape of the desks and tables in its classrooms to the color of the students sitting at them. I also use the term 'aesthetic' because I believe it underlines the ineffectiveness of racially discriminatory admissions in actually helping those who are truly underprivileged.... It must be remembered that the Law School's racial discrimination does nothing for those too poor or uneducated to

participate in elite higher education and therefore presents only an illusory solution to the challenges facing our Nation." *Grutter v. Bollinger*, 539 U.S. 306, 355 no. 3 (2003) (Thomas, J., dissenting).

14. Allison Schroeder and Theodore Melfi, *Hidden Figures*, directed by Theodore Melfi (20th Century Fox, 2016).

15. *Grutter v. Bollinger*, 539 U.S. 306, 378 (2003) (Thomas, J., dissenting).

16. Michael Shaara and Ron Maxwell, *Gettysburg*, directed by Ronald F. Maxwell (New Line Cinema, 1993).

17. "What the Black Man Wants: An Address Delivered in Boston, Massachusetts, on 26 January 1865," *The Frederick Douglass Papers: Volume 4, Series One: Speeches, Debates, and Interviews, 1864–80*, ed. J. Blassingame & J. McKivigan, (New Haven, Connecticut: Yale University Press, 1991), 59, 68.

18. In *Fisher*, the Court held that the University of Texas–Austin had not narrowly tailored its affirmative action policies, and so the policies were unconstitutional. Justice Thomas concurred, reiterating that affirmative action is "categorically prohibited by the Equal Protection Clause." *Fisher v. Univ. of Texas at Austin*, 570 U.S. 297, 315 (2013).

19. Dr. Ben Carson was the secretary of Housing and Urban Development during the Trump administration.

20. In *Department of Transportation v. Association of American Railroads*, 575 U.S. 43 (2015), Justice Thomas concurred with the Court's decision to remand the case, adding that it is unconstitutional to delegate lawmaking power to a private party. In *B & B Hardware, Inc. v. Hargis Indus., Inc.*, 575 U.S. 138 (2015), he dissented, arguing that an agency's adjudication should not preclude a party from seeking a remedy in federal court. And in his dissent to *Perez v. Mortgage Bankers Association*, 575 U.S. 92 (2015), Thomas argued that it is unconstitutional for a court to defer to agencies' interpretations of their own regulations. All three opinions exemplify how "[o]nly Justice Thomas has consistently questioned the constitutionality of the modern administrative state." Charles Cooper, "Confronting the Administrative

State," *National Affairs* (fall 2015), https://www.nationalaffairs.com/publications/detail/confronting-the-administrative-state.

21. "Frank Goodnow (1859–1939), an American legal scholar and political scientist…was influential in the development of the academic dimension of the progressive movement. An eventual president of Johns Hopkins University…he is perhaps best known as an early innovator in the professional study of public administration and administrative law." Jason R. Jividen, Introduction to Frank J. Goodnow, "The American Conception of Liberty," Teaching American History, https://teachingamericanhistory.org/document/the-american-conception-of-liberty/.

22. Woodrow Wilson was a leading Progressive in the late nineteenth century, a professor and president of Princeton University, and the twenty-eighth president of the United States.

23. When a party that has lost in a lower court requests that the Supreme Court review its case, it must submit a petition for the writ of certiorari. The petition will explain the facts of the case, say why the previous court decided wrongly, and argue why the Supreme Court should hear the case. The Court has the discretion to deny a petition, and it will adjudicate the case only if four justices agree to do so.

24. As this book went to print, Justice Thomas has been on the court for more than thirty years. Since he joined the Court in 1991, Justice Thomas has written 716 opinions on the merits (and many additional opinions on petitions for certiorari), the most of any sitting justice. "Clarence Thomas, Ballotpedia, https://ballotpedia.org/Clarence_Thomas_(Supreme_Court). Justice Thomas also averages more opinions per term than any other current justice. For example, Justice Sotomayor, since joining the Court in 2009 through the end of the 2020 term, has written 223 opinions, for an average of 20 per year. "Sonia Sotomayor," Ballotpedia, https://ballotpedia.org/Sonia_Sotomayor. In that same time frame since 2009, Justice Thomas has averaged 29 opinions per year. Since Justice Kagan joined the Court in 2010 through end of the 2020 term, she has written 106 opinions,

for an average of 11 per year. "Elena Kagan," Ballotpedia, https://ba llotpedia.org/Elena_Kagan. During that time same time period, Justice Thomas has averaged 30 per year. Justice Ginsburg wrote 467 opinions during her time on the court from 1993 until 2020, for an average of 18 per year. "Ruth Bader Ginsburg," Ballotpedia, https:// ballotpedia.org/Ruth_Bader_Ginsburg. During that same time period, Justice Thomas wrote 26 opinions per year. Finally, since Justice Samuel Alito joined the Court in 2006, he has written a total of 292 opinions through the end of the 2020 term, for an average of 21 opinions per year. During the same period, Justice Thomas averaged 27 opinions per year. For more on Justice Thomas's jurisprudence, please visit JusticeThomas.com, a website created and maintained by Mark Paoletta.

25. In 2020, because of concerns about COVID-19, the Court moved to virtual arguments, and the chief justice began asking the justices, in order of seniority, whether they had questions for the advocates. Since that change in procedure beginning in 2020, Justice Thomas has asked the first question in almost every case.

26. In *Citizens United v. Fed. Election Comm'n*, 558 U.S. 310, 480 (2010), the Court held that limiting independent corporate campaign spending violated the First Amendment. Justice Thomas voted with the majority but wrote a separate opinion to note that the Court's constitutional analysis did not "go far enough," and that other requirements risked chilling speech and violating the First Amendment.

27. In *National Federation of Independent Businesses v. Sebelius*, 567 U.S. 519, 708 (2012) the Court held that Congress had the power to enact the Affordable Care Act's individual mandate under the government's tax power but not the Commerce Clause. Justice Thomas joined Justice Scalia's dissent, which argued that Congress could not enact the mandate with either its power to tax or the Commerce Clause. He also dissented separately to argue that the majority's view was "inconsistent with the original understanding of

Congress's powers and with this Court's early Commerce Clause cases."

28. In *Obergefell v. Hodges*, 576 U.S. 644, 721 (2015), the Court announced that the Fourteenth Amendment protects the right to same-sex marriage. Justice Thomas dissented, calling the decision a "distortion of our Constitution [that] not only ignores the text, [but] inverts the relationship between the individual and the state in our Republic."

29. In *Kelo v. City of New London, Conn.*, 545 U.S. 469, 506 (2005), the Court held that the city of New London could use eminent domain to take property as long as the taking served a public purpose. Justice Thomas dissented, arguing that the Public Use Clause refers to the public's use of the property, not to the public's benefit from the property. In his words, the majority "erased the Public Use Clause from our Constitution."

30. In *Clinton v. Jones*, 520 U.S. 681 (1997), the Court held that presidential immunity from law-suits extends only to the president's official activities and not to his unofficial activities. Justice Thomas joined the majority.

31. In *Bush v. Gore*, 531 U.S. 98, 115 (2000), the Court held that the Florida Supreme Court's recount ruling violated the Equal Protection Clause. Justice Thomas joined Justice Rehnquist's concurrence, which would have reversed the Florida Supreme Court on the grounds that it did not respect the state legislature's role in presidential elections.

Chapter Ten: Legacy

1. Pauline Maier, *Ratification: The People Debate the Constitution, 1787–1788* (New York: Simon & Schuster, 2011).

2. Rick Famuwiya, *Confirmation*, directed by Rick Famuyiwa (Home Box Office, 2016).

3. Abraham Lincoln, Gettysburg Address, November 19, 1863.

4. In *Dred Scott v. Sandford*, 60 U.S. 393 (1857), the Court held that enslaved people were not citizens and did not have standing in a federal court and that the Fifth Amendment made it unconstitutional for Congress to ban slavery in any territory. It struck down the Missouri Compromise.

5. The Kansas–Nebraska Act created the states of Kansas and Nebraska. It allowed each state to choose whether to legalize slavery, unraveling the Missouri Compromise, thereby exacerbating the tensions that led up to the Civil War. Rose Drake, "The Law that Ripped America in Two," *Smithsonian Magazine*, May 2004, https://www.smithso nianmag.com/history/the-law-that-ripped-america-in-two-99723670/.

Appendix A: Excerpts from Interview with Ginni Thomas

1. S. S. Wilson and Brant Maddock, *Short Circuit*, directed by John Badham (Producers Sales Organization and the Turman-Foster Company, 1986).

2. The General Accounting Office is now called the Government Accountability Office.

3. Ginni Thomas served as Deputy Assistant Secretary for Congressional and Intergovernmental Relations at the U.S. Department of Labor from 1989 to 1992.

4. Juan Williams, "Open Season on Clarence Thomas," *Washington Post*, October 10, 1991, A23.

5. Charles Kothe was Dean of O. W. Coburn School of Law at Oral Roberts University in Tulsa, Oklahoma.

6. On Angela Wright, see chapter 8, note 18.

7. As we have seen, Anita Hill's opening statement to the Senate Judiciary Committee on October 11 was significantly different from the original September 23 statement she submitted to the Senate

Judiciary Committee and what she told the FBI in her September 25 interview.

8. Ginni Thomas, "Watch Shelby Steele Explain Race Issues in America," The Daily Caller, November 12, 2017, https://dailycaller .com/2017/11/12/watch-shelby-steele-explain-race-issues-in-america -video/; Shelby Steele, "The Freest Black Man in America," *National Review*, October 22, 2007, 36–39.

9. As we have seen, twelve women who had worked with Thomas testified in his support, with eight of them testifying after 1:00 a.m., and their panel closing out the hearing just after 2:00 a.m., October 14, 1991. *Nomination of Judge Clarence Thomas to Be Associate Justice of the Supreme Court of the United States: Senate Hearing 102-00* (Washington, D.C.: Government Printing Office, 1991), part 4, 585–64, https://www.govinfo.gov/content/pkg/GPO-CHRG-TH OMAS/pdf/GPO-CHRG-THOMAS-4.pdf.

10. Vincente Minnelli, *The Long, Long Trailer*, directed by Vincente Minelli (Metro-Goldwyn-Mayer, 1954).

11. Ed Rendell served as chair of the Democratic National Party from 1999 to 2001. He also served as the ninety-sixth mayor of Philadelphia (1992–2000) and the forty-fifth governor of Pennsylvania (2003–2011). Since 2015, Marjorie Rendell has served as a senior judge on the U.S. Court of Appeals for the Third Circuit. She served as a judge on the U.S. Court of Appeals from 1997 to 2015. Before that, she served as a federal judge on the U.S. District Court for the Eastern District of Pennsylvania. Ed Rendell and Marjorie Rendell were married in 1971 and divorced in 2016. "Ed Rendell," Wikipedia, https://en.wikipedia.org/wiki/Ed_Rendell; "Marjorie Rendell," Wikipedia, https://en.wikipedia.org/wiki/Marjorie_Rendell.

12. The Horatio Alger Association is a non-profit organization whose mission is "to provide scholarship assistance to deserving young people who have demonstrated integrity, determination in overcoming adversity, academic potential and the personal aspiration to make a

unique contribution to society." "About Us," Horatio Alger Association, https://horatioalger.org/about-us/.

Appendix B: The Litany of Humility
1.   Cardinal Merry del Val (1865–1930) is credited with writing this version of the Litany of Humility, a Catholic prayer asking for the virtue of humility, https://en.wikipedia.org/wiki/Litany_of_humility.

INDEX